INVESTIGATING THE
MARY CELESTE

a novel

D.LAWRENCE-YOUNG

CRANTHORPE
—MILLNER—
PUBLISHERS

Copyright © D. Lawrence-Young (2024)

The right of D. Lawrence-Young to be identified as author of this work has been asserted by them in accordance with section 77 and 78 of the Copyright, Designs and Patents Act 1988.

All rights reserved. No part of this publication may be reproduced, stored in a retrieval system, or transmitted in any form or by any means, electronic, mechanical, photocopying, recording, or otherwise, without the prior permission of the publishers.

Any person who commits any unauthorised act in relation to this publication may be liable to criminal prosecution and civil claims for damages.

First published by Cranthorpe Millner Publishers (2024)

ISBN 978-1-80378-171-6 (Paperback)

www.cranthorpemillner.com

Cranthorpe Millner Publishers

Other books by David Lawrence-Young

Fawkes and the Gunpowder Plot
Tolpuddle: A Novel of Heroism
Marlowe: Soul'd to the Devil
Will Shakespeare: Where was He?*
The Man Who Would be Shakespeare
Will the Real William Shakespeare Please Step Forward**
I, Master Shakespeare
Of Guns and Mules
Of Guns, Revenge and Hope
Arrows Over Agincourt
Anne of Cleves: Unbeloved
Sail Away from Botany Bay++
Catherine Howard: Henry's Fifth Failure
Six Million Accusers: Catching Adolf Eichmann
Mary Norton: Soldier Girl
Two Bullets in Sarajevo
King John: Two-Time Loser
Go Spy Out the Land
Entrenched

Emma Hamilton: Mistress of Land and Sea
My Jerusalem Book *(Editor)*
Villains of Yore‡
Wicked Women of Yore: Were they really wicked?‡
Colonel Blood: Soldier, Robber & Trickster‡
Kill the King & Other Conspiracies‡
Doctor Lopez: Trapped in the Royal Web

*Reissued as: Welcome to London, Mr Shakespeare
**Reissued as: Who *Really* Wrote Shakespeare?
++Reissued as: Away Away from Botany Bay
‡Also published by Cranthorpe Millner

As: David L. Young

Of Plots and Passions
Communicating in English *(Textbook)*
The Jewish Emigrant from Britain: 1700-2000 (contrib. chapter)
Out of Zion: Collection of essays. (contrib. chapter)

Website: www.dly-books.weebly.com
Email: dlybooks15@gmail.com

Contents

Prologue 1
Chapter 1 3
   A fatal precedent
Chapter 2 19
   Hopes for the *Mary Celeste*
Chapter 3 31
   To New York
Chapter 4 42
   Captains Briggs and Morehouse and a new crew
Chapter 5 61
   Last-minute details and downtown shopping
Chapter 6 74
   The *Mary Celeste* prepares to leave New York
Chapter 7 85
   The voyage of the *Mary Celeste* begins
Chapter 8 96
   The *Dei Gratia* leaves New York
Chapter 9 105
   Morehouse investigates the *Mary Celeste*

Chapter 10 122
   Salvage speculation
Chapter 11 133
   The enquiry opens in Gibraltar
Chapter 12 147
   The enquiry drags on
Chapter 13 157
   Enter Mr Winchester
Chapter 14 169
   The sword and the cuts
Chapter 15 183
   The verdict
Chapter 16 196
   The *Mary Celeste* sails again
Chapter 17 205
   The final voyage of the *Mary Celeste*
Other ghost ships 217
   Carroll A. Deering – January 1921 219
   SS Baychimo – October 1931 222
   MV Joyita – October 1955 225
   High Aim 6 – October 2003 231
   Jian Seng – Spring 2006 232
   Bel Amica – August 2006 233
   Kaz II – April 2007 234
   North Korean ghost ships 238

The *Mary Celeste* in print and in literature	239
Theories for disappearance – Human	265
Pirates and mutiny	266
Insurance fraud	271
Captain Briggs' cousin, Oliver Cobb's, theory	273
Captain Briggs's brother James's theory	276
The burning ship theory	277
The solution at last?	278
Theories for disappearance – Natural and supernatural	280
Giant sea monsters	280
Vanishing islands	282
Mermaids	285
The Bermuda Triangle	286
UFOs	286
Waterspouts	287
A 'seaquake'	289
This Author's Perspective	290
Author's Note	i
A Personal Request from the Author	iv
About the Author	v
Bibliography	vii

Dedicated to my ever-supportive wife, Beverley, who was always on hand to help her 'non-techie' husband with computer problems.

Also to my twin brother, Michael, who suddenly died during the writing and preparation of this book.

Prologue

"Hello, son, what have you been doing?"

"I've been talking to Uncle Nat in the garden."

"Uncle Nathan, Billy. Uncle Nathan."

"Yes, Pa."

"And what did you talk about?"

"Oh, the usual things. He was telling me one of his sea stories again."

"Which one this time?"

"Oh, like when he started off as a deckhand on a cargo ship sailing to Bermuda when he fell down an open hatch. Stuff like that. He told me that there was this area in the Atlantic Ocean between the coast of Florida and the island of Bermuda which sucks ships down to the bottom of the sea and that there were giant monsters and squids and, well, you know him, Pa, all sorts of scary stories like that."

"Oh, is he *still* telling those stories, Billy?"

"Yes, Pa, but when I asked him if he had seen any pirates, he said that those days were long gone. He said that the navy had killed 'em all off or that they had all killed each other."

"I'm not sure if that's exactly true, son. From time to time you do hear about pirates, but never mind. By the way, did he tell you his favourite story, the one about the missing crew on a ghost ship called the *Mary Celeste*?"

"No, he said he was going to tell me that one next week when I see him again. But what do you mean, Pa, a missing crew? What happened to them? When did this happen? Can *you* tell me, or is he the only one who knows?"

"No, no, son. Everyone knows the story of the mysterious *Mary Celeste*. It's one of the best-known sea stories ever. And it's all true. Every word of it."

"Really? Are you sure, or is it just another one of Uncle Nathan's stories?"

"No, son. This time it's true. I promise you. So listen carefully because everything I'm going to tell you really happened. It all started in the far north, in Nova Scotia in Canada to be exact. So this is how the story begins. It was in 1861, that is, May 1861…"

Chapter 1
A fatal precedent

A painting of the Mary Celeste

"Is that your ship, Josh?" George Bathurst asked, pointing across the water at the *Amazon* as it bobbed up and down in the calm waters of Spencer's Island harbour. To him, one ocean-going ship looked like any other. He had come to Spencer's Island for a few days to visit his brother, and before returning to Philadelphia he thought that it would be a good idea to look up his old friend, Joshua Dewis.

"What do you mean, my ship, George?" Joshua replied,

sucking on his favourite briarwood pipe. "I don't own it but, yes, I built it, so you could say that in a way that it is my ship. But," he continued proudly looking at the square-sailed vessel, "although I own some of her, I'm just a shareholder. The real owners are a bunch of businessmen somewhere to the south of here, near St. John."

"Hmm, strange how life turns out, isn't it?" George mused. "Although we are both from up here in Nova Scotia, our lives have followed completely different routes. I sit in my conveyancing office in Philadelphia all day, organising the buying and selling of houses and shops and property, while you have remained up here in the frozen north, not far from where we were born, making and repairing ships."

"It's not frozen, but anyway, are you jealous? Don't you like what you are doing?"

"No, no, it's nothing like that. I'm not jealous, at all. I enjoy very much what I do, although sometimes I feel it wouldn't do me any harm to get away from the office more and breathe in some of this cool country air of yours. That's all. But tell me," he continued, "what sort of ship is that *Amazon* of yours? A brigantine? A schooner? A barque? I know it's not a clipper because it's not big enough, right? And it doesn't have enough sails."

"Aye, you are right, there. The *Amazon* is a brigantine. A square-rigged brigantine, to be exact. If you look carefully, the main mast, that is the one at the back towards the stern, is carrying triangular fore and aft sails as well as its regular square sails, and the foremast just has the usual number of square sails, in this case, four of 'em."

"And there are two triangular sails in front of them, right?"

"Right."

"How much does she weigh?"

The stocky shipbuilder drew on his pipe for a minute and then answered. "She weighs nearly two hundred tons and that's quite some weight to be sure. Now, my landlubber friend," he said, pointing to a small building on the quayside. "Do you have any more questions or shall we walk over to the Jolly Sailor and have a meal and a drink?"

"No, no more questions, but just tell me, is she big enough to cross the Atlantic, or are you going to use her just for coastal voyages, from up here to New York, say, or further south to the Carolinas?"

"Oh no, George. The *Amazon* is big enough to sail the Atlantic and she'll easily be able to carry a decent cargo to England or anywhere in Europe. That's why these businessmen paid me to build her. I mean, she is nearly one hundred feet long, that is, from stem to stern and twenty-five feet wide."

"And how deep is she?"

"Almost twelve feet. Eleven and a half to be exact. Now does that satisfy you?"

"Aye, aye, captain," George saluted. "So now let's go and have a drink. A toast to your new ship and to all who sail in her."

The two men made their way over to the Jolly Sailor, a popular seamen's tavern on the waterfront. It was a half-timbered building with a sloping roof and two tall brick chimneys. It was a local landmark which, according to local gossip, had been built with timbers that had come from three old ships which had been broken up some fifty years ago.

As the two men entered the weather-beaten tavern, Joshua

Dewis was greeted by three of his other shipbuilding friends, who moved over to make room for him and George at their table. Dewis kindly declined their offer, saying that he had an important meeting with his friend and that he would happily join them for a drink on another occasion. Then he escorted George over to an unoccupied table in the far corner by a window where they could look out at the bustling harbour. Over a meal of meat pies and vegetables, washed down by the tavern's own dark amber ale, Dewis told his friend how he had built the *Amazon*.

"It was like this, George," Dewis began as he speared a potato with his fork. "I set up my business here, my shipbuilding yard, together with two brothers, Isaac and Jacob Spicer. They are local boys and they own a two and a half thousand acre timber farm nearby."

"Which they can use for masts and shipbuilding."

"That's right, so I began to work on the *Amazon* last year, when I laid the keel down and had it finished just before the bad winter weather set in. Then we had to leave it over the winter and started again as soon as we could in the spring. After that we worked hard for the next two months until May and that's when we launched her."

"What, the whole ship, masts and all?"

"Yes, the lot. And those masts you are talking about are nearly as tall as the *Amazon* is long. And to slow down any rot – that's a permanent problem with wooden ships – we packed a lot of rock salt between the boards."

"I see, and from what I can tell from here, she looks like she has a smooth hull."

"Oh yes, George. We worked hard on that. We made the planking smooth and fit flush, you know, not overlapping.

That way she will sail better and perhaps a little faster."

"And what's she like inside? All carved wood patterns and the like?"

"No, no. She's very simple. Remember, my friend, she's been built for trade, not as a rich man's fancy ship for cruising up and down the coast. No carving or decorative stuff like that. The *Amazon* is going to be a hard-working cargo ship. The only ornamentation I allowed was a decorated bowsprit."

"That's the front end, right? Like where they have the decorative carved figureheads; women or dragons or things like that that I've seen on those naval warships, yes?"

The shipbuilder nodded. "Yes, that's right. And so, George, after we've finished here, say in the next day or two, if you want, I'll take you aboard so you can admire my yard's first ship. How does that sound? Do you have the time?"

"Yes, I have to go back to Philly for an important meeting with a client on Saturday, so any time between then and now will be good for me. And if you agree, I'll bring my brother, Tom, with me so he can admire your ship as well."

Two days later, on a sunny afternoon, George, Tom and Joshua all climbed aboard the *Amazon* and the shipbuilder proudly showed them around.

"How many men will there be in the crew?" Tom asked. "Half a dozen? More?"

Joshua nodded. "Yes, I guess a number like that. Remember, the bigger the crew, the more the owners are going to have to pay out in wages, so they'll do their best to keep the crew at a minimum."

"But George told me that you are also an owner as well as the builder of this ship," Tom said.

"That's true," Joshua Dewis replied. "I own a quarter of

the shares, the Spicer brothers own another quarter and the businessmen who commissioned her own the remaining half. One of them is called Captain Robert McLellan. Maybe you've heard of him."

"Captain Robert McLellan? Of course, I've heard about him. I've read about him in the papers. It said that he's a good fellow. Knows his stuff. A good ol' sea-salt."

"Aye, that's also what I've heard. Anyway, he's going to captain the *Amazon*, at least for its first few voyages. After that we'll see what happens."

But, as the old saying goes, 'Man proposes, but God disposes'.

*

In June 1861, one month after she had been launched, the *Amazon* sailed out from her Nova Scotia harbour on her maiden voyage to cross the Atlantic. She was bound for London and was carrying a cargo of local Nova Scotia timber. After unloading it in London, it was intended that she would continue south to Lisbon in Portugal carrying an as yet unspecified cargo and then return home. It was planned that, altogether, this whole voyage to Europe and back would take about three months.

With the fanfare that usually accompanied the maiden voyage of any ship, and especially one that had been built locally by the Spencer's Island's men, the *Amazon*, now captained by Robert McLellan, slid down the slipway into the Minas Channel. Then after her cargo and stores had been securely loaded, her crew boarded her. This event too was accompanied by more cheers, waving flags and farewell hugs and blessings from the crew's wives, sweethearts and families, before she sailed out of the harbour and headed for the open sea. As the ship's crew took their last look at the harbour they saw the brightly coloured flags and bunting fluttering in the breeze, and as all sailors tend to do, they thought about all of the people they had left behind and when they would see them again. In addition, the sailors naturally thought about their forthcoming voyage and how this brand-new ship would behave in the North Atlantic's fearsome gales. These they guessed would be a part of the voyage that they would encounter in the next week or so. But this was not to be.

"What's the matter, captain?" the helmsman asked McLellan the following morning. The two men, the bulky, young-looking helmsman from Prince Edward Island and the slimmer captain, were standing by the helm on the foredeck as the *Amazon* sliced through the choppy seas of the western Atlantic. "You don't look so well, cap'n. A bit pale, if you ask me."

"You're right, lad. I think I've picked up a wee bit of a cold" – McLellan sniffed – "even before we set out. But fear not. After a few days at sea, especially if this good weather holds, I'll be all right. It's happened to me before, several times in fact, so don't worry, we'll be seeing London before you can say Jack Robinson."

But as the new ship braved the waves for the first time, the captain's cold grew progressively worse.

"That's a terrible hacking cough, you've got there," Fred, the first mate, said as McLellan spat a large gob of phlegm into a large handkerchief.

"Aye, but, it'll be over soon, man. You know, the dark

before the light. I'll be as right as rain in a day or two. Fear not, it won't be long before the pair of us will be sharing a drink in a nice pub I know in London near the Tower."

An hour later Captain McLellan collapsed on the deck and three of the crew carried the shaking and feverish man to his small cabin in the stern and put him to bed. Once they had seen he was comfortable, they closed the door and started discussing what they had seen.

"I tell you, Fred, he's got pneumonia," squinty-eyed O'Leary from Newfoundland said. "I've seen it before. He's breathing badly and he's feverish like. Y'know, all hot and sweating like my ol' gran'ma was before she passed away last year."

"Don't be soft, man," Joe, the tallest sailor on board replied. "It's just a bad cold. A couple of days in bed and a tot of brandy or two and he'll be all right. Just you see."

"No, I agree with O'Leary," fat Marlowe, the ship's cook, added. "That's no ordinary cold. You can see that the ol' boy doesn't have any energy. Why, man, he hardly touched his food these last two days. No, no, the cap'n's got pneumonia. That's what I say."

"Well, what do you think we should do? Turn back or risk sailing on?"

"It's not up to us to decide, is it? Let's ask the first mate and see what he says."

The first mate, Bob Collins, a weather-beaten old salt who had spent the last thirty years at sea, came to the captain's cabin and, after a quick look at his superior officer, stepped out to find himself surrounded by most of the *Amazon*'s crew.

"Well, what's it to be?" O'Leary asked. "Are we going to turn back or not? Will the ol' boy make it?"

The first mate shook his head. "No, lads. I don't think so. He could hardly answer when I asked him how he felt. He just lay there looking at me. And that cough of his. Terrible it was. And the fever. I put my hand to his forehead and he was burning hot. No, men, I don't think we've got any choice. We are going to have to go back and take him home."

"But what will the owners say?" asked Richard, the first mate's best friend, a sailor who had been with Bob for the past twenty years. "They are not going to be pleased about this."

Collins scratched his head and shrugged. "I know that, Rich, but do you think they'll be pleased if we come back with a dead captain on board?"

"Why, man, d'you really think he's that bad?"

"Aye, I do," the first mate said. "I've seen pneumonia before. It's a killer. Don't you remember, Rich, when we were sailing home from Brazil a few years ago? But here it's diff'rent."

"How so?"

"Luckily, we're only a couple of days or so out at sea, so if we turn back now we may be able to save him." First mate Collins looked around at the men standing with him on the foredeck. "So this is what I've decided. We're going to turn around right now. You men, make the necessary preparations and let's get moving. I just hope that the captain will hang in there 'til we get back."

Fortunately, although they were now sailing against the prevailing westerly winds, the return to harbour went as smoothly as the outward journey had gone. After the *Amazon* had drawn alongside the quay, the dying captain, now on a stretcher, was carefully carried to a waiting carriage and taken to the house of Jacob Spicer. There McLellan's loving wife, Mary Ann, looked after him, but there was not much she could do for the sick mariner. Despite the warm bed, wholesome food and prescribed medicine, two days later Captain Robert McLellan departed this world. Even though he had always boasted that he would die and be buried at sea, it was not to be. His death was the first to be linked with this ship. There would be quite a few others.

Apart from the natural sadness that attends the death of a local notable in a small community, Captain McLellan's demise cast a pall over the name of the merchant brigantine, the *Amazon*.

"That ship must be cursed," was heard to be whispered more than once in the Jolly Sailor and other local harbourside taverns.

"Och, don't be stupid, man," Jack Norton, a large retired first mate from Glasgow who had spent over thirty-five years at sea, gruffly replied. "Cap'n McLellan could have died anywhere, or on any ship. It just so happened that he was sick on the *Amazon*, that's all."

"Well, you can all say what you like, but I heard this morning that yon Joshua Dewis has had the *Amazon* registered now at Parrsboro and she's going to take a cargo of wood to England."

"The same cargo?"

Jack Norton's drinking partner shrugged. "I don't know, but so what? There's gonna be a new captain, a Captain Jack Parker..."

"Who? Jack Parker from Walton? That tall feller? I know him. He's a good man."

"Yes, him. He's looking for a new crew now and they

hope to be off by the end of the week. The owners have said that they've lost enough time as it is."

For most of the local people that was the end of the story. Captain Robert McLellan had died, a new captain had been found and the *Amazon* would set sail for England again. As it happened, she crossed the Atlantic without any serious problems. She delivered her cargo in London and the crew spent an alcoholic weekend there. On a fine day at the end of June 1861, the *Amazon* set off again, this time from London, and sailed down the Thames carrying a mixed cargo of sheepskins, agricultural machinery and barrels of good Scotch whisky. She arrived in Lisbon as planned and then returned to Nova Scotia loaded with several hundred barrels of Portuguese wine and sheets of cork.

But despite this financially successful first voyage, the *Amazon*'s problems were not over. There was talk that, while the ship was in Eastport, Maine, it had rammed a row of weirs in the harbour and had to delay sailing for a few days while the damage to the hull was repaired. Then there was more talk that after the ship had delivered her cargo in London, while sailing off the white cliffs of Dover, she had rammed another brig. Apparently this was not a minor collision as the second ship had sunk almost immediately. The crew of the *Amazon* then had to rescue the other ship's crew and take them back to Dover. There, more repairs to the *Amazon*'s hull had to be carried out in the harbour under the shadow of the famous white cliffs before she could continue with her voyage.

"I'm telling you, men," an old sailor with a leathery skinned face, kept repeating to anyone who would listen to him in the Jolly Sailor. "That *Amazon* is cursed. For a start, its first captain, yon McLellan, died soon after setting off with her to London and since then it hasn't had one voyage yet without someone else dying or causing itself and others damage. You mark my words. That ship's next voyage is going to end with the deaths of its own crew or another one. Oh yes, I will swear to that on the Holy Bible. Oh yes, I surely will."

But the old sailor was wrong. For the next few years, the *Amazon* crossed the Atlantic without any particular problems. George Spicer, the young man who had rushed over to inform Mary Ann McLellan that her husband was "mighty sick and fev'rish", joined the crew as the brigantine sailed regularly from New England to Europe and the Caribbean. She carried and delivered her usual cargoes of wood, fruit and coal, bringing her owners a fair if not spectacular financial return on their investment.

The *Amazon* spent the next seven years doing what she had been built to do. Captain Parker left after two years to become the master of another ship, and his place was taken by one of the original investors, William Thompson. Then in 1867, the new captain had a noisy argument with Joshua Dewis.

"We're not making enough profit," Thompson said. "You should have made the hold bigger so we could carry a larger cargo."

The shipbuilder held up his hands. "Sorry, William. It can't be done. If you change the internal structure or carry any more cargo than you've been doing up to now she'll sink like a stone."

Thompson stood up, stared down at Dewis and smacked his huge fist on the table. Their empty beer glasses jumped up and one fell to the floor, its shattered shards flying everywhere. "That's rubbish, man. She could easily carry a few more tons."

"No she can't, William, and just you remember who built the *Amazon*. You or me? Don't you think if I could have made the hold bigger, I would have done so? I've got shares in her profits as well as you, just remember that."

Thompson did not reply. He just got up, left his drink on the table and marched out. The following day he went to Dewis's office and told him that he would no longer work with him. "If you want a new captain for your cursed ship, young man, then you're going to have to find him. For me, sailing on the *Amazon* is finished."

The next dramatic news that Joshua Dewis received about the *Amazon* came in November of 1867. A strong gale coming up the New England coast had blown the *Amazon* onto the rocky shoreline of Big Grace Bay.

"It was like this, Father," Dewis's son, Robert, told his father when they met in Joshua's harbourside office later. "The winds were howling like you've never heard before and it was impossible to steer her. I was trying to help the helmsman hold the wheel steady all the time, but we had no chance. In the end we were driven onto those rocks near where they are building that new dock and…"

"And were the crew all right? Did anything happen to any of them?"

"Don't worry, Father, they all survived, but the *Amazon* was left stranded with some huge holes in the side of her hull. I don't know if she'll be able to be saved."

"Hmm," Dewis said at length. "It looks as if I'm going to have to go to Big Grace Bay and see what's to be done, doesn't it?"

His son nodded in agreement and the two of them finished off their meal in thoughtful silence.

The result was that, after Dewis had investigated the situation and assessed how much it would cost to repair the damage, he and his fellow owners decided that it was not worth repairing the *Amazon*. They had invested enough money so far and felt that any future returns would not justify the cost of carrying out the critical structural repairs. Therefore, as a way of cutting their losses, they sold the *Amazon* to a hopeful investor from Cape Breton Island. Although the Dewises, father and son, did not know it at the time, and not that it would have made much difference, the Cape Breton man had bought the damaged ship for purely speculative purposes. Soon after he signed the papers, he sold the *Amazon* again and as far as Dewis was concerned, that was the end of his connections with the brigantine that was later to become one of the world's best known nautical mysteries.

It sounded like there was to be a rather ignoble end to the *Amazon*. She had served her owners faithfully for over six years but now it seemed that she was to be broken up and sold for spares, or else just lie abandoned somewhere on the stormy coasts of the Nova Scotia coast.

For a year nothing more was heard of the *Amazon*. Her new owners repaired her, but it seemed that they did not do a very good job. In November 1868, Richard W. Haines bought the ship at an auction for the ridiculously cheap price of $1,150. Soon after this he invested another $9,000 to replace the sails, rigging and spars, as well as giving the *Amazon* a brand-new stern and keel.

"Richard, do you think it's wise spending so much on that old boat?" a friend of his asked. "Are you sure you're not flogging a dead horse?"

"Don't you worry about that, my friend, you'll see," Haines smiled. "Once I get a new captain and crew, fill up the hold and start sailing and selling, you'll be asking me if you can invest in the *Amazon* as well."

"I hope you're right, but before you make any profit, you're going to have to pay back the loans you've taken out, no?"

"You don't have to worry about that one either, my friend," Haines said. "Once the money starts flowing in, those loans will start flowing out. Think big. That's what I always say. Think big and be optimistic. Now come, let's have a drink on it – it's my turn to pay. And just to show you that the *Amazon* is going to turn a corner, so to speak, I am going to give her a new name."

"What are you going to call her? Florence, after your good lady-wife?"

"No, no, I'm going to call her the *Mary Celeste*."

"The *Mary Celeste*? Why that name?"

Haines shrugged. "I don't know. No special reason. I just like it, that's all. It has a nice sound to it Yes, the *Mary Celeste*, she's gonna be from now on," he announced.

"But are you sure that your wife won't be suspicious? Y'know, naming her after another woman instead of her?"

"Who, my wife? Don't worry, man, she knows me better than that. Besides, I don't know of any Marys, that is, apart from Mary Flexner and her I haven't seen for years. She was in the first grade with me and then her family moved down south to North Carolina when we went up to second grade.

Now, how many years ago was that?"

"Yeah, but still…"

"Don't you worry, man. *Mary Celeste* she's going to be. Heavenly Mary. I'm sure with a beautiful name like that she'll be remembered for the profitable ship that she will be."

But Haines's optimism failed him. In the early winter of 1869, when the storms were blowing around the Canadian Maritime Provinces of New Brunswick, Prince Edward Island and Nova Scotia, Richard W. Haines's creditors closed in on him like circling vultures and seized the newly named ship. He had not been able to repay the hefty loans he had taken out. As the newly christened *Mary Celeste* was his collateral, to recoup their investment, the ship was put up for auction once again, and the New York company, J.H. Winchester & Co, Ship Owners & Commission Merchants, bought her. Their plans were like everyone else's who had owned the square-sailed brigantine: invest in her, make her shipshape, carry cargo and above all else, make a handsome profit. Would J.H. Winchester & Co. succeed where the previous owners had failed? Would the *Mary Celeste*, as Haines had prophesied, prove to be a heavenly investment whose profits and name would be remembered forever?

Chapter 2
Hopes for the *Mary Celeste*

"There she is, Captain Briggs," James Winchester, the portly ship-owner of J.H. Winchester & Co. said, pointing to the clean lines of the ship. He had arranged to meet the semi-retired captain and businessman Briggs a few days beforehand, when he had heard that the man was looking to invest in a merchant sailing ship which he could captain at the same time. "In that way," the bearded mariner had said to the Winchester man, "I'll be able to look after my investment more personally, won't I?"

"Aye, and have you ever seen such a fine-looking ship in your life?"

Captain Briggs, otherwise known as Benjamin Spooner Briggs, nodded and said that the new ship he thought of commanding certainly looked most pleasing. He added that if he took out shares in her, he would be very proud to take the newly repaired vessel on her maiden voyage to Genoa that November.

"So tell me something about yourself," James Winchester said. "All I know about you is that you have a good reputation, that you are a married man aged thirty-seven and come from a seafaring family."

"That's right and—"

"Ah yes, and I heard that you were a merchant ship captain on the Union side during the Civil War."

"All that's true enough." Briggs smiled modestly. "But I wasn't up to much during the war. I didn't see much action if the truth be told. I just captained the *Sciota*, a naval gunboat, off the coast of Texas. I did chase a suspected enemy ship away."

"Why do you say 'suspected'? Wasn't it an enemy ship?"

"No, in the end it turned out to be one of ours, but later I gave chase to a rebel blockade runner. When we caught it, we took the crew prisoner and then burned the ship, and that, I'm afraid, was my only contribution to the Union winning the war."

"I see, so tell me more about yourself, such as where were you born? Where have you sailed to? What about your family? It's important for us to know something about the captains we're employing. And... you know what?" Winchester said, relighting his pipe for the hundredth time that morning. "Let's go to that tavern over there, the Home from the Sea, on the corner by the ships' tackle store and you can tell me everything over a meal and a beer. I hear that their ale isn't too bad and that they serve a very tasty meat stew. That way you'll be able to tell me everything and we'll be out of this confounded wind."

Briggs nodded in agreement and a few minutes later the two men were to be found sitting at a table next to a front window in the tavern known by the locals as 'the Home'. From there, they had a good view of the blue-grey skies and the harbour where the waves crashed loudly against its rough walls; waves that occasionally broke over the top spraying the small boats bobbing up and down where they had been anchored by their owners seeking protection from the powerful Atlantic rollers.

As they waited for their meal, Briggs looked around. The walls were covered with pictures of brigantines, schooners and large yachts, while an old sextant lay on the windowsill. A highly polished wooden steering wheel was attached to the wall opposite the entrance, its handles covered with shiny brass grips. Winchester noted that Briggs smiled approvingly, and he commented that although most of the taverns near the harbour were similarly decorated, the Home seemed to outshine the others. Then after being served generous helpings of steaming beef stew and vegetables on thick china plates together with large tankards of ale, the two men resumed their conversation.

"Well, it's like this," Briggs began. "I was born Benjamin Spooner Briggs in Wareham, Massachusetts in 1835. My parents were called Nathan and Sophia and I was their third child, that is, their second son. Both my father and my grandfather had been sailors and… Do you really want to know all this?"

"Yes, yes, Benjamin. I'm always interested in the people I employ and work with. Please continue."

Briggs shrugged. "All right, if you insist, I'll tell you everything, but don't tell me afterwards that you were bored. Agreed?"

"Agreed." Briggs's new employer smiled. "Please continue."

Briggs finished swallowing a piece of meat and continued. "As I said, I was born in New England some thirty-five years ago, a little more, in fact, and by the time I made my entrance into this world, my father had quit his seafaring days and had become a businessman. Then my parents had two more sons, Oliver and James, and then my father's business collapsed."

Winchester stopped eating and looked up. "So what happened then?"

"He did the only thing that he knew. He sent us five children and my mother to live with my grandparents and he became a sailor again. His aim was to make as much money as he could, and after five years of hard work, he left the sea once again after having risen in the ranks, as they say, to become a first mate. Then with his savings he built a new house which we later called Rose Cottage. This was because of the garden that was full of rose bushes. And, yes, if you really want to know about all the details of my past life…"

"I do."

"We used to use maritime words to describe the various parts of the house."

"Such as?"

"Such as calling the front porch the 'quarterdeck', and the upstairs rooms being 'aloft'. Of course, as we were growing up and living in such a small town on the coast, we boys had a very limited choice of which career we could follow. You could be either a sailor or a businessman. That is, if you wanted to keep on living in Wareham."

"And you chose to be a sailor," Winchester said as he signalled to the waitress to bring over another two tankards of ale.

"Right. I sailed my first voyage as a deckhand, and a few years later – when I was twenty – I served as a first mate on the *Hope*. The ship sailed around Cape Horn and my father, who had gone back to sea once again, was my captain."

"Was that a good idea, serving under your father? Weren't the other men jealous that you would receive special favours?"

Briggs shook his head as he thought back to those days. "No, sir. Far from it. He made me work as hard as all the rest of the crew, perhaps even harder. I must admit that I wasn't very pleased about this, but I have to say that in the long run, it was probably a good idea. This way I learned everything about running a ship. After that I sailed on the *Sea Foam*, which was another merchant brig. I kept working my way up the ladder, so to speak: sailor, second mate, first mate, and then I got my certificate and became a captain."

"Also on a brig?"

"No, something larger than that. The *Forest King*, a three-masted schooner."

"*Forest King*? Now that's a strange name for a ship, no, Benjamin? Sounds more countryside than maritime."

"Yes, I thought about that several times, but no matter, she served me well. I sailed across the Atlantic and back several times on her without any mishap, and it was about this time, in 1862, that I married my wife, a Miss Sarah Elizabeth Cobb. And you know what? If it had been my father who had been my captain once, now it was Sarah's father and it was he who married us. I had known Sarah since I was very young – in fact, we are first cousins. After we were married I took her on a honeymoon voyage to the Mediterranean on the *Forest King*, and she often used to come with me on voyages after that."

"Wasn't that a little strange? You know the old sailors' superstition about having women on board, and all that?"

Benjamin Briggs shrugged his wide shoulders. "It never

made any problems. Sometimes I'd overhear a crewman say something, but it never came to anything. Besides, as Sarah said more than once, this way we'd be together instead of her being a typical sailor's wife sitting at home wondering what was happening to her old man all the time. And as for my family, the idea of sailing with a woman on board wasn't a new one. Sometimes my mother would accompany my father and no-one said anything."

"And what about your children? Did they ever sail with you as well?"

"Oh yes. As soon as my first-born child, Arthur, was old enough, he would sail with us, but as time passed and he started his schooling, then I'd go off on my own, without Sarah or my son."

"So that brings you up to the present day, does it not?"

"Yes, more or less. But in the meanwhile, my father died and my daughter, Sophia Matilda, was born soon after. She came just in time, I'm telling you. I missed my father a lot and little Sophia really took up the slack. It was at about this time that I was thinking of giving up the sea. You know, settle down on land and use my savings to open a business of my own. Perhaps selling supplies for ships or something like that. In that way I'd be on dry land and yet still have a connection to the sea."

"Why, had you had enough of the ocean?'

"No, no, it was nothing like that. It was the constant stories of accidents happening to sailors being washed overboard during storms – things like that. I began to wonder if it was responsible on my part to keep crossing the Atlantic aware, you know, that I might not come back home, and so I'd leave my wife with two small children behind."

"So couldn't you have become a captain of a trading ship that plied the coasts of America instead, not keep crossing the Atlantic?"

Briggs shrugged and finished off his ale. "Perhaps, but that was less profitable, and I didn't want to penny-pinch and have to save all the time. I had got used to having a good life, but besides, that question is now irrelevant."

"Why?"

Briggs smiled. "Because you and your company came along and are trying to persuade me to buy a one-third interest in the *Mary Celeste*."

James Winchester smiled back. "I see, so that by your agreeing to captain the *Mary Celeste*, as you said before, you will be looking after your investment. Very smart."

"Yes, I guess so, but no-one's forcing me to do so. I still love the sea and I still love being in command of my own ship. And you know that, if occasionally, I'll be able to take Sarah and my children on board with me, then I suppose that I'll have the best of both worlds, no? The sea and my family."

"And tell me something, Captain Briggs," Winchester said, leaning forward as if his next question was a great secret. "Someone in my office told me that you are a very religious, I mean, a God-fearing man."

"Well, I wouldn't put it as strongly as that, sir. It is true that I am a God-fearing man, but I wouldn't say that I am *very* religious. That would be somewhat of an exaggeration. But yes, it's true, Mr Winchester, I do try and read my Bible once a day and I take my father's old family Bible with me on every voyage. And of course, I insist that the crew do not blaspheme or use profane language."

"Hmm, that must be hard at times, especially in a storm

or in any other difficult situation at sea."

"Yes," Briggs agreed, "but sometimes I turn the other cheek."

"Or the other ear," Winchester smiled.

"Aye, and I don't say anything when I hear a sailor sound off when he's hurt his hand or leg or failed to tie a tight knot properly when necessary."

Briggs's new employer nodded and was just about to ask him if he wanted anything else to eat or drink when Briggs, looking out of the window over the harbour, said, "By the way, tell me something about my new command. You haven't told me very much so far. All I know is how big she is, the size of her hold and a couple of details about her former owners. As you know, I've seen her in the harbour but so far I've taken quite a few things from you on trust. So what more is there for me to know?"

Winchester held up his hand. "All right, so here we go. Here are some more details about her and I'll also fill you in about her background. After that we'll go on board and I'll show you around. How does that sound?"

Briggs nodded and pushed his empty plate aside.

"She was first built up here in Nova Scotia in 1861 when she made her maiden voyage to Europe. But she was called the *Amazon* just then and…"

"The *Amazon*? Wasn't that the ship whose first captain, a Captain McLellan, died? Of pneumonia or something like that?"

"That's right. How did you know?"

"Oh, that sort of news spreads like wildfire in small communities like mine. That and the usual village gossip."

"I see. Well as you already know, she is just under one

hundred feet long, about twenty-five feet wide and weighs two hundred tons, more or less. She was severely damaged a few years ago and my company bought her after a few other people had done so, one as a speculative investment. We, that is my company invested quite a lot in rebuilding and repairing her, and so now she is, as they say, shipshape and ready to go. Does that satisfy your curiosity?"

Briggs shook his head. "No, not really. I want to go on board and see her for myself.".."

Winchester nodded and stood up to pay the bill. Then the two men took their hats and coats and made their way across the harbour in the light wind to where the *Mary Celeste* was gently riding at anchor. It looked as if she were trying to free herself from the hawsers tying her to the black iron bollards on the harbour wall. As Briggs followed his employer up the gangplank, he made a sign of the cross and looked around.

"Well, the first thing I can tell you," the ship's new captain said, "is that she looks tight and clean and I like the lines of her. But now I'll have an even closer inspection than before, if you don't mind."

He walked off in the direction of the bow, looking, touching and inspecting the state of the wood, the rigging and the joints. He saw that much of the original planking had been replaced and so too had several of the stairways. The forward and main hatch covers looked as though they fitted well, and he couldn't see any harmful effects of saltwater on the rigging or on the lower sails. He then looked up at the two masts, nearly eighty feet high, and at the yardarms. They all looked to be in good shape and Winchester saw Briggs smile to himself.

"Now let us go below," Briggs said, climbing down the

stairs to the cabins and the hold. "If they look as good as what I've just seen on deck, then this *Mary Celeste* will be one of the finest ships I'll ever have sailed on."

The two men went below and made their first stop at the two cabins, one each for the captain and the first mate, which had been built under the boom. Briggs nodded approvingly as he inspected them, already imagining himself and Sarah using the cabin where he was now standing.

"Someone told me, in the harbour after I first saw her, that some other changes were made. Can I see them?"

Winchester nodded and Briggs inspected the enlarged space at the bow end which would be used for the crew's sleeping and living quarters.

"And what other changes have you made? I see that there are two lifeboats on board."

"Right, but of course I hope that you won't be needing them."

Briggs nodded and noted that the smaller one looked in a better state than the main one.

"That's true but they are both seaworthy as you will see," Winchester said. "And yes, when we were repairing her after she'd been washed onto the rocks at Big Grace Bay, we added another four feet to her length and the same to her draught. Then we decided that if we were going to increase space, we would add more storage room at the stern end, you know, for the crew's food and other supplies."

"I see, and what about the hold?" Briggs asked. "Is that the same size as it was before the repairs were carried out, or have these other extensions been done at the expense of the hold?"

"No, no. The hold has also been increased so that you'll

be able to carry another seventy-five tons of cargo."

Briggs smiled. "I see. More cargo, more profits."

Winchester smiled in return. "Of course, that's what we're here for, no? And if you are going to be a shareholder you should be pleased as well. And if you looked at the trade papers recently, you'll have noticed that we said that the *Mary Celeste* will be able to carry up to three and half thousand barrels in the hold."

Briggs whistled in appreciation. "And what other changes have you made?"

The ship owner took out a page from his pocket and consulted it. "No, I think I have told you everything, that is, here inside the ship. So, now let's go outside and I'll show you what we did to the hull." The two men then climbed from the gloomy hold onto the sunlit deck and then walked down the gangplank. As he did so, Briggs looked carefully again at the hull.

"Yes, I like that you've covered the lower half of the hull with metal sheeting," he said.

"That's right. Although it cost quite a packet, we thought it would be worth it, as it will save us from dealing with the usual marine growth that can be expensive to remove."

"And it's copper?" Briggs asked.

"Of course, captain. Nothing but the best," his fellow shareholder smiled. "I just hope that all of this pays off. I must admit that the company spent much more on repairs than we originally intended, but I hope that after a few voyages we'll get a good return on our investment."

"Well, looking at the ship now, I'm sure you will. I'm telling you," Briggs said, "after looking around I have to say that this is one of the finest ships I've ever seen. So with a full cargo, good seas and a hard-working crew, we should be able to make a goodly profit very quickly."

"By the way, what are you going to do about the crew? When and where will you find them?"

"Oh, don't you worry about that. I already know a few of the men I'm planning on taking, that is, if they're not working at the moment. And as for the rest, well, I'll see about them later. They'll be the least of my problems."

"How so?"

"Because I have control over the crew. At least I hope so. But with the weather, I have to take what the Good Lord provides."

"That's true enough," Winchester nodded. "Now let's go back to the tavern to drink to our success and your first voyage on your new ship. I've worked up quite a thirst."

Briggs smiled. "I'm not really thirsty and, as you may know, I'm not really a drinking man. But to have a drink to our success is certainly a good idea. To the *Mary Celeste*," he said. "Let's go and have a wee one to her. But just a very wee one."

Chapter 3
To New York

Captain Benjamin Briggs

After Captain Briggs's meeting with his employer, the last important thing he had to do was to have a good meal with all of his family before setting off on his next transatlantic voyage. In the family circle, they called this the Last Supper, although they hoped that this would not be so, of course. This time he would be taking his wife, Sarah, and his two-year-old daughter, Sophia Matilda with him so that this meal would really be for his parents, his siblings and his son.

"Where are we having our Last Supper?" Arthur asked. "Here at home or are we going to eat in a hotel like we did once last year?"

"Why, Arthur, which do you prefer?" Briggs asked his son as he ruffled the boy's thick curly locks.

"In a hotel, Father. I like the bright lights and the feeling that I am the president and all the waiters are there to serve me."

"Well, Arthur, that's what's going to happen, except that this time, we are going to eat in a hotel in New York."

"In New York! Wow, that is so exciting!" The seven-year-old boy could hardly stop himself from jumping up and down in his chair. "Which hotel, Father?"

"The Washington, son. It's a new one on Fifth Avenue. I've been told it's very grand."

"But won't it cost a fortune, darling?" Mrs Briggs asked.

"Maybe, my dear, but the ship's owners have promised me that they will pay for half of our meal."

"When are we going, Father? I can hardly wait."

"Yes, Arthur, I can see that." Captain Briggs smiled. "We'll pack tomorrow and set out for New York the day after. We are due to sail on or about the fifth of November, that is if the winds are favourable, and, of course, if I find myself a good crew."

"When are you going to do that?" Mrs Briggs asked. "When we're in New York?"

Briggs nodded. "While you take young Arthur

sightseeing. I'll have to miss out a bit of that as I'll be in the office seeing about the crew and the cargo and all sorts of other things."

"Will we be able to go shopping as well, Benjamin?" Mrs Briggs asked. "There are some things I want to take with me when we sail."

"Yes, I'm sure there will be enough time for that, my dear, but, as I said, I won't be able to be with you all the time."

"And will Mother be able to buy me some things before we sail?" Arthur asked. "I would like some new toy soldiers and a model boat and—"

"Arthur, didn't Mother tell you that you are not coming with us?"

"What? I'm not coming?"

"No, son, you'll be at school when we're away."

"But, Father, that's not fair!" the somewhat deflated Arthur said. "Last time you promised me that I could come with you the next time you sailed to England."

"I know that, son, but first of all, we're not going to England, but to Genoa and—"

"Where's Genoa?"

"It's in Italy, and secondly, I promised you that you could come on this next voyage if you were on vacation from school."

"B-but Father," the boy protested, his eyes beginning to fill with tears. "My friend Johnny Desmond's father's taking him out of school next week when he sails to South America. He's going to Brazil and Argentina. Johnny told me that his father said that he will learn more on board than sitting in a stuffy old classroom."

"I'm sorry, son, but your mother and I have discussed this

and we think that, despite what Johnny Desmond's father thinks, it will be best for you if you wait until the summer to sail again with me. And then you'll have the time to go on a really long voyage."

This last sentence did not seem to mollify Captain Briggs's oldest child. However, the young boy wiped his eyes with the back of his hand and asked, "And where am I going to stay and who is going to look after me?"

"You'll be staying here, Arthur, in this house," his mother replied, gently putting her hands on his shoulders. "And your grandma and Uncle James will move in and be here all the time we are away."

"But I don't like Uncle James very much, and besides, he smells."

"What do you mean, he smells?"

"That awful tobacco that he smokes. It's horrible."

"Well, Arthur, he won't be here all the time and—"

"And Grandma doesn't cook as well as you do, Mother. She often forgets that she's left what she's preparing on the stove and then it tastes burned."

"Well, I promise I'll tell her to be careful, but think, you are still coming with us to New York and—"

"And is Sophia going with you to this Genoa place?"

"Yes, Arthur. She doesn't have to go to school and besides, she's much too young for me to leave her behind with anyone. Remember, she's only two."

"Well, I still don't think it's fair and all the other boys in my class will think that I'm a softie because my father isn't taking me," Arthur said, sticking out his tongue at his father when his back was turned.

"Now, now, Arthur, that's enough," his mother said,

catching him. "Tomorrow we'll pack and when we're in New York I'll let you buy the biggest box of toy soldiers that F.A.O. Schwarz sells."

"Do you promise?"

For an answer, he received a strong hug from his mother as she whispered, "I promise," in his ear.

"And a model boat?" Arthur asked, exploiting the situation.

"Maybe, son, if your father agrees."

The next day in the Briggs household was one of organised chaos. It was not a new scene and the whole family was used to it. Clothes were wrapped and packed and Mrs Briggs's special kitchen utensils were put in boxes and labelled. As usual, the careful Sarah Briggs left notes dotted around the house as well as a page full of instructions for Arthur. Naturally, these included reminders about washing, homework and feeding the dog and cats. In addition, detailed lists of European addresses and instructions on how to look after young Arthur were written out for his grandmother and Uncle James, as well as the dates when the *Mary Celeste* was expected to make landfall in Lisbon and Genoa. Another page consisted of the names and addresses of the Winchester ship owners in New York, although, naturally, Benjamin and Sarah hoped that this information would never be needed. By the time the sun set that evening over Rose Cottage, Marion, Massachusetts, and all the various boxes, trunks and bags were tied up, locked and labelled, everyone in the Briggs family was exhausted.

They were even more so than expected because in the middle of their packing, neighbours kept popping in to wish them 'Bon voyage', while some gave them packages to send to their friends and family once the *Mary Celeste* had reached one of its destinations. Other neighbours also asked the captain and his wife whether they could buy a few things for them while they were in Genoa.

The following day, Captain Briggs, Sarah, Arthur and Sophia, together with Uncle James, who would bring Arthur home again, left Rose Cottage early in the morning. Taking a farewell look at their home and waving to a few of the neighbours who had got up early that October morning, they climbed into the carriage with their cabin trunks securely strapped onto the back rack and set off. From their home it rumbled and rattled over the stony route that would take them from Rose Cottage to the main road. Despite his disappointment about not sailing with his parents this time, Arthur was still excited at the prospect of the journey to New York and the fact that he had been promised a huge box of toy soldiers and a model boat.

"I want it to be like your *Mary Celeste*," he kept telling his father. "So whenever I play with it, I will think of you."

"That's nice, son," his mother said, ruffling his hair for the hundredth time that morning. "And I have packed a picture of you which I will hang up in our cabin so that I will think of you all the time."

"How long will it take us to get to New York, Father?" Arthur asked.

"Well, we're not in too much of a hurry, son, so I guess it will take us about five to seven days."

"And will we sleep in hotels and taverns like we did last time?"

"Yes, we'll probably stop in Providence, New London and New Haven before we arrive in New York."

"So that means we'll go through a few different states as well," Arthur added. "I'll be able to add them to the list of states I've already been through."

"Which ones are those?" his mother asked as she moved young Sophia to prevent her knocking her head on the inside frame of the carriage.

"Well, I went to New Hampshire and Vermont last summer, and yes I also went to New York and Maine and so now I'll be able to add some more."

"That's right, Arthur," Uncle James said. "You'll be able to add Connecticut and Rhode Island to your list. So with your home state of Massachusetts, you'll have been to seven altogether. That will be seven out of thirty-seven."

"Yes," his mother smiled. "Only another thirty to go."

"*Thirty!* I'll never do that."

"Oh, you never know what will happen in life, son. One day when you grow up you might move from Marion and the north-east to one of the newer states out west such as Nebraska or Nevada."

Arthur shook his head. He did not think that that was likely. Just as he was going to say so, his father said, "But come, let us first offer up a quick prayer to the Good Lord for our journey to New York and our voyage on the *Mary Celeste*."

The first two days' journey went quickly enough. They stayed in hotels in Providence and New London and Arthur was very happy to see the blue-grey waters of Long Island Sound out of the carriage window as they made their way west. It was some two hours after they had left New London that they encountered their first problem. As they were leaving a small village, their carriage lurched to the right and the three adults and their children all fell onto each other. Sophia woke up and started crying as she lay sprawled out over her mother.

"What happened?" Arthur asked.

"I think one of the back wheels has come off," Uncle James said. "I'll try and get out and have a look."

Pushing and heaving his portly frame over Briggs, he kicked the carriage door open with his foot and slid out onto the side of the road. He brushed the dust and bits of grass off his trousers and called out, "I'm right, Ben, one of the rear wheels has come off. The one on the right-hand side."

"Is it broken? Is the driver all right?" Briggs shouted back to him as he manoeuvred himself out of the carriage.

"Yes, the driver is all right. Just winded that's all. But now I can see what happened to the wheel. The locking pin came free. It's over here. Luckily it didn't snap. It's just bent a little."

By now, Briggs had joined Uncle James and the two of them were wondering how they and the driver would refit the wheel.

"You'll have to lift the carriage up," Sarah said, stating the obvious as she joined them, holding Sophia on her hip. "Will you be able to do that?"

"No," Briggs and Uncle James answered in unison. "It's much too heavy. We'll have to get some help."

Half an hour later, after flagging down a cart carrying some local farm labourers, they managed to lift up the rear end of the carriage and push the wheel back onto the axle.

"I'd go back to New London if I were you and have it fixed properly," the foreman said, a burly man who had been using some pretty ripe language to his workers, wiping his dirty hands on a piece of rag. "There's a good wheelwright just off the main road behind the Blue Ship saloon. Tell the owner, Jim Stanton, that I, Bob Halliday, sent you and he'll see you right. But take it carefully," Halliday added. "That locking pin don't look too good, so just be ready for that wheel to come off again."

"Yes, I can see what you mean," Briggs said, pointing to the mangled piece of metal. "But we've got no choice, have we?"

After a round of handshakes, "Thank yous" and wishes of "Good luck", the Briggs family and their driver set off back to New London at a very sedate pace.

"Well, at least ships don't have wheels that fall off, that is, apart from the steering wheel," Arthur said, "and I've never heard you speak of that before."

"That's right, Arthur," his father said, "but sails have been known to blow away in storms and have had to be replaced."

"Does that mean that the sailors have to climb aloft and repair them high up there?"

"Yes, Arthur, and it's not easy. I'm telling you, from personal experience, it is much easier to fix a carriage wheel down here on the ground than replace a torn sail up aloft in a high wind."

"Why, when did it happen to you? That is, when did you have to fix new sails to the yardarms?"

"Oh, quite a few years ago, Arthur," Briggs replied. "It was once when I was caught in a storm off the coast of Texas. During the war. The wind blew so much that it ripped off one of the topsails, which had to be replaced as soon as possible."

He then went on to tell his son about how long it had taken the crew to replace the sail and how one of the sailors had missed his footing and fallen into the sea.

"Were you able to save him?" Sarah and Arthur asked together.

"Oh, yes." Briggs smiled at the memory. "Luckily he was a good swimmer."

"Aren't all sailors?" Arthur asked.

"No, son. Quite a lot can't swim at all," he replied, leaning out of the carriage window to look at the rear wheel that they had replaced.

"Is the wheel and locking pin all right?" an anxious Sarah asked.

"From here it looks so, my dear. Let's pray that it gets us back to New London without falling off again."

Their prayers were answered and they found the wheelwright that Bob Halliday had told them about. He was a tall thickset man with bright eyes and tanned muscular arms. As soon as Briggs had shown him the problem and explained that Bob Halliday had helped them, the wheelwright told them to go over to the restaurant on the other side of the street and come back in an hour's time.

This they did, and while they were having a light meal of eggs, buns and coffee, Briggs and Sarah decided that because it would be late afternoon when they would be ready to move off again, they should spend another night in New London and set off early the following morning instead.

"It's lucky we've got time for that," Uncle James said. "Otherwise you would have had to hire a horse and rush off to New York on your own or send a telegraph."

The owner of the Madison Hotel was pleased to see them come back for another night and gave them the same rooms they'd had the previous night.

"You're lucky that wheel business didn't happen in the summer," he said, handing them the keys. "Now it's off season, but in the summer I can be booked up for weeks."

They left early the following morning, and with a few more shouts of "Good luck" and "Have a safe trip", they were on their way.

Luckily, they had no more difficulties en route, and after a pleasant stay in New Haven, they arrived in New York the following evening. There they stayed at the Hotel Washington as planned. This was one of the newest and most opulent hotels in town and Arthur seemed to spend most of his time with his head thrown back and his mouth wide open saying, "Look at that. Look over there," as he pointed to gilt fittings, large windows or gold-tasselled drapes.

The following morning after breakfast they left as planned and, while Briggs went to meet his friend Captain Morehouse, Sarah and Uncle James took the children to walk around the centre of New York. Here Mrs Briggs and Uncle James took baby Sophia and young Arthur to F.A.O. Schwarz to buy his promised box of toy soldiers and model ship.

"Doesn't she look like Father's ship? I mean, just look at those masts and sails," Arthur kept saying after he had walked out of the store proudly holding his new toy ship under his arm. "I hope mine sails as well on the pond back home as Father's real ship does."

"I'm sure she will, Arthur," his mother said. "And yes, she certainly does look like Father's ship. Now what are you going to call her?"

"*Mary Celeste II*," Arthur replied at once. "What else can I call her?"

Chapter 4
Captains Briggs and Morehouse and a new crew

"Hello, David," Briggs said, holding out his hand to the huge man standing in front of him. "How are you, and what have you been doing since we last met?"

"Me? Well, I've been quite a busy fella. I've been to London twice, once to Gibraltar, once to Genoa and I've got another trip to Lisbon planned soon."

Briggs looked at the man facing him and took in the swept back hair that was growing grey, the bushy somewhat unkempt beard and his fellow captain's friendly dark brown eyes. Morehouse was wearing a thick wool jacket and waistcoat, the latter adorned with the chain of a gold pocket watch that was stretched across his chest.

"Genoa, David, why there's a coincidence for you. That's where I'm off to in a few days. What's it like there? I've never been before."

"Wait a minute, Ben, let's go and sit down over there in that restaurant, the Ship and Anchor, and have us a meal and a drink. I hear they serve some pretty good fish there."

"No, no, David, I'd prefer meat. I'm sure we'll have more than enough fish once we're at sea. And Sarah will be cooking them and not—"

"What, you're taking your wife with you this time?"

"Yes, her and little Sophia. Sarah has never been to Genoa and she said she'd like to see the place. She says, since Christopher Columbus came from there and we are a seafaring family, she should really see it."

"Fair enough." Morehouse smiled. "That's a good enough reason. But how will she be if it gets stormy? And your little one?"

"I'm sure she'll be all right," Briggs replied. "She's been to sea before with me. The last time she was on board and a storm blew up, she remained very calm."

The two men entered the Ship and Anchor, looked around and then walked over to a table near the window from where they could watch over the busy harbour and sat down. They both ordered meat soup, beef and mixed vegetables and while Morehouse ordered a tankard of ale, Briggs asked for a large glass of lemon juice. While they were waiting for their meal, Morehouse started telling Briggs what he had been doing.

"Oh, Ben, you should see London. That sure is some town. The buildings there," he enthused, "they are so high class, so magnificent. Why, their Buckingham Palace where their Queen Victoria lives is so big. And you know, I was told, that what we common folk see from the street is really the back of it. It makes our White House in Washington seem somewhat small. And their Houses of Parliament and that clock tower thing, Big Ben. That's truly something special."

"Yes, I've seen pictures of it, David. And did you hear it sound the hour?"

"Did I? Of course I did. I waited for ten minutes so that I could hear it. What a sound. I'm telling you, my friend, we should have one of those here in America, say here in New York or near the White House and—"

"Ah, here is our food," Briggs interrupted as the waiter approached their table carrying a large tray. "Come, let's get tucked into this afore it gets cold."

The two men stopped talking for a while as they ate and drank until they were satisfied. Then at the same time, they both pushed their chairs back, rubbed their stomachs and resumed their conversation.

"No, no, you first, David," Briggs said. "Tell me about your next voyage. Where are you going and in what?"

"Well, my friend, my ship is going to be the *Dei Gratia.*"

"The *Dei Gratia*? Why, I've heard of her. She's a brig like the *Mary Celeste* I'm going to be sailing in a day or two."

"That's right, Ben," Morehouse said, signalling the waiter to bring over another round of ale. "She is nearly three hundred gross tons and over one hundred feet long"

"That's a bit larger than the *Mary Celeste.*"

"Right, and about twenty-five feet wide"

"Also like the *Mary Celeste*"

"Aye, also true," Briggs agreed. "She *is* like your new ship in many ways although I think that the *Dei Gratia* may be able to take a somewhat larger cargo. But no matter. So tell me, how old is she and where was she built?"

"Well, she is quite new," Morehouse replied. "In fact, she was built last year at Bear River in Nova Scotia."

"Ah, that's where the *Mary Celeste* comes from, Nova Scotia, from Spencer's Island, but she's now over ten years old. But that shouldn't be a problem – she was rebuilt last year here in New York."

"Who rebuilt her?"

Briggs shrugged. "I don't know. But what I do know is that they did a good job after she had run aground onto some rocks in Big Grace Bay. I can tell you that now she is a good clean ship and whoever did the rebuilding, didn't do a cheap patch up job either. Do you know, they even used copper sheeting to cover the hull? So as far as having problems on that score, I should be all right."

"Who was responsible for that? The Winchester Company?"

"Yes, they are my new employers and I'm also going to be a part shareholder in this ship. I'll be going to their offices first thing in the morning to see about my crew. I'll be seeing Mr Winchester in his office on Fifth Avenue."

"How many are you signing up?"

"I told him that I want to take seven men with me. I hope I get a good crew because you know what it's like when you've got a few lazy ones. They can turn a good voyage into a floating hell."

"Don't tell me, Ben," Morehouse said. "I remember on one of my voyages to London from New York, I had to put three men ashore in Boston who were almost mutinous in their laziness. I don't even know why they bothered to sign on."

"Maybe they saw it as a cheap way to get to London," Briggs suggested.

"Maybe, but I was sure glad to see the back of them. But tell me, do you know what cargo you'll be taking with you and to where?" Morehouse asked as he finished off his tankard of ale.

"We'll be taking seventeen hundred and one barrels of some sort of industrial alcohol, and the barrels will be of the red oak type. It's true that that won't be a full hold, but it should be enough to make a tidy profit. We'll be sailing to

Genoa and then we'll sail south down the Italian coast to Messina. There we should be able to pick up a new cargo but I don't know anything about that one yet."

"Oh, I like that," Morehouse grinned as he wiped the ale off his bushy moustache. "Seventeen hundred and one barrels. Not a drop more or a drop less. That's just like you, my friend. Being exact with the details."

"Well, you did ask, David."

"True, but alcohol. I hope your crew will be made up of teetotallers."

"Fear not, David. This alcohol isn't to be drunk. It's the industrial sort. You know, the heavier style stuff that'll be used in factories or breweries over there in Italy, but don't ask me how" – he shrugged – "because I sure don't know. All I know is that the barrels had better be sealed properly or we'll have problems with escaping fumes. Industrial alcohol has a fearful smell and it can catch fire just like that," Briggs added, snapping his fingers loudly.

The two men were silent for a moment as they imagined a burning ship in the middle of the ocean. They both knew that fire was the greatest danger that they could ever face while in the middle of sea. It was even worse than the threat of a mutinous crew.

"But tell me, Ben," Morehouse said, breaking the short heavy silence that had descended upon them.

"Is that all you're going to carry, alcohol? Aren't you going to have any ballast on board?"

"Of course I am. Thirty tons of rocks and stone. That should be enough if we encounter any storms. But tell me, my friend, something about the *Dei Gratia*, that is, apart from being similar to the *Mary Celeste*."

"Well, I'll also be carrying over seventeen barrels of alcohol like you and I'll also have almost five hundred cases of petroleum."

"Well, you shouldn't have any problems with that, David. Your ship is a bit bigger than mine and she's also newer, no?"

Morehouse nodded. "Aye, as I said, she's only one year."

"And when and where are you due to sail? And you're also sailing from New York?"

"Yes, on November fifteenth—"

"About ten days after me."

"That's right, and we are bound for somewhere in Italy. I'll know exactly where next week for all this petroleum."

"Yes, a dangerous cargo if you're not lucky."

"True, but I've carried stuff like this before so I'm not too worried. As usual, I'm more concerned about the crew," Morehouse added.

"How many will you have?"

"Seven or eight, I guess. I'll see in a few minutes when I go over to the owner's offices."

"David, before you go, which route are you going to take? The northerly or the southern?"

"The southerly one. I'm hoping that even though it might take a little longer, it will mean that I miss out on some of the storms that tend to blow further to the north at this time of year."

"Good idea. I was thinking the same. The fewer the storms, the better is what I always say, even if it does add a few days onto the voyage. At least that way, you stand a better chance of getting to your destination in one piece."

At this point, Captain Morehouse stood up, pushed his chair back and thrust out a hand.

"Well, good luck, Ben, but I've got to go. I've that meeting now with my owners about the crew and the supplies. So if I don't see you again before you sail, I hope all goes well with you, and no doubt we'll meet up somewhere in Europe."

"Aye, probably in London or Genoa or some such place," Briggs replied taking his friend's outstretched hand. "Goodbye, David, and I hope you too have a good voyage." After another hearty handshake, the two men separated.

Two hours later, Captain Benjamin Spooner Briggs was sitting in the spacious office of the J.H. Winchester and Co. shipping company. Standing or lounging against the walls outside in the corridor were seven men who were hoping to be signed on as crew.

"Well, Captain Briggs," James Winchester began. "I hope that you are looking forward to your first voyage with us."

"Yes, sir, after checking out the ship a few days ago I am. So too is my wife, as a matter of fact. And yes, we'll be taking our daughter, little Sophia with us as well. This will be the second time I'm sailing with such a young one on board, that is, apart from the time I took my son, Arthur with me when he was also very young."

"Isn't he going with you this time as well?"

Briggs shook his head. "No, sir. Not this time, to his great disappointment. He'll be at school, and his grandmother and his Uncle James will be looking after him while we're away. And," Briggs added, "he's not very pleased about that either."

"Because he won't be sailing with you?"

"Partly that, but also because his grandmother is a very strict disciplinarian. If you ever thought that I might sound a bit tough, you should see his grandmother. She could take on a Confederate cavalry regiment and beat them."

"I see," Winchester said. "But now, let's get down to brass tacks and see about your crew. The board of directors has decided that you'll take seven men with you. And, if that is all right with you, I suggest that we start choosing them now."

"Yes, sir. I saw them waiting in the corridor when I arrived. I think we should call in the man who may be first mate and see what he's like."

Winchester nodded and walked over to the door. He opened it and called out for Master Richardson to come into the office.

A medium-sized man with sleek back hair, sharp eyes, a dark thin moustache and an equally dark thick square beard entered. He was wearing a royal blue coat and holding a flat black hat as he came to a halt in front of James H. Winchester's cluttered desk.

"Yes, sir," he said in a rich voice. "Here I am, sir, at your service. Albert G. Richardson."

"Ah, good to see you again, Albert," Briggs said, standing up and shaking hands with the slimmer man. "Sit down and tell me what you have you been doing since we last sailed together?"

Richardson shrugged. "Nothing special, sir. When we parted company after our last voyage, I went back home to Stockton in Maine for a while and there I became a father for the first time. A boy, sir, and everybody says he looks like me."

"Ah yes, I'd heard that you had got yourself married."

"Oh yes, sir. That's right, sir. I married Mistress Frances Spates, y'know, Captain Winchester's wife's niece. And a fine lady she is too, if I may add."

"I'm sure she is, Albert," Briggs replied as he pulled a piece of paper out of his satchel and placed it on the desk in front of him. "Now, you know why I've asked for you to come here, don't you?"

"Yes, sir. I was told that you want me to serve you again as the first mate on your company's new ship, the *Mary Celeste*."

Briggs nodded. "That's right. Are you agreeable?"

Richardson nodded back. "Yes, sir. I was thinking that it's time I went back to sea. The money's beginning to run out at home and so it'll be good to be earning again, sir."

"And you'll be ready to set sail at the beginning of November, on the fifth if the winds are good, leaving from here in New York?"

"Yes, sir. That will be no problem at all."

Briggs rubbed his hands together and leaned over to shake Richardson's hand. "Good," he said. "Then if that is all right with Mr Winchester here, that's settled."

Briggs turned to look at his fellow ship owner. Winchester smiled, stood up and leaned over the desk to shake Richardson's hand. "Just make sure that all your papers are sorted out with my office," he said, "and Captain Briggs will see you in a few days."

The newly commissioned first mate of the *Mary Celeste* stood up and made a casual salute. "Yes, sir."

"Ah, and when you leave, please ask Master Andrew Gilling to step in, will you?"

Richardson nodded, took his hat and left the room. A moment later a tall, broad-shouldered man in a dark coat who, like Richardson, also held a flat black hat stepped into the room.

"Captain Briggs?"

"Right, and you are Master Andrew Gilling?"

"Yes, captain. The one and only, at least, as far as I know from around these parts although there are some Danish connections in my family. And who may I ask is this other gentleman?" he asked as he looked at Winchester.

"He is the owner of this company, Master Gilling, and also part-owner of the *Mary Celeste*."

"Oh, please accept my apologies, sir," Gilling said quickly. "I didn't mean to offend you."

"No offence taken." Winchester smiled. "Now where did you say you were from?"

"Sir, I'm a New Yorker through and through. Been one since I was born here twenty-five years ago."

Briggs looked at Gilling's ruddy, weatherworn face. If Briggs had been asked to guess his prospective second mate's age, he would have replied that the man facing him was at least thirty years old. Wind, waves and salt had certainly left their mark. "I see, so sit down and tell me how many of those twenty-five years you've been at sea."

"I'd say nearly most of them, captain. I first served as a deck hand on the *Leviathan* when we sailed to Rio de Janeiro, just before I turned fourteen. Then after that I sailed to London and Cadiz and a couple of times to France, that is, to Cherbourg, and I've sailed to some places that I've forgotten the names of in West Africa. So you see, captain, I've been busy."

"Yes, I can see that," Briggs replied, pulling another piece of paper out from a pile and placing it in front of him. "And I see here, from the company's records that you became a second mate two years ago."

"Yes, captain, that's right. And after this next voyage with you, I aim to get my certification to become a first mate."

"That's good to know. I always like to hear about crewmen trying to improve themselves. That way, they usually work hard and do a good job. So now tell me, Master Gilling, a little more about yourself. Are you married?"

The tall man looked down for a moment and fidgeted with the peak of his hat. "No, captain, I'm not married. I thought I was going to be last year when I was walking out with a young lady from upstate New York, but her family were against it. They thought that having a sailor who was merely a second mate for their precious Evangelina wasn't good enough, so they forced her to break off our relationship."

"I'm sorry to hear that."

"Yes, captain, and so was I. I really loved that woman, but I'm over it now and I've got myself a new young lady, a Mistress Josephine Lawrence."

"Well, I hope you have better luck with her, and, perhaps I should add, with her family as well. Now tell me, how do you get on with other crewmen on board?"

"Well enough, captain. I've never heard of any complaints, and I believe my record is clean with this company and with the other companies and captains I have worked with."

Briggs looked at the page in front of him. "Yes, your record is clean as you say, that is, apart from that one time when you were too drunk to do a good day's work in Cherbourg."

Gilling paused and looked down. Then he looked at Briggs straight in the eye and said, "Oh, yes, captain. I was celebrating my younger sister's wedding. I couldn't be there, seeing as it was here in New York and I was over there in France, so I did the next best thing. But that's the only time that has happened. God's honour it is, sir, getting too drunk to work, sir. Of that I can assure you."

"Yes, yes, I can see that. So, are you ready to become the second mate on my new ship, the *Mary Celeste*?"

"Yes, captain. And may I ask when we are due to sail and where we will be sailing to?"

Briggs gave him the necessary information and then Gilling left after saluting Briggs and Winchester.

"He sounds quite a character," Winchester said when he heard the door click. "I hope for your sake that what he said about getting drunk only once is true."

"Fear not, Mr Winchester," Briggs said. "I won't let any of the crew get drunk. I haven't done so up to now and I don't intend letting drunkenness on my ship start."

"Good, so let's see the Lorenzon brothers, who I believe are waiting outside."

Briggs stood up, walked over to the door and asked the two brothers to come into the office. On hearing their names, the two men sitting nearest the door stood up and followed Captain Briggs, the taller one coming first.

"You are Boz and Volkert Lorenzon, I believe," Briggs said to the two similar looking men facing him.

"*Ja*, yes, captain, we are. I am Boz," the bearded one answered, "and this is my brother, Volkert."

"I see, and where are you from?"

"From *Deutschland*, er, from Germany, captain. From Fohr. It's a small island in the North Sea near Denmark," Boz replied.

"I see Briggs," said and pointed to a couple of chairs.

"Please take a seat," he said and began asking them the usual questions about themselves, their sailing record and if they planned to return to New York with him or if they wished to remain in Europe once they arrived.

"*Nein, nein*, sir. I vish to stay in Europe at the end of ziss voyage," Volkert said in his heavy German accent, "to be with *mein* vife, Ilse, and *mein* little girl, Heidi, but *mein bruder* here vishes to come back to New York, *ja*?" he asked, turning to the younger-looking man."

"*Ja*," Boz nodded. "I want to live in America. You see *Ich bin mit fräulein* er, I am engaged to be married to an American *fräulein* after this voyage and the money you pay me will be used for our wedding."

"Congratulations," Briggs smiled. "And who is the lucky lady?"

"Her name is Emily, sir. Emily William. She comes from a family of sailors from Nantucket, and so they know about ships and sailing."

"Excellent," Briggs smiled. "So if you are good, you will save me looking for another sailor for the return crew, won't you?"

"*Ja*," Boz replied.

"And do you know the other two German crewmen waiting outside? That is, I presume that they are also German as I heard them talking when I came in."

"*Ja*," Boz replied. "That is, *Ich bin einmal mit ihm gesegelt*, er, I have sailed with Arian Martens before, but I don't know the other man. I sailed with Martens once to Cadiz. That was two years ago. He's a good man, Captain Briggs. He works hard."

"Hmm, that is good to know," Winchester said, looking at Briggs. "So, you two sign here and make sure that you are ready to leave on November the fourth or fifth, that is, if the winds are in our favour. Check with this office; probably late at night on the third is best. I'll post a notice on the door outside."

Volkert nodded and then asked, "Vat time, sir? Ve vould not want to miss your ship."

"Be here at this office at half past five in the morning," Winchester replied. "On time and with all your gear."

The two German seamen nodded and stood up. Briggs then checked the relevant documents, and they reached across the desk to shake hands with their new captain and left. As they did so, Arian Martens and Gottlieb Goodschaad entered.

Briggs looked at them closely as he had done with the other two Germans. He was a great believer in the axiom that first impressions counted. The fair-headed one of the pair, who Briggs was to learn was Arian Martens, stretched forward and thrust out his hand. Briggs shook it and felt its rough texture, the hand of a practiced sailor. The other man quickly followed suit and then they both sat down, as shown by Briggs and Winchester, in the chairs facing him.

"Good afternoon, gentlemen," Briggs began, looking at the list in front of him. "And which one of you is Arian Martens and who is Gottlieb Goodschaad?"

"I am Arian Martens," the smaller man said, "and this is *mein freund*, Gottlieb Goodschaad."

"And you are both from Germany, like the other two who I just spoke to?"

"*Ja, ja*," Martens replied. "*Ich bin* from Berlin and

Gottlieb is from Hamburg."

Briggs scribbled something down on the page in front of him and turned to Goodschaad.

"Master Goodschaad," he said, "or should I call you, Herr Goodschaad?"

"*Nein*, Master Goodschaad is good enough. I live here now in America, in New York, for several years and so everyone calls me master."

"I see," Briggs replied. "But Goodschaad is a Dutch name, no?"

The sailor nodded. "*Ja*, that is right. You see my family moved to Hamburg from Rotterdam a long time ago. We have been sailors for many years and one of my family was even a pirate in the Caribbean over one hundred years ago. The English hanged him, but all the others were good sailors. I hope I am as well. You see, I have been a sailor for nearly *twintig*, er, twenty years." And while saying that, he took out his papers from his coat and gave them to Briggs to inspect.

After he had done so, Briggs inspected Goodschaad more closely. He saw a dark-brown-haired, round-faced man, his face lined by his years at sea, and with a scar stretching from below his right eye across his cheek down to where it cut through his moustache making a small break above the man's upper lip. The German sailor's eyes were dark and piercing and somehow Briggs was not sure of him. But his papers were in order and there were no negative comments in them regarding his past behaviour. From the list of ships he had worked on it was clear that he was an experienced sailor and had sailed with the Winchester company in the past. *I cannot turn him down*, Briggs thought, *just because he looks a little threatening and one of his forebears was a pirate. That would be most un-Christian of me.* And thinking thus, he turned to face Arian Martens.

He too passed his papers over to Briggs who read through them quickly, made a few notes on the page in front of him and returned them to Martens. He then passed another document over to his two new crew members to sign which he had forgotten to give them earlier. They did so, Martens with a flourish and Goodschaad with a small round-lettered signature. They stood up, shook hands with Captain Briggs and James Winchester and left the office.

Winchester then turned to Briggs and said that he thought employing four foreigners would not be a problem Briggs agreed and said that he saw nothing wrong with this and that many of the merchant fleet crews were made up of foreigners, that is, non-Americans, and that this had not posed any major problems for him in the past. Hearing that, Winchester walked over to the office door, opened it and called for the last man waiting outside in the corridor, Edward William Head, a New Yorker from Brooklyn.

"Ah, Master Head, I've heard about you," Briggs said, as a slight, red-headed, smooth-faced man entered the room. As Briggs pointed to one of the chairs he noticed that the man was walking with a slight limp affecting his left foot.

"Has anything happened to your foot?" Briggs asked.

"No, sir. It's been like that for a long time. Since I had an accident on board the *Mary Elizabeth* in sixty-seven, sir. A box full of iron parts for an engine dropped on it and it's been like this ever since."

Briggs was about to say something, but Head continued, "But don't you worry, sir. It hasn't stopped me from sailing. See." He handed a document over to Briggs to prove it. "In all the past five years, the only time I've taken off was to marry my wife, Emma, and that was just two weeks, sir."

"Well that's good to hear, and I understand that," Briggs said, glancing at his list, "you want to sign on the *Mary Celeste* as the steward and cook."

"Yes, sir. I love cooking and I love travelling, so by sailing on ships like yours, this is a good way of doing both. And as I've just said, sir, I got married recently so I need the money." His eyes sparkled and it was clear that he was speaking the truth and not just saying this in order to get a job.

"So are you sure that this will be all right – being away from home for a couple of months or so? Is she happy that you want to go to sea so quickly after tying the knot?" Winchester asked. At the same time, Briggs was thinking the same, while aware that this time his own wife and baby daughter would be sailing with him.

"She doesn't mind, sir. She knew about my work before we got married, and besides, she has her own family close by in Brooklyn. But, I might add, I hope we're back before April, sir, because we're due to have a baby then."

"Congratulations, man, and good luck," Briggs said. "And yes, I do plan to be back here before then, as, apart from other things, I'm leaving my own son, Arthur, behind. I don't want to leave him for too long."

"Yes, sir. I see, sir."

This meeting ended soon after like Briggs's other meetings with the rest of his new crew. Briggs told Head as he had told the others to be by the ship at half-past five on the following morning and then Head signed the necessary papers and left after a vigorous handshake with his new captain.

The next official duty Briggs carried out was to sign the bills of lading, before he went to the New York Custom House where he had to complete various other forms. These included signing the Articles of Agreement and recording the final list of crewmen who were to sail with him. He also took the opportunity to write to his mother about the forthcoming voyage. Among other things he wrote:

I hope we shall have a pleasant voyage. Baby Sophia calls for Arthur constantly and wants to see him in the album, which by the way is a favourite book of hers. She knows your picture in both albums and points and says Gamma Bis [Grandmother Briggs]. She seems real smart and has got over her bad cold... We finished loading last night and shall leave on Tuesday morning if we don't get off tomorrow night, the Lord willing... hoping to be with you again in the early spring, with much love I am yours. Affectionately. Benj.

*

That night in his hotel room Briggs told his wife that he had written to her mother and that he had also spoken to each of the crew and was pleased with what he had heard and seen of them.

"They all look and sound all right," he said, "except this German-Dutch one, Gottlieb Goodschaad. I must tell you, my dear that the first time you'll see him, he'll look a bit frightening because of a long scar down the right side of his face. But don't you worry. From what he told me and from what I read in his papers he sounds experienced and he has a good record, so I decided to sign him on. There were one or two that I rejected but now I'm satisfied with who I've got."

"Well, I hope you are right, Ben," Sarah said. "Remember, I'm coming with you this time. Myself and baby Sophia."

"Fear not, my love," Briggs said, putting his arms around her. "There's no reason why we should have any trouble with this crew. The men look as good as any others I've sailed with. If we put our trust in them and in the Good Lord, then we should have a safe voyage."

"I'll say amen to that," Sarah said and after checking that Arthur was sound asleep, they went to bed for their penultimate night's sleep in New York.

Chapter 5
Last-minute details and downtown shopping

Sophia Briggs (left) and Sarah Briggs (right)

The following day, Briggs had decided with Sarah, would be one of business and pleasure. The business part would be spent at the Winchester company office and the harbour going over the last-minute details while the pleasure part would be going into the centre of New York with the family. Uncle James had declined to join them as he had planned to meet an old friend, a sergeant who had been in his old New York infantry regiment during the Civil War. So as a result, Briggs and his wife decided to have a farewell meal with Arthur in a fine restaurant.

"I'll meet you back here," Briggs said to his wife, kissing her and the children goodbye. "I should be finished by one o'clock, but if I am late, I'll send the office boy to tell you when I'll return."

Saying that, he walked briskly through the grey morning to J.H. Winchester's offices on Fifth Avenue. There he was promptly met by James Henry Winchester himself.

"How are you, Captain Briggs? Is everything ready?"

"Yes, I think so, sir. But I just want to check up on a few details here and then go over to the harbour to see again how the cargo has been loaded. I tend to be a bit pernickety about details like that even though I was there yesterday."

Winchester nodded and then asked, "So, captain, what do you need from this office?"

"I want to take my copies of the necessary charts, sir, especially the ones about the route from the harbour to the sea. I don't want to hit anything before I start, do I? After all, the *Mary Celeste* has done that before, no?"

"That's all right, captain. I'll ask my secretary to bring the charts here. Now is there anything else?"

"Yes, sir. I'd like to take a final look at the lists of supplies."

Winchester jotted this down and called for his assistant. "Take Captain Briggs to the office at the end of the corridor and give him everything, that is, all the paperwork and copies of the charts that he needs for the *Mary Celeste*."

"Now, sir?"

"Yes, now. He's sailing tomorrow to Genoa."

Just as Briggs was about to follow the assistant out, the ship owner called him back. "When you've finished with the paperwork, Briggs, and you've made your final check of the ship, come back up here to have a toast. We often do that when we send one of our ships on a long voyage."

Briggs saluted. "Yes, sir. But you know me. Just a wee dram. I don't really drink and I've arranged to meet my family downtown for lunch." And with that he followed the assistant to his office.

One hour later, Briggs and the assistant were on board the *Mary Celeste*. Briggs made as thorough an inspection as possible above decks before descending into the hold to see how the barrels of industrial alcohol were stored.

"We can't have them rolling around in a storm, can we?" he said half aloud as the assistant dutifully walked behind him in the gloomy hold making notes. The assistant was a young man, aged about twenty. He had smooth skin, a short brown beard and side whiskers, and his pale complexion indicated that even though he worked in a shipping company, he spent most of his time indoors. He looked keen and Briggs noted that he showed an intelligent interest in everything, both in the office and now on board the *Mary Celeste*.

The two men carefully made their way between the rows of stacked barrels as Briggs checked that they were stowed tightly in position and that they were all sealed. From time to time he would pull on a rope or two to see that they were sufficiently taut. At the same time he was aware of the smell of the fumes that the barrels were giving off as they lay there in the hold. But however close he pushed his nose to the sides of the barrels, especially the somewhat stained ones, he could not find any signs of leaks, either from the barrels themselves or on the floor below. A few barrels were stained around the bungholes, but when Briggs touched them, they felt as dry as a bone. *Probably from past use or from when the alcohol was poured into them*, he thought as he continued inspecting the other barrels.

"I suppose the fumes come through the wood," he said at last.

"Yes, captain," the assistant said. "It was the same on the last ship the company sent to London carrying alcohol like this. It also had this smell, but no-one could find a trace of a leak, and I assure you, we looked most thoroughly."

"Yes, I'm sure you did," Briggs replied. "But if you don't mind, I want to check up just one more time."

The two men repeated their inspection tour below, but as already noted, apart from a few stains on some of the barrels, they could find no hint of leaking alcohol.

"Well, to be on the safe side," Briggs said, "when the weather permits, I'll open the hatches from time to time to let any fumes out. That should cure any problem. Nothing that a good whiff of sea air won't clear up, eh? Now, let's go back to the office."

Briggs remained in the office for another hour finishing off the paperwork and then told Winchester that he would be leaving to meet his wife and children downtown.

"We're going to have a good meal and perhaps buy another toy or two for my son as compensation for not sailing with me this time," Briggs said.

"Ah, but before you go, I just remembered something. I

want you to look at these papers I received from the Atlantic Mutual, our insurance company. I picked them up this morning from the offices of the United States Shipping Commissioner."

He slid the papers over the desk and Briggs noted that the ship and her cargo were insured for about fifty thousand dollars.

"Is that a fair sum?" Briggs asked.

Winchester nodded. "Yes, I think so. Anyway, I hope we won't have to worry about that, Captain Briggs. I also hope these papers prove to be just another example of the rules and regulations that the authorities and the insurance companies impose upon us poor seafarers and that we don't really need."

Briggs smiled back. He did not like dealing with all the necessary documentation, but he knew that he had no choice. "Yes," he added. "I often leave the finances at home to my wife. She's a very capable woman and has more than once spotted a mistake that I'd overlooked."

"Ah, talking of family," Winchester asked, "are you pleased with the cabin you'll be using with your wife? Is there enough storage space? We've installed another bed for your wife. I know from my own experience that the ladies tend to bring more on board than their husbands. The last time my wife travelled with me, about four months ago in the summer, she brought enough with her to fill another hold if we had had one."

Briggs replied that he was pleased with his cabin, its size and its décor, and the two men shook hands.

"Will you be coming down to the harbour tomorrow morning to see us off?" Briggs asked, picking up his dark blue captain's cap and heavy winter coat of the same colour.

"Of course, I will, captain." Winchester smiled. "I always make a point of seeing the company's ships off before they sail if I can. Especially if it is a long voyage like the one you are going to make. It makes me feel safer to see that everything is as ready as it should be."

"Good, then I'll see you tomorrow morning. I'll be down at the harbour at six and I hope all the crew will be there on time. I told them to be there for half-past five just to be on the safe side."

Winchester nodded in agreement. "And I think you've got a good crew, and I suspect by the time you reach Genoa you'll be speaking fluent German."

Briggs smiled. "Yes, or their English will improve."

"So, Captain Briggs, I think that we have seen to everything that needs seeing to," Winchester said looking once again at one of his checklists. "Do you have any more questions?"

"Yes, sir."

"Hmm, there always is. What?"

"There is just one thing I'd like to ask you about the lifeboats. One of them appears to have a hole in it near the stern. It looks like the planking was pushed in when they loaded it on board. Will there be time to repair it before we leave?"

"I doubt it, but where is the hole exactly? Above the waterline?"

"That's a bit of a difficult question to answer, sir, for it depends on how many people will be in it, if it comes to that."

"But there is a second lifeboat, and if necessary, you'll be carrying some spare wood with you, so you'll be able to repair it at the beginning of the voyage. Also, if you have to use the lifeboats, which I obviously hope not, then you'll load most of the people or even all of you onto the other one, yes? That means that the one with the hole in it will be lighter."

"Yes, sir, I had thought of that, and from what I saw, it shouldn't be so hard to jury-rig some sort of repair during our first days out at sea."

"That's right, captain, but let's pray that you won't need the lifeboats anyway."

"Yes, sir. I most heartily agree with you there."

"Good," Winchester said, standing up. "So on that optimistic note, let's wish for a safe and successful voyage."

And with a small toast, handshakes, pats on the back and an agreement to meet the following morning, Briggs left the office. He hurried back to the hotel and was pleased to be there on time. He told Sarah that everything had gone smoothly, both in the office and on board. "We should have a good voyage, I think," he added, "that is, if the weather doesn't become too stormy. We will be sailing across the North Atlantic in the winter so it's very possible we'll meet a storm or two even if we will be using the southerly route."

"Yes, I know that, my dear, and don't forget, I've sailed with you in stormy weather before."

"Yes, but this time we'll have little Sophia with us."

"Don't you worry about her, Ben. If you look after the ship, I'll make sure Sophia is well looked after even if it becomes stormy."

Briggs shrugged. "I just thought that I'd mention it in case you had changed your mind and had decided not to come. But you know, I'm very happy that you're coming on this voyage, and I know young Arthur here would also have been very happy to come."

As he said this, Briggs could see his son looking up at his mother hoping that she would change her mind.

Mrs Briggs looked down lovingly at her son, ruffled his hair for the hundredth time that day and said, "I'm sorry to disappoint you, Arthur, but we are going to join your father this time. But fear not, we'll all be together again and then you'll be able to sail with your father next summer when school is over and the weather is better." She pulled the stocky seven-year-old close to her, ruffled his hair yet again and gave him a big hug.

"So," Briggs said. "If everyone's ready, let's go downtown and buy Arthur another set of soldiers and have a good meal. I'm feeling hungry and could happily finish off a large piece of beef or something of that sort."

"And I want some meat pies," Arthur said. "That and lots of French-fried potatoes."

Half an hour later found the Briggs family and Uncle James in the centre of New York's shopping area.

"Pa, everything is so big here and the buildings are so tall," Arthur said, looking up and gawping at the tall buildings surrounding Union Square. Look" – he pointed – "that one over there is over six stories high, and it's got a very high pointed roof on top. Just imagine if we had buildings like that at home."

"Yes, but then our town wouldn't be like it is, right? But come, let's go to Macy's and buy you some more soldiers. I know you say that you never have enough of them."

They set off and began to make their way to Central Park. "Pa, is that a zoo over there?" Arthur asked, pointing to a large notice on the right.

"Yes, do you want to go there before we go to Macy's?"

"Yes, yes, and do they have lions and tigers there?"

"I don't know," Briggs replied. "Mother, do they have lions and tigers there?"

"I'm not sure, but I know they have bears, monkeys and all sorts of fish and some peacocks."

Ten minutes later, the Briggs family were to be found wandering around the zoo, which was officially called the Menagerie. As soon as little Sophia saw the bear rear up on its hind legs, she burst into tears and wouldn't stop crying until they showed her the monkeys. Fortunately their swinging around in their huge cage distracted her enough to cause her to smile and clap her hands with joy instead. After that they continued on their way to Macy's, where they headed for the toy department. For Arthur this was paradise.

"Oh, Ma, there's so much here I don't know what to choose," he said, his eyes darting from one dramatic display to another. "Just imagine if I was rich and could buy all these toys, I'd be so happy."

"Well, son, go over there and pick out which box of soldiers you want." Mrs Briggs smiled. "Perhaps you'll buy some with blue jackets and tall hats this time so you can have two different armies."

Arthur walked over to where the boxes of toy soldiers were displayed and stood there open-mouthed.

"Oh, it's so hard to choose," he kept saying aloud. "I don't know what I want."

"Well do you want more of those English soldiers in their red tunics or those blue American Civil War ones – the Union ones?" his father asked.

Arthur hesitated. "I'll take the Union ones this time," he said at last. "I like their dark blue uniforms and their long rifles and bayonets."

From here they moved over to a display of large model ships. It contained models of single sailed Viking ships, Spanish galleons and all sorts of other square-sailed ships.

"Pa," Arthur said pointing to an impressive sailing ship with two masts and several square and triangular sails. "I think this one looks like your new ship. One day when I'm older I'm going to make a model of a ship like your *Mary Celeste*, but in the meanwhile I'll play with the one you bought me already and that will remind me of you when you're away."

"That's a nice thought," Briggs said and looked at the display more carefully. "Ah, here's one that looks even more like the *Mary Celeste*." He pointed out another model. "Yes, that really does look like my new ship."

Arthur nodded happily. This stay in New York was turning out to be even better than he had hoped. Buying toys, going out for a meal *and* going to the harbour to see his father's ship. Apart from not joining his family for the voyage, what more could he ask for? But there was one thing he did not like about this huge city.

"New York is so smelly," Arthur said, holding his nose. "It's not like this at home."

"That's because of all the horses and their droppings," his father said. "You've always got to be careful walking around big cities. They're all like this. When I was in London, Paris and Berlin they were all the same. Horses and their smells."

Sometime later as they continued their walk and were strolling alongside the Hudson River, Arthur stopped admiring the many boats he saw and cried out, "Look at that bridge over there! Isn't it big?"

"That's right, son. That's the High Bridge. It's the oldest bridge here in the city, and look over there, downstream. Can you see those two tall towers they're building on either side of the river?"

Arthur strained his eyes. "Yes, they're very big. Are they going to be part of a bridge one day?"

"Yes, Arthur. One day those towers will be part of the new Brooklyn Bridge, but come, let's get moving. First I want to show you my ship and then we'll go and eat. I must say that I'm very hungry and I'm sure that you and your mother are, so let's go quickly."

An hour and a half later, the Briggs family climbed up the gangplank onto the deck of the *Mary Celeste*. First mate Albert Richardson was there to greet them.

"What are you doing here. Albert?" Briggs asked. "We don't sail until tomorrow."

"I know that, captain, but I just wanted to make sure that my cabin was all right and that everything on board, above deck and in the hold, was shipshape."

"Very commendable," Briggs commented. "And are you going to sleep here in your cabin tonight?"

"Yes, captain, that is, if you have no objections. I'll stay on watch till midnight, if that's all right with you."

Briggs did not object and since Sarah said that she wanted to sit down, Briggs took Arthur for a tour of the *Mary Celeste*.

"And is this where you and Ma and Sophia will be sleeping?" Arthur asked as he stepped into the small cabin near the bow end of the ship.

"Yes, Arthur," Briggs replied and added, "and when I take you with me next summer, you will sleep in this little cabin next door. At the moment it's full of food and supplies, but don't worry, by July it'll be ready for you."

Arthur smiled in anticipation of this summer vacation voyage and then asked if he could go down into the hold. "Uncle James says that it's full of alcohol."

"That's right, but not the sort you drink. It's for factories in Italy."

"Why, what are they going to do with it? You always say, Father, that drinking alcohol leads to sin."

"I know that, son, but this alcohol is going to be used for cleaning liquids and pharmaceuticals, not drinking."

"What are pharmaceuticals?"

"Drugs, Arthur," his mother replied. "Drugs and medicines. So you see, your father will be taking cargo to Italy which will help sick people. Now isn't that good of him?"

Arthur nodded and they finished their tour of inspection, then from the harbour they continued on their way to the restaurant. They were all very hungry and were very happy half an hour later to face a tasty meal. This consisted of vegetable soup, roast beef and vegetables, followed by apple pie and cream. Briggs and Uncle James washed theirs down with beer while Sarah and the children drank some apple juice.

It was a very happy but tired family that returned to the Hotel Washington that night. There, Briggs and Sarah tucked the children into bed. Sophia fell asleep immediately, but Arthur was still so excited after his day in New York. As Briggs sat on the side of his bed, he told his son what they would do together after he returned from the coming voyage. But in the end, despite Arthur's attempts to fight off sleep, the seven-year-old boy slipped into the arms of Morpheus and was soon gently snoring.

Briggs pulled the blanket up to the boy's chin, bent over and kissed his forehead. Mrs Briggs followed suit, leaving their son dreaming about himself commanding the *Mary Celeste* under full sail. In his dream she was ploughing through the North Atlantic waves, flags flying from the tops of her masts as the coast of Italy came in sight. He, Captain Arthur Briggs, was standing proudly on the top deck by the steering wheel pointing the beautiful brigantine to Genoa and the future.

While their children were asleep in the room next door, Captain Benjamin Briggs and his wife undressed and got into bed. There they talked about the *Mary Celeste*, her voyage, her new and untried crew and their own future plans. Sarah Briggs's last words that night were, come what may, they must make sure they kept their promise to Arthur and let him join his father for a voyage on the *Mary Celeste* the following summer.

Chapter 6

The *Mary Celeste* prepares to leave New York

Early the next morning, Sarah Briggs entered Arthur's room and tapped the sleeping boy on the shoulder. "Come on sleepyhead, time to get up and go."

"To go where?" He opened his eyes, yawned and pulled himself up in bed.

"Downstairs for breakfast, of course."

"But it's so early, Ma, and look, it's still dark outside."

"I know that, son, but you've got a long day ahead of you," she said pulling the bedclothes down. "Remember, Uncle James is taking you home today. You've got school next week and I promised your teachers that you would be back by then."

Half an hour later the Briggs family were sitting down in the hotel dining room having their breakfast. The night before, Briggs had notified the hotel that he and his family would be wanting a very early breakfast. At first, the hotel manager was not too pleased about this, but after Briggs had agreed to pay a few extra dollars this had been arranged. As soon as he finished eating, or rather wolfing his food down, Arthur asked permission to be excused and then ran upstairs to spread his new toy soldiers over the quilt in his bedroom for a final battle before packing them away in their boxes. As he was directing the final stages of the battle he heard his mother call out for him to come downstairs to the lobby. A carriage was waiting to take them and their luggage down to the harbour. Hearing this, Arthur threw his troops into their boxes and ran downstairs. This time it was a more subdued young boy who now realised that he would soon be separated from his parents.

"Do you have to go?" he asked for the hundredth time that morning, hugging his mother. "Can't someone else take the *Mary Celeste* to Italy?"

"No, Arthur," his father replied, gently pulling his son over to him. "This time it has to be me, and besides, we've been through all this before, haven't we?"

Arthur nodded. Deep down he knew that he had no choice.

"And now," Briggs said. "Before leaving, we are going to church to pray that we have a safe and successful voyage."

Sarah nodded in approval. "Which church do you have in mind, Ben?"

"Trinity, my love. It's not far from here. It's where Broadway and Wall Street meet. I've been there before so I know the way."

They arrived at the impressive Gothic Revival building some ten minutes later and all young Arthur could say as he gawped open-mouthed at the tall spire atop the square tower at one end of the church was, "Wow, it's so tall. It must be the tallest building in America."

"It was, once," Uncle James said, "and it's still the tallest building in New York."

They went inside and stopped to stand at the back for a few minutes to get used to the semi-darkness. This was relieved by the weak early morning, coloured light streaming in from the huge stained-glass windows at the far end. Briggs then directed his family to a pew halfway down the length of the building and there they prayed for a safe outward voyage and a speedy return home to America. As they walked out, Briggs took his son's hand and led him to the cemetery outside. They stopped after a few moments and faced a large oblong white marble memorial topped with a white pyramidal structure. After reading the inscription that had been carved on its base, Arthur asked, "Who is this Alexander Hamilton, Pa? What did he do? Why does he have such a huge grave?"

"He was one of the founders of this country, son, and he was killed by a rival politician nearly seventy years ago," Briggs explained. "You see, there was this other politician called Aaron Burr and he and Hamilton had a big argument and then they fought a duel."

"With swords? Like in that picture that I've got in my book at home?"

"No, Arthur, with pistols. And so you see, this Aaron Burr shot and wounded Hamilton, who died the next day. So what do you learn from this? You learn that you must always try and reason with people even if you don't like them. Violence is never the answer. Remember that when you are in school playing with your friends. You must never hit or hurt anyone else. As Jesus said in the Sermon on the Mount, 'Turn the other cheek'. Remember, son, we are all God's creatures."

"But what did Hamilton and Burr argue about, Pa?"

"Oh, the usual things that politicians fight about: money and power. The two men hated each other and Burr was insulted when Hamilton wrote an article saying that he, Burr, was not the right man to have an important job in New York."

"Yes, but—"

"Come, everybody," said Sarah, who had by now joined them. "Let's return to the hotel. Enough of sad stories for today. Today we should be happy. We're going on a sea voyage, which, if the weather is nice, should be fun."

They returned to their hotel and after a quick midday meal, went for a gentle stroll around the neighbourhood, where Briggs pointed out some of the more interesting buildings to his wife and son.

"Hmm, I'm going to miss my daily walk when we're on board," Sarah said.

"Yes, so am I," Briggs admitted. "Strolling around the deck is not quite the same."

Arthur, of course, saw this as an opportunity to try and persuade his parents once again not to leave him behind.

"So stay behind and let someone else sail your ship to this Genoa place. Then you'll be able to stroll here at home."

"You don't give up, do you?" Briggs smiled. "But fear not, son, we'll have lots of opportunities when we come back to go out for a stroll, just you see."

Then after buying Arthur some candies from a sidewalk stand, they walked back to the hotel. There they all climbed aboard the carriage and half an hour later they were standing at the foot of the gangplank of the *Mary Celeste*. They went aboard and Briggs introduced his wife, children and Uncle James to the first mate, Albert Richardson, and to Edward Head, the cook, who were already standing on the foredeck.

"Is everything all right," Briggs asked as he shook their hands.

"Yes, captain. I was just checking out a few things," Richardson said. "Everything, except that hole in the small lifeboat, is just shipshape."

"Aye, and I wanted to see the galley and how the food and other things have been stored," Head added.

"Have you met the rest of the crew?" Briggs asked.

"Yes," Richardson replied, pointing to a small building not far away. "They're buying some last-minute things, tobacco and pipes. Look, they're coming over to us now. They must have seen you come aboard, cap'n."

A few minutes later, the rest of the crew had joined them and Briggs realised that the time had come to set sail. This was preceded by yet another round of hugs and kisses between Arthur and his parents and Uncle James. Briggs and Sarah promised to write letters as soon as they reached Genoa and then the Briggs family split into two parts: those who were off for the high seas and those who would return to the family home at Rose Cottage, Marion, Massachusetts.

*

At the same time that a tear-stained mother, son and small daughter were saying goodbye to each other, on the other side of the harbour, Captain David Reed Morehouse was busy interviewing men to crew the *Dei Gratia*. He was using the New York office of his ship owner, George F. Miller of Nova Scotia. His ship was due to sail on fifteenth of November, ten days after the *Mary Celeste* had left port. The *Dei Gratia* was to journey to Gibraltar where Morehouse would receive further instructions about more cargoes and about which route he should use to return to New York. In the meanwhile, he would be carrying over seventeen hundred barrels of petroleum, a cargo he was not happy taking due to its inflammable nature. However, he knew that even though he was the captain of a merchant ship, he had no say in what he was taking. His job was to deliver the cargo and make sure that the company's ship and crew returned safely to port.

As he was thinking about this next transatlantic voyage and checking through a list of supplies, he heard a knock on the door. Calling out, "Come in," Morehouse expected to see the weather-beaten face of his employer, Mr Miller. But it was Oliver Deveau, the *Dei Gratia*'s first mate.

"Ah, Mr Oliver Deveau, is it not? Please sit down."

"Yes, captain," the man answered, pulling up a chair. "I believe you wished to see me."

"That's right. I'm busy signing up my new crew for the company's ship the *Dei Gratia* and I was thinking of taking you on."

"As first mate, captain? Like I've been on my last voyages."

"Yes, Mr Deveau, as first mate. Would that be agreeable with you?"

"Yes, captain. That's the job that I was hoping you would offer me."

"Even though you've sailed before as a captain, yourself?"

"Yes, sir, but let's just say, unofficially."

"I see. You mean that even though you were in command, you weren't paid for being so?"

"Yes, captain. That's about the size of it. However, it is true to say that even though I've spent many years at sea, I have never received my Master's Certificate. But fear not, I believe my years of experience will overcome any lack of a piece of paper, sir."

On hearing this, Morehouse looked at the man more carefully. He was impressed by his honesty. He noticed that Deveau did not have a commanding physique – the sort that makes other men immediately respect you. However, his sharp eyes, square black beard and lined face showed that he was a man who you did not argue with. He was wearing a dark brown winter coat over a deep blue jacket and trousers, and Morehouse could see that his white shirt was clean. In addition, Morehouse noted, Deveau's shoes were highly polished. *This is a man who looks after himself*, Morehouse thought. He asked, "Mr Deveau, how old are you?"

Deveau told him and Morehouse smiled. "Why, you are nearly one year older than me. So why did you never receive your Master's Certificate?"

The future first mate of the *Dei Gratia* shrugged. "I don't know really. It's just one of those things, I guess. I suppose one day I'll get round to it, but in the meanwhile, I'm enjoying being first mate." He paused for a few moments. "Perhaps I like being in the middle. On the one hand I'm not just a simple sailor taking orders, and on the other, I don't have to shoulder all the responsibility that a captain like you does."

Morehouse liked the honesty of his answer. "And will you be wanting to return here with me on the *Dei Gratia*?"

"Yes, captain. I will want to get back here as quickly as possible. You see, I recently had a baby son and I don't want to miss seeing him grow up. I mean, that's what my own father did with me. He was always away at sea and I hardly saw him until I was ten years old when he had an accident and he couldn't sail anymore."

"What happened to him?"

"Some piece of iron machinery fell on his shoulder and crushed his arm when they were loading his ship. He couldn't work after that so the company paid him off with a few dollars as compensation and that was the end of his sailing days."

"So what did he do after that? I mean, he still had to earn his living, didn't he?"

"Yes, captain. So he bought a tobacconist's shop near the harbour where we lived in Nova Scotia. This way he was able to make enough to live on and at the same time he stayed in touch with the sailors who came into his shop. But anyway, captain, enough about me and my family. Please could you tell me about the *Dei Gratia*, what will be in the hold and where we'll be sailing to?"

Morehouse told him about the cargo and the forthcoming voyage and then for the next ten minutes they talked about their past experiences at sea. Just as Deveau was going to tell his new captain about a particularly long, drawn-out storm he had survived in the Bay of Biscay, there was a knock on the door.

"Come in," Morehouse called, and John Wright stuck his tousled head around the door.

"Are you Captain Morehouse?" he asked, stepping into the office.

"Yes, and you are?"

"John Wright, captain. I heard you were looking for a second mate for your next voyage."

"You heard right," Morehouse said. "And it's good that you are both here so if I sign you on, then you can meet your first mate here, Mr Oliver Deveau." The two men shook hands, exchanged a few words and then Deveau left, his sea story unfinished.

As Wright sat down where Deveau had been a few minutes earlier, Morehouse compared the two men. Whereas the slight yet confident Deveau had easily made his presence known, Wright seemed to have an apologetic air about him despite being much larger. However, Morehouse noted that he looked sharp and intelligent and that he too wore clothes that were in good condition, not frayed or worn out. He had fine grey-blond hair, narrow cheeks and a well-clipped moustache. He was not bearded.

"Have you been a second mate before?" Morehouse asked.

"Yes, captain. Several times, and after this voyage I'm planning to get my papers so I can sail as a first mate."

"And have you crossed the Atlantic before?"

"Yes, captain, at least a dozen times, and my last few voyages were as a second mate on merchant ships like the *Dei Gratia*."

"How do you know about the *Dei Gratia*?" Morehouse asked.

Wright tapped the side of his nose. "I try to keep abreast of what is happening in the harbour, captain. I'm hoping to get married soon, perhaps after this voyage, and so I need to save up as much as I can and keep working all the time. I don't like hanging around the harbour watching other fellows work and myself doing nothing."

Morehouse was surprised by this answer. Despite his quiet air, this man was determined to better himself. "So you are an ambitious fellow?"

"Yes, sir, and here are my papers. You'll see that I have a good record. I'm sure you'll be pleased with me."

All in all, Morehouse was quite surprised by the way Wright spoke.

"And will you be wanting to return with me to New York?"

"Yes, captain. As I said, I'm hoping to get married by the summer and my young lady lives here in the city. So as for the return journey, most certainly yes, that is, if you are pleased with me."

Morehouse nodded and wrote a few notes down on the paper in front of him. They then talked a little about Wright's past career and the future voyage. The result was that ten minutes later the new second mate of the *Dei Gratia* left the office with a document confirming his new appointment. Then each in turn, the other crewmen, John Johnson, Augustus Anderson and Charles Lund came into the office and were interviewed and taken on by Morehouse. As with Deveau and Wright, they were each told to be ready to sail from New York on the fifteenth of November. None of the crew, to Morehouse's surprise, made any remark about how there would be only six of them on the *Dei Gratia*. He assumed that the men knew that the ship owners always liked to keep the number of crewmen down so that they would have to pay fewer expenses. However, this also meant that the crew would have to work hard, especially if they ran into any squalls or storms, and that there would be few opportunities for rest during the voyage. Morehouse had talked about this with Briggs, who told him that the crew for his own upcoming voyage on the *Mary Celeste* would number only eight men, including himself.

By the time that Charles Lund, the last member of the crew, had been interviewed, Morehouse was feeling satisfied.

He sat back in his chair and took out a bottle of rum he had in his bag and gulped down a good swallow. *I seem to have a good bunch of men this time*, he thought, even though Johnson, who originally came from Russia, spoke very poor English. *But at least his papers are good and he seems to know his way around a ship. Well, I hope he and the others are better than the last crew I had. Bunch of ignorant ne'er-do-wells*, he remembered. *I had to be on the ball for the whole voyage and that first mate, Harrison, was a useless idiot, especially when we were sailing off the coast of Portugal in that storm. I'm glad I sacked the lot of them as soon as we went ashore. Now I think I have learned from that experience and if I'm lucky I'll be in for an easier time. That Deveau and Wright seem to know what they're doing, and if so, this next voyage should be as easy as sliding down the ratlines on a calm day.*

Chapter 7
The voyage of the *Mary Celeste* begins

19th Century painting of New York Harbour

The early morning of 5 November 1872 found Captain Briggs and first mate, Richardson, leaning over the side rail on the top deck of the *Mary Celeste*. They were looking at the familiar buildings and harbour installations of New York as they sailed past, exploiting the fast wind which blew under the heavy grey sky.

"I don't like the look of those clouds, captain," Richardson said. "They look pretty threatening to me. Not a good way to start out on a voyage is what I say."

"Yes, I agree with you, but perhaps they'll clear once we've left the coast behind. I know that's happened more than once. And don't voice your feelings to Mrs Briggs, all right?"

"Yes, captain, but where is she at the moment?"

"She's in our cabin with my little girl making it ready for the voyage. Unpacking clothes and preparing my daughter's cot and taking out her dolls and things."

"I see, but look over there, captain. There's the *Osprey*, she's setting off as well. I was talking to her first mate yesterday and they're also bound for Europe. To London, he told me."

"What are they carrying?"

"Like us, captain. Barrels of industrial alcohol. Two thousand five hundred of them. But talking about barrels, I think I'll go below and just check once more to make sure ours are all lashed down tightly. We don't want that lot rolling around if a storm breaks out, and I must confess, captain, I don't like the look of that sky at all."

At this point, Richardson went below and called for the second mate, Gilling, and Arian Martens to join him in the hold. Twenty minutes later, Richardson came back on deck to find Briggs looking concerned.

"Are the barrels all safely stowed, Richardson?"

"Yes, captain, but you look worried."

"I am. The clouds are worse and the wind has got stronger since you went below. Now what I want you to do is to have the rest of the sails unfurled and we'll see if we can beat this storm and make for the channel. The quicker we get away, the better."

"Yes, captain." Richardson wheeled around to tell the crew to unfurl the sails and see if they could benefit from the rising wind and escape any possible oncoming storm.

But Briggs's plans came to naught. The strong winds frustrated them and soon he found himself beaten back by a powerful headwind. It was so forceful that in the end the *Mary Celeste* was forced to anchor off Staten Island and wait for the storm to blow itself out.

"How long are we going to have to wait here, my dear?" Sarah asked her husband. She was carrying little Sophia and the pair of them were wearing heavy winter coats and thick woolly hats and mittens. Sophia kept putting her covered hands in front of her face to protect herself from the cold winds.

Briggs shook his head. "I don't have an answer for that, my dear. We'll just have to wait patiently, that's all. This has happened to me before and there's nothing you can do about it but pray. Just ride out the storm and pray that there's nothing worse awaiting us out on the open sea these next few weeks."

"Yes, I guess you're right, Ben, but it's still annoying, isn't it? We've got a fine ship and a good crew, no? and now we're stuck here waiting around Staten Island. It just doesn't seem right."

"Well, let's just hope that it's the only bad luck that we have on this voyage. I'd prefer that, if we are going to have any, we have it now and be done with it."

Sarah nodded and then took her daughter below to their cabin. There they took off their hats, heavy coats and mittens before they moved over to the portholes to look at the wintry scene outside. She ran her fingers gently through her daughter's curly hair and then sat down to look at the latest edition of *The New York Times*, which she had bought that morning before coming on board. A few minutes later her husband came to join her. He too removed his cap and coat and sat down next to his wife.

"I've left Richardson and Martens up on deck by the wheel," he said. "If there's any news about the storm, they'll let me know."

Sarah nodded and then asked, "Who do you think is going to win the election, my dear? Grant or Greeley?"

"Sarah, I think it's going to be Grant. At least, that's what all the papers are predicting. I mean, he's worked hard to rebuild the economy after the war and he's even begun to take in black people to work for the government. Now that's a first, isn't it?"

"I agree, my dear, but Greeley has promised to fight corruption and that's also important."

"I know, but we're going to have to wait until we get to Europe to see who our next president will be," Briggs said. "More of Grant or have a new broom with Mr Horace Greeley."

Soon after that, an impatient Captain Briggs put his cap and coat on again, kissed his wife and daughter and then went back up on deck. Sarah took the opportunity to write a letter to her mother-in-law, which she would mail to her from the post office on Staten Island.

Dear Mother Briggs,

Probably you will be a little surprised to receive a letter with this date, but instead of proceeding to sea when we came out Tuesday morning, we were forced to anchor about a mile or so from the city. This was because there was a very stormy headwind and B. said it looked so thick and nasty ahead we would not gain much if we were beating and banging about at sea.

She added some details about Sophia and how she was enjoying herself in her cabin and about a meal that they had eaten which had included some rather sour baked apples. She added an affectionate message for Arthur and hoped that he would behave himself and do well in school. Although she could not know this, this was to be the last letter that would be sent from the *Mary Celeste*.

The storm took two days to blow over before the weather brightened up again, and in the meanwhile everyone on board – both the Briggs family and the crew – were becoming progressively more impatient. Even little Sophia kept asking when they would start sailing again. "I don't like waiting here," she pouted at her mother as she held her favourite dolly. "It's not fair. Can't papa do something? He's the captain."

Her mother agreed but told her that her father, like everybody else on board, would just have to be patient and wait for the storm to end. When this happened and they began to haul up the anchor in preparation for sailing east out into the Atlantic, the crew cheered and little Sophia, warmly held in her mother's arms, clapped her hands as well. Then the sails were unfurled, and the *Mary Celeste* set off again on her voyage, smoothly entering the Narrows between Brooklyn and Staten Island.

"That saved us a few miles, captain," Richardson said, "but we must make sure we don't get stuck on any sandbars before we hit the open sea. I've been on ships that have done that before. The time they saved going through the Narrows without watching carefully enough what they were doing cost them later. One captain told me that they had to wait for hours for the high tide to come in before they could get off those sandbars."

"Well, we should be all right," Briggs said, standing by the wheel. "This ship has a shallow draught and so I think we'll be safe taking the risk."

Briggs was right. They cleared the Narrows without any problems and after paying their guide, a past acquaintance of Briggs's who knew the area around New York well, they set off for the open sea. With the beaches and fine houses on Long Island on the port side, the *Mary Celeste* now began her voyage out into the huge expanse of the Atlantic Ocean. As the sea was not too choppy, Sarah brought Sophia to stand close to her by the side rail to point out the various sights on the shore. All was going well until Sophia accidentally dropped her favourite dolly overboard.

"*Wah!* Mary-Lou was my best dolly," the little girl wailed as she saw it drift away on the waves. "She was my best dolly. You gave her to me for Christmas. Can't papa stop the ship and pick it up?" she appealed to her mother as she watched the red and green dolly bobbing up and down in the water, rapidly falling further and further astern as the *Mary Celeste* picked up speed.

"No, Sophia, the wind's too strong for papa to stop the ship," Sarah replied, hugging the sad little girl to her chest. "But don't you fret so, you've got two more dollies downstairs, and I promise you that when we arrive in Genoa I will buy you a beautiful new one even nicer than Mary-Lou. Now how does that sound?"

"Do you promise? A real promise?" Sophia insisted as she wiped her eyes.

Sarah nodded and took her daughter below before there were any more tearful scenes.

The next few days passed uneventfully. The *Mary Celeste* seemed to positively swallow up the miles under the westerly winds so much so that they managed to make up for the two-day delay hanging around waiting, anchored off Staten Island. The first and second mates carried out their duties without any problem and the rest of the crew worked well in unison with their officers and with each other. Orders and instructions were given in a mixture of English, Dutch and German while Edward Head, the steward and cook, provided good meals so that no-one had any cause for complaint. Even little Sophia was pleased with the special meals he served her, and the incident with the lost dolly seemed to be completely forgotten.

It was on the third night on the ocean that this idyllic situation came to an end. Sophia was asleep in her cot, Sarah was in bed reading a book and Briggs was sitting at his desk writing up the daily log. Suddenly he felt jerked out of his chair and the small lantern on his desk slid across it and smashed to the floor, its light extinguished, causing the cabin to be plunged into semi-darkness.

"What the...?" he asked, though no-one replied. But by

the time he had picked up the broken lantern and made sure its flame was completely out, he understood that the *Mary Celeste* was sailing into a typical North Atlantic storm. Grabbing his heavy coat and pulling on his cap, he shouted to Sarah above the noise of the wind to stay below and keep the cabin door shut. He rushed up onto the deck to find second mate Gilling fighting to hold the wheel steady. Briggs shouted for Volkert Lorenzon to help Gilling with the wheel, before yelling instructions to Volkert's brother, Boz, and the other crewmen.

"Get those topsails reefed!" Briggs shouted above the roaring wind. "*Now!* Leave the lower ones. We'll see what happens later."

Hoping that his voice carried above the stormy winds, Briggs then turned around and ordered Volkert to stop helping the second mate at the wheel and go with the other men, who were now climbing to the tops of the masts. Briggs made his way carefully over the slippery deck and stood with Gilling as they held the wheel steady. "We don't want to let those waves catch us side on," Briggs said as he and Gilling did their best to keep the *Mary Celeste* on an even course. "If they do, they'll swamp us."

Gilling nodded and the two men tightened their grip on the wheel as the winds and waves tried to wrest it from their hands. After some twenty minutes, Gilling tapped on Briggs's shoulder and looked up at the sky.

"I think it's lifting, captain. I saw a patch of blue sky."

Briggs looked up and nodded. "I think you're right but I'll stay here with you for a bit longer and then I'll go down to see how my wife and daughter are doing." Ten minutes later, Briggs called out to Richardson to stop working on the rigging and take his place at the wheel with Gilling. Once the first mate was there, Briggs gingerly crossed the still heaving deck and made his way down to his cabin. There he found Sarah sitting in a padded chair, holding little Sophia in one arm while she gripped the side of the bed with her other hand.

"How are you?" he asked, lowering himself into his own padded chair.

"We're surviving." She half smiled. "But Sophia wasn't happy, actually, she was very scared when the storm was at its height. It seemed as if the whole floor would rise up and tip us over."

"Yes, I was thinking about you when I was on deck, but there was nothing more that I could do. But I think that the worst part is now over. I sent the men aloft to furl the topsails and since then the ship has been easier to control." Briggs stood up, crossed over to his wife and kissed her on the forehead and then picked up his daughter. She looked up, held out her arms to him and he kissed her on each cheek.

"Papa," she said quietly, "I was so scared." Briggs handed her back to his wife. Sophia closed her eyes and quickly buried herself in the warm safety of her mother's arms and was soon fast asleep.

A few minutes later, Briggs was standing by the wheel.

"How is it?" he asked Richardson and Gilling.

"The wind has certainly dropped, captain," Gilling said.

"But just as you went below," Richardson added, "we caught a huge wave which washed over the foredeck."

"Did it do any damage?"

"No, captain, not really, but it washed overboard a box of fruit that hadn't been lashed down properly."

Briggs shrugged. There was nothing that he could do

about it. "No use crying over spilt milk," he said. "Just make sure that it doesn't happen again. That's all."

He shouted up to the Lorenzon brothers, Head and Martens, who had returned to their positions high up where the topsails' yardarms met the masts, and told them to unfurl the topsails. A few minutes later he heard the heavy cracks as the topsails opened to catch the wind. He smiled as he felt the forward surge of the *Mary Celeste* cutting through the waves as if she wanted to make up for lost time. Then the men climbed down, and Briggs told Head to rustle up some hot coffee and warm cookies to give to the crew.

"I think we all deserve it tonight," the captain said, clapping Richardson on the back. "Gilling," he called out. "Stay by the wheel while I check out the hold. I hope those barrels didn't come loose in that storm."

Briggs went below to find that the barrels were still firmly tied down, although as soon as he entered the hold he became aware of the strong alcohol fumes that filled the air. Swinging his lantern carefully from side to side, he looked around to see if any of the barrels had split open or if one of their corks had become loose. With one hand holding the lantern and the other holding a handkerchief covering his nose to keep out the worst of the heavy fumes, he made as thorough a search as he could to see if he could find the source of the smell. He pulled on ropes, checked knots and the wooden wedges holding the barrels in place, but he could not find anything amiss. He only stopped when his lantern started flickering unevenly, warning him that it was running out of fuel. He climbed back up on desk, glad to breathe in the fresh salty tang of the North Atlantic. However, he was determined to go below again later to see what was causing such a build-up of fumes in the hold. As he was thinking this, he remembered that yesterday he had seen a damp patch on the floor of the hold near the door. What had caused it? Seawater from the sea's tossing and turning during the storm, or had one of the barrels started leaking, a leak he had not yet found? Whatever the reason, it would have to be investigated very soon.

But for the time being, now that the storm had abated, he would have to check out his ship. He would make sure that if the Atlantic wanted to show its tempestuous face again, then the *Mary Celeste* and her crew would be ready to take on any challenge.

Chapter 8
The *Dei Gratia* leaves New York

It was 4 December 1872 and the skies over the North Atlantic were dark grey and threatening. The *Dei Gratia* was ploughing her way through the white-capped blue-grey waves as her bow pointed east. All her sails were unfurled and catching every blast of wind they could as Captain Morehouse wished to make up time, days that he had lost fighting several short storms and squalls since he had left New York nearly three weeks earlier.

"Shall we put up any more sail, captain?" first mate Deveau asked.

Morehouse shook his head. "No, no, man, not at the moment. Too much up there and we'll keel over. If the wind slackens off a bit, then we'll put up some more. So, Deveau, have the men ready if necessary."

"Yes, captain," the first mate saluted and, after telling the crew to be prepared to hoist some more sails soon, he went down below to the galley to warm himself. He knew that this was the warmest place on board, and it was from here that John Johnson was quietly and efficiently providing everyone with enough food and drink. *It is good to be below*, he thought as he climbed down the narrow stairs. A warm fuggy feeling of shelter and protection enveloped him as he left behind the cold damp winds, which had been blowing for the past few days up on deck. And of course, the smell of sizzling bacon and strong coffee also helped that good feeling. Deveau then asked Johnson for a coffee.

"Aye, I think I have another one myself," Johnson said in his heavy accented English, pouring himself a mug out of a chipped metal coffee pot. "You can never have enough of this I say, although in Russia we often added something extra."

"Vodka?"

"*Da*, yes, or something like that."

"Yeah, I agree with you," Deveau nodded. "Especially sailing day after day in this drizzle. The cold fairly seeps into your bones, at least, that's what it does with me."

Johnson nodded. "Yes, you are right, but I lucky spending most of my days down here in galley. I must tell you, Mr Deveau, this sort of weather I hate most when I on ship. Cold and damp. At least, in storm, you get wet, the storm goes away and then you get dressed warm and dry. In this weather you are cold and wet all the time."

Deveau was surprised at hearing Johnson talk like this. Normally the tall blond sailor said very little, and when asked how he was he would nod and grunt, "All right, I guess," and continue with what he was doing. Deveau decided to ask the normally taciturn Johnson a little about himself while he was in such a talkative mood.

"Where you from, Johnson?" he began. "Someone told me you are from Norfolk."

Johnson shook his head and sipped his coffee. "No, no, they wrong," he said. "I from Baltimore but I born in Russia. But, Mr Deveau, you want a biscuit? I made some this morning."

Deveau took a couple and the two men munched in companionable silence. Then Johnson said, "This is second time I sailing with Captain Morehouse. He a good man and knows what he doing."

"Yes, I've heard that," Deveau said. "And of the crew aboard now, I've sailed with John Wright before. That is, before he became a second mate. He's a good man to have around in times of trouble. Solid, y'know. Solid and reliable."

"*Da*, but I don't know anything about those other two, Anderson and Lund. I never been on ship with them before."

"Neither have I," Deveau said, "but they seem to be pulling their weight as much as anyone else. Especially last week when we had that big storm."

"But they had to, no?" Johnson said. "Especially as we only small crew. No time or place to be lazy while everyone working hard. I don't like ship bosses having small crews. I know why, but it can be very bad. Bad for all. Bad for men and bad for ships."

Deveau put down his empty coffee mug and nodded. "I've heard of more than one ship that went down in a storm because there weren't enough on board. Have you heard of the *Warfield*?"

"*Warfield*? Yes, I heard of her. Sailed from Boston, *da*, yes?"

"Aye, that's right," Deveau said. "Well, she went down a couple of years ago near the Azores because she was undermanned. She was a brig like this, even a bit bigger if I remember right. She had a crew of just six and one of them was a fourteen-year-old boy. I heard that they didn't stand any chance at all of riding out the storm they got caught in."

"Served owners right, is what I say," Johnson said. "Trouble is, it's always simple sailors like me that get killed and drown because owners not pay for more men. That's what I say."

Deveau nodded, thanked Johnson, and putting on his heavy coat again, he climbed back up onto the foredeck. Taking care not to slip on the wet planking, he made his way over to where Captain Morehouse was standing at the wheel.

"D'you want me to take over for a while, captain, while you take a rest?" Deveau asked.

"Good idea, man. I'll go below and start writing up today's log. I hate getting behind with jobs like that. It means that I have to remember what happened each day, and with all the things going on around me all the time, that's not always possible." And saying that, the captain with his thick, grey flecked beard, handed the wheel over to his first mate. "Don't hesitate to come for me if necessary. I don't want any heroes thinking they can do everything themselves," Morehouse added as he too made his way carefully over to the stairs below. "I don't expect this weather to change soon but you can never tell, especially at this time of the year."

Deveau then rested his hands on the wheel and began thinking of all the voyages he had made over the Atlantic. He quite enjoyed serving as a first mate on ships like the *Dei Gratia*. On the one hand it gave him some authority and responsibility, but on the other, if anything did go wrong, the blame would always be on the captain's head, not his. He knew that his wife wanted him to become a captain.

"More money," she kept saying.

"Aye, lass, and more problems," was his usual reply.

"But you've sailed as a captain before," she would say.

"I know, love, but I'm quite happy being first mate, at least for the time being. So don't pester me anymore, and we'll be all right. Just you see."

As he saw a picture of his wife and his small son in his mind's eye, he was also aware of the vast scene surrounding him. The ever-moving sea out to the distant horizon whichever way you looked. At the same time he was aware of the constant splashing of the waves on the sides of the ship, and the ever-present sound of the wind in the large square and triangular sails above him. Those sounds, together with the flapping of the company's flag on the main mast and the wind whistling through the rigging and the rope ladders up to the topsails, were an integral part of life at sea.

How many times have I climbed up those ladders in a storm? he asked himself, and thought back to the days when, as a sixteen-year-old cabin boy on his first voyage, he had been sent aloft to help some of the other men furl up a mainsail in a storm in the South Atlantic. He had been terrified. Until then the voyage had been idyllic: smooth seas and regular winds, hot meals on time and friendly chats with the rest of the crew. During those first two weeks he had learned more and more about the business of being a sailor every day. But then suddenly the winds had changed and so had everything else. The days of smooth sailing were over. The merchant ship he was on, the *Lady Catherine*, was bucking and jumping through the blue-grey mountainous waves and deep dark troughs, like a bronco on his uncle's farm in Texas.

"You, Deveau," the captain had shouted at him. "Get yourself up aloft and help Smith and Haynes up there. Looks like they need a hand."

"But, captain—" the young Deveau replied.

"Quick, man and don't argue."

The frightened cabin boy began the perilous climb up the rope ladder, hanging on for dear life. The ropes were cold, wet and slippery and it was hard for the inexperienced sailor to climb. Terrified of looking down, he approached the mainsail's yardarm, and Haynes, a large bully of a man, shouted at him, "C'mon, man, can't you make it any faster? I need you to grab that rope and now!"

A few minutes later, Deveau was up there, standing on the line of rigging under the yardarm fighting the rough heavy sail, the raging wind and his own terrible fears. Doing his best to be useful and not to fall, he grabbed alternately at the sail, the ropes and anything he thought would help him finish off the fearful task as quickly as he could. All he had wanted to do was to be able to climb back down to the swaying deck below and hope that he would not sick up his last meal.

Now, as he looked ahead and tried to see where the choppy grey ocean and the sky met at the horizon, Deveau smiled to himself. *I made it that time*, he thought, *and countless other times after that. No doubt I'll have to do it again before my seafaring days are over, but the less I do so, the better.*

Calling for Augustus Anderson to come and replace him at the wheel, he turned to go down below to see that the *Dei Gratia*'s cargo and ballast had not shifted in the storm.

Down in the hold he checked that the barrels were sitting tightly on each other and none worked themselves loose. Walking around in the gloom, the only light coming from his swaying lantern, he pulled on the various ropes, ties and wooden wedges to see that they had not worked loose. He saw a small red-brown stain on the floor and bent over to check it. It was dry. "Hmm," he said to himself. "That must have come from one of this ship's earlier voyages," and he continued his inspection.

Ten minutes later, and satisfied that the cargo was being held firmly in place, he climbed back up the ladder onto the deck. Just as he was going to ask Charles Lund what he wanted to do when they reached dry land, Captain Morehouse called him. "Deveau, come here. Take a look at that strange shape over there. There, that thing that looks like some sort of ship. What do you think it is?"

Morehouse handed his prized telescope, the one he had bought when he had first become a captain, over to his first mate and waited for his answer.

"You are right, captain. It *is* a ship. At least it looks like one. But it's certainly moving in a strange way."

"Aye, that's what I thought," Morehouse said. "Now look at its sails. The topsails, I mean. There seems to be something peculiar about them. Don't some of them look torn to you? All ripped up? Take another look."

Deveau put the telescope to his right eye again. "Yes, captain, I think you're right. Only the foretop stays and lower topsail jib look all right. The rest of them are still furled, or else torn and flapping in the wind."

"Well," Morehouse concluded. "That will explain why she's moving like that. Like she's not under any control."

"Yes, captain. That's just what I was thinking. By the way, can you make out her name?"

The captain of the *Dei Gratia* took hold of his telescope again and had a long hard look at the mysterious ship wallowing in the seas perhaps a mile away from him.

"No, Deveau. She's too far away from us. I wonder what's wrong. It's like there's no-one in command." Then he turned in the direction of his helmsman. "Lund," he shouted. "Can you see that ship over there on our port side?"

"Aye, captain."

"Then change course and make for the port bow."

"Aye, aye, captain," Lund shouted back and began turning the polished wooden wheel to the left.

As he did so, Morehouse and Deveau kept passing the telescope between them as they made comments on what they could see.

"There's only three sails which are still set."

"Aye, and it looks like two other sails have been blown away."

"Look below. There's a sail lying loose, sort of half reefed."

"True. And look how she's moving. Like a man who's had too much to drink."

"Can you make out her name now?" Morehouse asked as he handed over his telescope to Deveau.

The first mate took a long look at the ship with its half-torn sails moving drunkenly now less than a mile to port.

He handed back the telescope and said, "No, captain. We're still too far away. We'll have to wait until we can get closer."

By this time, the rest of the crew who were not busy had joined their captain and first mate at the side rail and were discussing what they could see.

"Looks like there's no-one in charge," Anderson said.

"Don't be soft, man. There must be, but where's the captain?"

Deveau shrugged, "I can't see him, and come to that, I can't see anyone on board, captain or not."

"Can't you see anyone by the wheel at least?" Lund persisted.

Deveau shrugged again. "No, I can't see anyone on deck but we're still too far away. Wait until we get closer. Maybe they've all gone down below for whatever reason. Here captain, see if you agree. Take another look."

Morehouse lifted his telescope again and took another long sweeping look.

"You are right, Deveau. I can't see anyone on board or by the wheel. That's most strange. I wonder what's up."

"Where are they all?" second mate Wright called out. "It don't make no sense. Surely they can't all be below."

"P'rhaps, the crew have abandoned her," Lund suggested.

"What? Right here, in the middle of the ocean? Don't be daft, man."

Just as his crew were wondering what had happened to the ship that they had unexpectedly come across, Morehouse aimed his telescope so he could look at the hull more carefully. He was trying to make out the name of this mysterious ship and where she had come from.

"Deveau, I think I can see what she's called now," Morehouse called out after a couple of minutes. "It's the… wait a minute. I know that ship. Yes, it's the *Mary* something. Aye, it's the *Mary Celeste*."

Chapter 9
Morehouse investigates the *Mary Celeste*

A brigantine ship, similar to the Dei Gratia

"The *Mary Celeste*, captain? Didn't she leave New York a week before us? She should be much nearer to Europe by now, not sailing out here in the North Atlantic."

"Yes, Deveau. You're right. She left New York on the

fifth and her captain, Captain Briggs, told me that he was bound for Genoa. Aye, that's what's so strange in this business. What's she still doing out here? Here, get me a megaphone and I'll call over to them to see if they need any help."

Deveau was back in a few minutes with a megaphone. He handed the polished brass instrument over to his captain.

"*Ahoy there!*" Morehouse called out. "Is anyone on board? Do you need any help?"

All the crew stood on the side of the *Dei Gratia*, waiting. Waiting for a reply that would explain the mystery of the *Mary Celeste* sailing apparently unmanned in the middle of the ocean. None of the *Dei Gratia* men spoke as they all leaned expectantly towards the merchant brigantine with its torn sails. The only reply they received was the sound of the waves slap-splashing against the hulls of the two ships and the whistling of the wind in the rigging as the two brigantines drew closer to each other.

"*Ahoy there!*" Morehouse shouted out again even louder, thinking that perhaps the crew on the *Mary Celeste* had not heard him.

By now the two ships were more or less parallel, but neither Morehouse nor any of his crew could see anyone on board the *Mary Celeste*. The crewmen continued to pass Morehouse's telescope among themselves to see if any of them could see any movement on board. However, each man said that he could see no-one at all.

"Deveau," Morehouse said after a few minutes. "I think you should take a couple of men and go over there and see what's happened. I certainly don't like what we are looking at."

"Neither do I, captain. I've never seen anything like this before in all my years at sea. Who shall I take with me?"

"Take Wright and Johnson. They're good men. And take a gun or two with you. I don't know if you'll need them, but it won't hurt to be armed."

"Yes, captain." Deveau turned to make the necessary arrangements to lower one of the small lifeboats mounted on the rear deck of the *Dei Gratia*. Then he, Wright and Johnson took their caps and heavy sea-coats and made ready to row to the *Mary Celeste*.

Ten minutes later, the crew of the *Dei Gratia* were leaning over the side rail watching their small lifeboat bobbing about on the waves as Johnson rowed the first and second mates over to the *Mary Celeste*.

"Row all the way around her," Deveau told Johnson as they approached the wallowing ship. "Let's see if we can see anything before we go aboard. Look out for any holes or signs of damage or fighting." Deveau watched the top of the ship's uncontrolled rudder as it bobbed up and down in the water, moving aimlessly from side to side in the ever-swirling waves.

Johnson did so, but none of the three men could detect any clue as to what had happened to the ship whose dark hull now loomed high above them. Following Deveau's instructions, Johnson circled the *Mary Celeste* a second time and then pulled up alongside. Once their small boat had stopped rocking enough for Wright to stand up, he did so and grabbed a loose rope hanging from a handrail on the ship and tied it to a rope that they had brought with them.

"Johnson, you wait here," Deveau said as he checked that his revolver was firmly pushed into his belt, "and I'll go aboard with Wright. Be ready for anything – especially if we have to return to the *Dei Gratia* in a hurry. Wright, you brought a gun with you, didn't you?"

"Aye," the second mate replied, and he pointed to the revolver pushed down inside his own wide belt. "Aye, armed and ready to use it."

"And I'm as steady as I can make it," Johnson called out above the noise of the waves, looking at Deveau and doing his best to prevent the lifeboat from banging against the hull of the *Mary Celeste*.

Deveau then carefully hoisted himself up and climbed out of the bobbing lifeboat. When he thought that he had a good hold on the upper part of the hull, he grabbed a beam sticking out of the side of the ship and swung himself over the side rail onto the deck.

"Now you do the same," he shouted down to John Wright. "But watch your footing. It's very slippery."

The second mate followed Deveau's lead, and soon he too was standing on the swaying deck of the *Mary Celeste*.

"Is anyone there?" Deveau called out as soon as he saw that the second mate was safely aboard and that Johnson was waiting below. He and Wright waited, each holding their revolvers ready. "Can anyone hear me?"

The only sounds were of the loosely flapping sails above them and a door or two below decks banging repeatedly as the ship lurched and swayed in the Atlantic waves.

"Is anyone there?" Deveau called out again.

As before there was no answer. Just the sound of the wind whistling through the rigging and the sails.

"That's strange," Deveau said after calling out yet a third time and getting no response. Can you see anything that will tell us what's happened here?" he asked Wright.

Wright shrugged. "No, not so far, that is apart from those torn sails. And, man, if she's been abandoned, why hasn't the wheel been lashed down? No wonder she's been sailing as she is. It's the wind that's been pushing her. And hey, look at that rigging over there by the port bow. It doesn't look right. Something's happened to it, but I don't know what."

"Yes, I can see that, but tell me, where is everybody? They can't just have disappeared into thin air. I mean, we're in the middle of the ocean."

"P'rhaps they're all below for some reason, though I don't know why. I suggest we go below and see what's happening there."

Deveau nodded in agreement and the two men, still with their revolvers at the ready, prepared to climb down to the lower deck. However, just before doing so, Deveau leaned over the side and shouted down to Johnson.

"We're going to have a look below. There's no-one up here on the top deck, so just stay ready."

"*Da*," Johnson shouted back in Russian. "Yes."

Then Deveau turned to Wright. "Can you see a lantern anywhere? No doubt it'll be as black as pitch down there."

The two men looked around and then Wright called out. "Here, I've found one. By this locker."

He lit it and the two men then climbed down the short staircase and stood in the gloom of the lower deck. Carefully, and with their revolvers still drawn, they looked around but could not see anything out of the ordinary at first glance.

"Look, here's another lantern, Wright, so now we've got one each," Deveau said. "Light it and then you start looking in that direction" – he pointed to the bow – "and I'll go to the stern end. But whatever you do, be careful."

"Aye, aye," Wright said, and now that his eyes had become used to the gloomy light and the jumping shadows caused by his lantern, he headed for the bow. Like the first mate, he wanted to see where all the crew of the *Mary Celeste* were and what had happened to them.

After a few minutes, the two men met up in the centre of the hold.

"Did you see anything unusual, apart from that we haven't seen anyone on board?" Deveau asked. "It's really strange. I've looked in the captain's and crew's cabins and I didn't see anything strange in them except that the bedding is soaking wet and that there's quite a lot of seawater in the galley."

"Are you sure that it's not water that the cook spilt or something like that?"

"No, no, Wright. It's seawater all right. It's all over the floor. I dipped my finger in it and tasted it. It's salty."

"But where is everybody?" Wright said again. "You don't just abandon ship in mid-ocean without a good reason. It just doesn't make any sense, does it?"

Deveau nodded and continued poking his lantern in more dark corners.

"It's really weird, scary if you like. I didn't see no hide nor hair of them. No-one, dead or alive. Tell me," Wright asked, "did you see any clues anywhere else that might explain what has happened? You know, anything broken or bloodstains anywhere? Because I haven't."

Deveau shrugged. "Apart from a couple of damp patches on the floor and a fairly strong smell of alcohol, I couldn't see anything wrong in the hold. All the barrels are still in place and I didn't see any broken ones. Did you?"

"No. That was one of the first things I looked for. But I did see some stains on the floor under some of them."

"Were they wet or dry?"

"Dry, but they could have been from some time ago, y'know, the alcohol itself having evaporated."

Deveau nodded and looked around again. "Wright, I suggest that we go and see what the situation is like further down below, you know, with the bilge water. That might tell us something. Yes, and we might find something there that'll tell us about what's happened to the captain and his crew. I'm telling you, I still can't get it out of my head that we haven't found anyone on board, no-one at all or what might have happened to them."

"Yeah, I agree with you," Wright said, and the two men clambered up the steps again. They then made their way down another flight of stairs to the ship's two pumps, which were situated behind the main mast. Deveau took hold of the ship's sounding line – a long length of rope with a heavy rod tied to its end – and dropped it down the hole that led to the bilge water at the bottom of the hull. After a few moments, he hauled the wet rope back up.

"How much water is there?" Wright asked.

"Three and a half feet," Deveau replied, as he studied the rope and measured it off.

"That's not so bad," Wright said. "A bit much maybe, but the pumps should have been able to empty that out. Without any problems. That's not enough to make anyone abandon the ship, is it?"

"You're right, so let's go through the cabins again and see if we have missed anything."

The two men retraced their steps and carefully searched the cabins again. Apart from the wet bedding they found no signs of fighting or violence, and so they decided to check the decks and hatches once more. Again they did not find anything unusual, and Deveau suggested that they return to the *Dei Gratia* and tell Captain Morehouse what they had seen. Wright agreed and they climbed back up to the top deck.

Just as they were taking their last look around, Wright told Deveau that he could not see the lifeboat.

"Aye, you're right," Deveau said after looking around carefully. "It's not here."

"Well, I wonder where it is?" Wright asked. "I mean, you're not going to abandon ship in a lifeboat in the middle of the ocean unless you've got a very good reason to, are you? It just doesn't make any sense."

"Well, you might if you were sinking," Deveau replied as he looked around once again. "But, man, this ship, apart from those torn sails and some problems with the rigging, is in fair condition and doesn't look like it was going to sink, so where is the lifeboat and why is it missing?" He paused and looked towards the stern of the ship. "Hmm, maybe they moved it for some reason, although I can't think why. So come on, Wright, let's have one more look around and then, if we don't find it, we'll tell Captain Morehouse."

"Aye, we'll have to tell him about that and everything else here that's not right, especially that there's no-one on board. I'm telling you, man, I don't like it and I don't feel good about all this. It's just not right."

Deveau nodded vigorously in agreement and the two men spent the next ten minutes making a thorough search for the missing lifeboat on the upper and lower decks. After they had failed to find it Deveau leaned over the starboard rail and shouted down to Johnson.

"Bring her as close as you can and then we'll go back to Captain Morehouse."

Twenty minutes later, the first and second mate of the *Dei Gratia* were telling their captain and the rest of the crew what they had seen.

"It was really strange," Deveau began. "Weird, in fact. The ship is basically in good condition and yet there's no-one on board."

"No-one?"

Deveau and Wright nodded vigorously. "Yes, captain," Deveau continued. "No-one at all. We searched her from the top deck down to the bilges, from stem to stern and we couldn't find a living soul."

"Aye, and not even a dead one," Wright added. "It's sure weird considering she is in good condition."

"What do you mean, she's in good condition?" Morehouse asked. "The topsails are all ripped up."

"Yes, captain, I saw that, but, basically, the rest of her is all right. And yes, we found some seawater in the galley and the bedding in the captain's and the crew's cabins is soaking wet."

"Aye," Wright added, "and as for the ship itself, some of the rigging needs repairing. Not all of it, mind you, just some. Ah, yes, what was really strange, captain, was that if they had abandoned ship, why hadn't they lashed down the wheel? I'm telling you, I don't like it." He shivered. "It's weird, man. It really is. I didn't feel good at all on there. Like some sort of ghosts are prowling about. Real weird." And he shivered again.

"Captain," he added. "We couldn't even find her lifeboat. We looked hard for it, we did. I'm telling you, by rights it should have been on her deck but there was no sign of it."

Morehouse looked thoughtful. "Did you go below? Had they left it there for some reason?"

"Yes, captain, we went below and it wasn't there. It wasn't anywhere," Wright replied as he sucked nervously on his pipe. "The lifeboat should have been next to the main hatch, no?"

Deveau and Captain Morehouse nodded and then Morehouse asked, "And what about below? The hull? Did you see any damage there?"

"I not see any, captain," Johnson joined in. "While first and second mate were on board, I look at hull and she look good. Clean as whistle, as you say. I see no dirty marks or anything. Nothing."

Morehouse thought for a moment and then turned to Deveau and Wright. "And what about the hold? Did you go down there?"

"Yes, captain. Wright and I went down to see if the hold and the cargo were as they should be and they were. All the barrels were tied down tight and the ballast was also as we expected it to be, that is, also as it should be."

"And none of the barrels were broken or had leaked?"

"No, captain, although," Wright added, "there was a strong smell of alcohol and I saw a few stains where some of the barrels may have leaked, but that's normal when you think about how many she was carrying."

"But none had leaked out in any serious way?"

"No, captain. Not that we could see." And Wright looked

at Deveau for confirmation.

Deveau nodded and Wright continued. "And I couldn't see any wet stains on the floor. Well, not real ones. Just some dark reddish-brown smudges, that's all."

"And what about the bilge water? How deep was that?"

"Well, when we went down there, we found a sounding rod lying alongside the pumps so we lowered it down into the bilge water and there was about three and a half feet."

"Three and a half feet, you say," Morehouse said. "Well, that's not too much. Quite normal, in fact. That could easily have been pumped out."

"Yes, captain," Wright said. "That's what we said. But to be sure, we checked the pumps to see if they were working."

"And?"

"They were in perfect working order."

"Aye, but as Wright said before, some of the rigging looked in a bad way, captain," Deveau said. "The main peak halyard was broken off and I think a few other parts need repairing." Deveau looked over to the *Mary Celeste* sailing sluggishly alongside and continued. "I'm telling you, captain, if anyone is going to do anything with her, the sails and some of the rigging will have to be fixed immediately."

For a few moments all the men standing around Captain Morehouse were silent. What could have happened to the crew of the *Mary Celeste*? What could have made the captain, his family and everyone on board abandon ship in mid-ocean?

"Maybe it was monsters that killed the crew," Augustus Anderson said, his eyes shining. "You know, some great big slimy octopus creature or giant squid that swam up to the ship, slithered on board and then picked off the crew one by one."

"You've been reading too many dime novels," Morehouse said. "I think we can discount your monster theory, but tell me" – he turned to Deveau – "were there any signs of violence on the ship? You know, blood or damage?"

"No, nothing big, really, although the binnacle box was all smashed up. The compass wasn't inside it and there were bits of glass all over the deck nearby."

"That's right," Wright agreed and then suggested, "Maybe she was attacked by pirates and—"

"Aye, or p'rhaps there was a mutiny on board," Charles Lund interrupted.

"Yes, or maybe they all succumbed to some sort of fever or madness and jumped off overboard," Anderson continued.

"Well, I'm sorry to disappoint you two," Deveau said looking at Anderson and Lund, "but we found no signs of fever, mutiny or pirates. No bodies lying on the decks and not a drop of blood."

"That's right." Wright nodded. "Everything in the cabins was all shipshape. We even found a few pieces of the captain's wife's jewellery lying around. I'm sure if there had been any pirates, they wouldn't have left stuff like that, now would they?"

"Yeah, I guess you're right," Anderson agreed.

"Besides," Captain Morehouse added, "there haven't been any reports of pirates around this part of the Atlantic for years. Aye, for about forty years, in fact. And as for mutinies on board, well, they're pretty rare, too."

"Why, when was the last one, captain?" Lund asked.

"Well the last one I heard of broke out on a schooner, the *Walter M. Towgood*, about fifteen years ago. Before that there was a French ship called the *Rosalie* found deserted in 1840."

"Yes, I heard about that one, captain," Deveau said. "It was a bit like this *Mary Celeste* ship, no? I mean, if I remember right, the *Rosalie* was crossing the Atlantic from Hamburg to Havana with a regular cargo. If I recall, she was seen sailing with all sails set but with no crew aboard and the only living things they found were a few canaries and a half-starved cat."

"And what about that Spanish one, the *Viego*? She was found deserted some four years ago," Anderson said.

"So tell me," Morehouse said, holding up his hand to silence his chattering crew. "What did you find in the cabins? Anything suspicious?"

"No, captain, not really," Wright replied, relighting his pipe. "It was all neat and tidy – really shipshape. I even found the captain's wife's gold locket on a small cupboard. In fact, the only thing not in order in the captain's cabin was that the bed hadn't been made."

"And yes, some of his little daughter's toys and dolls lay scattered about, but that you can expect when you have little children about, no?"

Morehouse nodded. "Yes, Deveau, that doesn't seem strange, but what about clothes and other things? Were they in order?"

"Yes, captain. And yes, there was a harmonium, or some such instrument in the cabin and some sheets of music lying on a table. There was also a large bag of dirty clothes in a closet. All the clean ones were folded as expected. Ah, and, captain, we found a sword in the captain's cabin. It was—"

"A sword?"

"Aye. It was in its scabbard and when I pulled it out to have a look I saw some reddish marks like bloodstains, but I'm not sure if they were really. Maybe it was just rust, y'know, like what the sea air does to metal."

"And there was a pair of India rubber overshoes near the bed," Wright added. "But in general, the captain's cabin looked quite normal. No signs of violence anywhere. No pirates and no mutiny." He looked at Anderson and Lund.

"What about crew's cabin?" Johnson asked. "What was it like?"

"As expected," Wright answered. "There was some washing hanging on the line and the usual things lying around – oilskins, boots, pipes and stuff like that. Nothing unusual."

"And what about food and water? Did you see if there was enough on board?" Lund asked.

"Yes, Charlie, I inspected their supplies as well," Wright replied. "They had a couple of weeks' of uncooked food and there was plenty of fresh water, so that couldn't have been a reason to abandon ship."

"Yes," Deveau added, "and all the pots and pans had been washed up. There was a barrel of flour in the corner that was about two-thirds full."

"And drink, you know, alcohol, did you find any signs of that?" Morehouse asked.

The two men shook their heads. "No," Deveau said. "Not a drop. No beer, no wine, no nothing. Just the alcohol in the hold, and as you said before, that stuff was undrinkable, y'know, made for industry."

"That's right," Wright confirmed. "But what we did see was that all of the ship's hatches were open, even the skylight in the captain's cabin and some of the other portholes."

"But that's crazy," Charles Lund said. "It would only take a couple of large waves coming over the bow and the whole ship would be swamped!"

"Aye," Anderson said. "Maybe that's why the bedding in the cabins was soaked and that's why you found some water in the galley."

The rest of the crew were nodding and agreeing about this strange fact when Morehouse interrupted. "Ah, but wait a minute," he said. "Did you find the ship's log?"

"Yes, captain," Deveau said. "Here, I've brought it with me." He rummaged around in his pouch for a moment and pulled out a half-completed ship's log.

"Where did you find this?" Morehouse asked.

"In the first mate's cabin. It was on top of a pile of papers, and seeing what it was, I packed it carefully as I knew you'd want to have a look at it," Deveau said handing it over to Morehouse who started reading it. "And if you look, cap'n, the last entry was made on November the twenty-fifth at eight in the morning, that is, nearly three weeks after she left New York."

"Aye, just over a week ago," Morehouse said. "Ten days ago, to be exact." He read the last three pages and then said, "Well, they don't seem to have met any particular problems. Storms and squalls, which is to be expected. There's no special trouble that's been recorded here, that is, anything that would have caused them to abandon ship."

"Yes, captain, I thought the same when I looked through it. I was hoping that the log would give us a clue, but it doesn't," Deveau said. "It seems that up until the twenty-fifth, it was plain sailing."

"And what about the chronometer and the sextant,"

Captain Morehouse asked next. "Did you find them? Were they in good condition?"

"Ah, that's another part of this mystery, captain," Wright replied. "We don't know. You see, even though we looked very carefully for them, we couldn't find them anywhere. Not the chronometer, not the sextant and no navigation book or the ship's register. I'm telling you, captain, it's most baffling, it is. Most baffling. All I can think of is that they took them with them or somehow they got washed overboard, but I don't really think that's what happened. I mean, it's not as if everything is wet like a huge wave came through the porthole, is it? Just the bedding and some water on the floor in the galley."

Deveau nodded in agreement and then added, "Captain Morehouse, apart from the ripped up topsails and the rigging that isn't as it should be, the only real sign of violence we saw was the binnacle box all smashed up."

"Aye, and the compass in it was missing, and there were bits of broken glass everywhere nearby, but we couldn't see any bloodstains on any of this."

"None at all?"

"No, captain. It was just all smashed up."

"Yes, captain," Wright added. "The binnacle looked as it had been forced out. There were these grooves around where it had been. Yes, sir, if you asked me, I'd say that someone had forced it out with a chisel or something like that."

"So in other words," the captain of the *Dei Gratia* concluded, looking straight at his first and second mates. "You are telling me that for whatever unknown reason, Captain Briggs abandoned a ship in more or less good condition in mid-ocean in November and took all the navigational instruments and the ship's register, the sextant and the chronometer with him, but not the logbook?"

"Yes, captain," Deveau and Wright said together.

"Well, I wonder what all this means?" Morehouse asked aloud. "I wonder what in the hell happened to the *Mary Celeste*?"

Chapter 10
Salvage speculation

An hour later, Captain Morehouse called his first and second mates, Deveau and Wright, to his cabin. After pouring each of them a tot of rum and one for himself he got down to business.

"Listen," he began. "I have no idea what's happened to the *Mary Celeste*, but what I do know is that we cannot just leave her there in the middle of the ocean and—"

"Do you mean, captain, that you want us to tow her to a port and claim salvage?" Deveau interrupted.

Morehouse nodded. "Yes, that's exactly what I was thinking, and the quicker we do so, the better. If we don't, any other ship coming along will do it and then we'll lose all that salvage money."

"Do you have any idea how much money we're talking about, captain?" Wright asked.

"No, not really, but all I know is that when I was talking to her captain, Captain Briggs, in New York just before he left, he said that the *Mary Celeste* and her cargo were insured for about fifty thousand dollars."

"So in other words," Wright said, "we're talking about salvaging a ship and cargo worth a small fortune."

"That's right," Morehouse said. "But the question is, what

are we going to do about it? I'm wondering if it's possible to tow her to the nearest port, or if we have enough men on this ship to put a few of you on the *Mary Celeste* and bring her in separately? I mean, we've still got quite some way to go to the Portuguese or Spanish coast."

"If you ask me, captain," Deveau said. "I think it would be nigh impossible to tow her for the rest of the voyage. We're still out in the Atlantic, it is November, and although the winds at the moment are in our favour, think what it'll be like when we get closer to the Bay of Biscay or the Portuguese coast."

Morehouse turned his back on his men and walked over to the porthole at the side of his cabin to think about this new, unexpected situation. Could he spare three men to put on board the *Mary Celeste* to sail her into port and claim a decent amount of salvage money, or would he be endangering his crew and both ships if he divided his forces?

"Yes, Deveau, I have considered that," Morehouse replied, turning back to face his men. "But the question is, can I still sail the *Dei Gratia* if I put three or four of you on board in order to bring in the *Mary Celeste*? I mean, you know what this would require, don't you?"

"Yes, captain," Wright said. "It means that each of the two ships would have only three or four men aboard. If you ask me I'm not sure that that will be enough, especially if we run into any stormy weather."

Morehouse and Deveau nodded in agreement. Wright had summed up the situation perfectly.

"All right," Morehouse said. "I think, in principle, it is worth the risk to bring in the *Mary Celeste*. However, the best way would be for some of you to sail her. It would also be best if she was kept as close as possible to the *Dei Gratia* and let's hope that the weather won't separate us too far if there are any more squalls or rough seas. But you realise, that if we do this, everyone here, that is, on both ships is going to have to work like hell for the rest of the time that we're at sea. Now what do you say about that?"

Wright, thinking about the extra salvage money he would receive, nodded and Deveau replied that he agreed with his captain. Morehouse, still thinking aloud, continued, "The trouble is, that I'll have to give those men some navigational instruments as well. And of course, I'll have to give them one of my own lifeboats, the smallest one, of course, since it's only going to take three men in it."

"And who are they going to be?" Wright asked.

"I think the best thing would be for you, Deveau, and two other men to sail the *Mary Celeste* into port. After all," he said, looking directly at his first mate, "you are the most experienced sailor here and even if you don't have the qualifications of a captain, you have at least served as one."

Deveau nodded as he accepted his captain's compliment. Morehouse continued, "You, Wright, will then become the temporary first mate on the *Dei Gratia*. How does that sound?"

Now it was Wright's turn to nod in agreement. He was ambitious and later, if he could say that he had sailed half across the Atlantic as a first mate, even as a temporary one, that would look good on his record.

"Good," Captain Morehouse said, rubbing his hands together. "Now that we've got that one sorted out, Deveau, which two men do you want to take with you?"

Deveau scratched his head and paused before answering.

"If you don't mind, captain, I'll take Anderson and Lund. They're good men and I know that I can rely on them. Is that all right with you?"

Morehouse said it was and sent Wright to bring Anderson and Lund to his cabin while he talked to his first mate. "Well, Deveau, all I can spare you, that is, apart from a small lifeboat, is a barometer, watch and compass."

"Yes, captain, and you know, I've got a few instruments of my own so I'm not too worried about that," Deveau said. "Besides, if I'm lucky, I'll be following you, so I shouldn't really get lost, should I?" He paused for a moment to clear his throat. "However, I think the main problem will be for the reduced crews of both the ships to stay awake while we're sailing. We'll have to do all the work with the absolute minimum of men and that'll mean very little sleep for all of us over the next week or so."

"Yes, I'd thought of that," Morehouse said. "But if we make a good few thousand in salvage money it will have been worth the risk, even though it may be tough as we get closer to the European coast. As it is, from what I've heard in the past, we will get about half of the combined value of the ship and her cargo when all this is over. Now that's not a bad sum, is it?"

Deveau and Wright nodded and then Deveau asked, "And you're still heading for Gibraltar, captain?"

"Yes, and I think you should do the same. I know it will add a few more miles than, say, aiming for Cadiz or Lisbon, but Gibraltar is where I'm due to deliver my own cargo, so I don't really have any choice, do I?"

Deveau nodded again. His captain was right.

"And by the way, Deveau," Morehouse said, "I'll ask the

cook to give you some of the food he has already prepared so you won't have to worry about that for a few days and I'll lend you my own pocket watch, which you can give me back when we get to Gibraltar."

Deveau thanked him and the men left to make their own preparations for what they knew would be a tough piece of sailing – sailing and navigating a two-masted brig for hundreds of miles across the Atlantic Ocean in winter with only a crew of three.

Two hours later, the *Dei Gratia*'s small lifeboat, now loaded with food, instruments and tools, was lowered over the side into the choppy waves. Deveau, Anderson and Lund then clambered down the side of the *Dei Gratia* into the rocking lifeboat. After waving to the rest of the crew and Captain Morehouse, Lund grabbed hold of the oars and started rowing. It took them only ten minutes to cover the short distance to where the *Mary Celeste* was rolling and swaying aimlessly in the blue-grey waves, entirely controlled by the speed and direction of the wind. In his final discussion with Captain Morehouse, Deveau had agreed that he and his crew would try and stay as close to the *Dei Gratia* as possible.

Once they reached the *Mary Celeste*, Anderson tied the lifeboat to the hull of the ship and the three men climbed aboard.

"This is weird," Lund commented as soon as he was on the deck. "It's like standing on a ghost ship, except that it's not one. Don't you feel that, Andy?"

Anderson shivered for a moment, nodded and then looked carefully around – as if he was expecting something or someone to suddenly appear. When nothing happened, he shook his head and walked towards the wheel. He asked

Deveau whether he should lash it down. Deveau said that he should, and Anderson took a piece of rope lying on the deck and tied the wheel into position. They immediately felt the effect as the strong westerly wind was caught in the mainsails and the rudder straightened out, guiding the now not-so-silent ship towards the horizon.

Deveau called the two men towards him. "Listen, we have got a lot of work to do, and fast."

"Aye, we've got to repair those topsails and the rigging immediately if we're going to be able to keep up with Morehouse," Anderson said, looking up at the masts.

"Yes, and we must see what can be done about that bilge water," Lund added. "If, as you said earlier, you measured about three and a half feet of it, that's not too much, but we don't really need it. The less there is the better."

"I know," Deveau said. "But go and check out the pumps anyway and see if they are really working properly. From what I saw when I came on board before, I think that they are. And yes, we are going to have to work out a rota for sleeping. There must be at least one of us awake at all times."

Anderson nodded. Lund returned a few minutes later to say that the pumps were working and that he had measured the depth of the bilge water below. He said that there was still three and a half feet of it, which was good news as it showed that the *Mary Celeste* was not leaking below the waterline. Knowing that, Lund spent the next two hours pumping the bilges dry. While he was doing so, Deveau and Anderson inspected the state of the sails, masts and rigging more closely.

"Have we got enough spare sails?" Anderson asked.

"I think so," Deveau replied. "I saw some when I came

aboard last time. They're below at the back of the hold. But for tonight we'll just tighten what we've got now and then start working on the topsails tomorrow when it's light. It will probably take us a day or two to replace those topsails and then, if the winds are fair after that, we should be able to keep up with Captain Morehouse as much as possible."

Deveau was right. The temporary sails enabled the *Mary Celeste* to stay near the *Dei Gratia* that night and the following morning. After lashing the wheel again into position and after only a couple of hours of fitful sleep in turns, the three exhausted sailors started working on fixing the new topsails for the almost silent ship.

It took them the best part of two days, between working and sleeping in shifts, to repair the *Mary Celeste*'s sails and some of the rigging, while doing their best to keep within sight of the *Dei Gratia*. At one point Lund nearly fell off the yard arm from where he was gripping on to tie a strong knot which would connect the new sail to the long spar. A sudden blast of wind blew against him and he had to lean forward quickly to grab a piece of rope to haul himself upright. He succeeded and soon the sail was in position, taking up the wind and helping the *Mary Celeste* sail even closer to the Portuguese coast.

Fortunately the three sailors got on well with each other and no-one complained about the hard work involved. In addition, Deveau found a spare trysail below deck in the hold and he had his two fellow sailors rig it as a foresail. It took them a couple of hours of hard work, ripe language and the bruising of Lund's left arm. However, when it was up, they immediately felt the difference in the ship's movements as she cut through the sea keeping as close as possible to the *Dei Gratia*.

"Well, I'm glad that job's finished at last," Anderson said as he poured out mugs of steaming coffee for the other two. "I thought we'd never get that first topsail in place on the foremast or that trysail, but we did. But Deveau, what are we going to do about that extra seawater in the galley? I don't think it's possible to pump it out."

"So let's go and see," Deveau said. Leaving Lund to steer the *Mary Celeste*, Anderson and Deveau entered the galley and soon saw that the pump they had used to empty out the bilge water was not suitable to get rid of the water swirling around on the galley floor.

"What d'you think we should do about it?" Anderson asked. "Can we live with this for a few more days until we reach land?"

"No, Andy, I don't think that's a good idea," Deveau replied, looking around carefully. "It might be all right now, now that the seas are calm, but think about what might happen if there's a storm. No, man, we must get rid of it."

"Aye, but how? Not with buckets I hope."

Deveau's answer was to drill some strategically placed holes in the ship's sides which succeeded in allowing the water to drain away leaving the galley dry but with a musty smell.

"Aye, and now I think we should start working out a proper timetable for sleeping," Deveau said after the freshly drilled holes had been plugged up. "Remember, we still have three or four hundred miles to go before we reach the Portuguese coast and we don't know what the weather will be like. I suggest that we divide up the day into four-hour watches and that we bring the wet bedding and mattresses up on deck to dry them out."

"Yes, and we've still got to deal with the rest of the rigging," Lund added, rubbing his bruised arm and hand, which he had cut while working on the topsail. "From what I have seen, some of it is going to have to be restrung and that could be quite a job."

"Yes, you're right there," Deveau agreed. "But we'll only try and repair the parts of the rigging that we have to. We'll just have to hope that what we don't touch will survive the rest of the voyage."

Anderson nodded and then asked, "I wonder what caused all the rigging to be in the condition it is now. It's weird."

"The whole thing is strange," Lund kept saying. "I keep thinking all the time about what might have happened to make Captain Briggs abandon ship in the middle of the ocean."

"Aye, and with his wife and baby daughter," Anderson added. "It just doesn't make any sense, does it?"

The other two nodded in agreement as they set to sorting out the various ropes for the rigging and laying them out on the foredeck as part of their preparation. For the next few hours, the *Mary Celeste*'s new crew attacked the problem of the rigging and by sunset it was in the best condition possible considering their situation. Of course, during most of this time, they took turns in manning the wheel and keeping as close as they could to the *Dei Gratia*. When a certain task needed all three of them, the wheel was lashed into position. On several occasions over the following week when they came close enough to the *Dei Gratia*, Deveau and Morehouse were able to shout to each other.

"I see you've fixed the topsails," Morehouse shouted through a megaphone after he had seen the new sails in position.

"Yes," Deveau hollered back, "and we've replaced some of the rigging, but only that which was really necessary."

"How are you off for food and drink?" Morehouse shouted again.

"We're all right for that," his first mate replied, "although we had to throw some of the fruit and potatoes overboard as they had gone rotten. And yes, we threw some of the fresh meat into the sea for the same reason. It was crawling, it was. Stinking as well. But don't worry, we've been eating lots of salt beef. That and onions."

"What about the broken binnacle? Did you find another?"

"No, we looked but we didn't have any luck. But don't worry, captain, we made a sort of temporary repair. And don't forget I've got my own compass as well. And, besides, if we stay close to you, we should be all right, no?"

The crews of the *Mary Celeste* and the *Dei Gratia* were lucky. For the following week the winds were light and soon the two ships were within sight of land. Then, just as Wright shouted that he could see Cape Spartel, part of the northernmost coast of Morocco, a sudden squall blew up which separated their two ships. The two crews had to work extremely hard that night to prevent the ships from being swamped by huge waves, and by the time they sailed into the calmer waters of the harbour at Gibraltar, the *Dei Gratia* one day earlier than the *Mary Celeste*, all the men on both ships were completely exhausted.

"What happened to you in that storm?" Morehouse asked Deveau once they were all reunited in a seafront tavern.

"We were nearly washed ashore onto the coast of Morocco," the first mate replied. "We had to turn east and add quite a few extra miles before we reached here, but we survived and that's the main thing, no?"

Morehouse nodded and then said, "And now we're going to have to face the authorities and tell them what happened. I mean, it's not every day that a ship is completely abandoned in mid-ocean and then turns up safe and sound in a harbour with another crew asking for salvage. I wonder what's going to happen. But I tell you what I'm going to do now. I'm going to wire a message to New York and tell them that we are going to start the procedure for a salvage claim."

And saying that, Morehouse scribbled down the message he wanted to telegram to New York.

Found fourth and brought here Mary Celeste abandoned seaworthy. Admiralty impost. Notify all parties. Telegraph offer of salvage.

"Aye," Anderson said, as Captain Morehouse put his pen in his pocket, "and I wonder how long that will take and how much we'll get. It should be quite a sum by my reckoning."

"Well, I hope it is," second mate John Wright said. "And I hope it won't take too long to get it. I could do with going home with a sackful of gold coins. I really could."

Chapter 11
The enquiry opens in Gibraltar

19th Century Gibraltar

"Ah, it's good to be back on dry land again," Captain Morehouse said to the official sitting opposite him. "Especially after a voyage like that."

"I wouldn't know," Thomas J. Vecchio, marshal of the British Vice Admiralty Court in Gibraltar, replied. "I'm not a sea-going man myself. I'm just a servant of Her Majesty whose job here is to make sure that everything runs smoothly and that justice is served."

Marshal Vecchio was the opposite of Captain Morehouse, the sailor. Whereas Morehouse was large, dressed in dark colours in tough seaman's garb, Vecchio was thin, fine-featured and wore a well-fitting light grey suit, a matching hat and beige cravat. As opposed to Morehouse's rolling gait, Vecchio had a slight limp and walked holding a silver-knobbed cane.

The admiralty official looked at the captain with interest. It was not every day that one ship brought in another from the middle of the Atlantic and claimed salvage money for having done so. In addition, the word had swiftly spread around the port that the *Mary Celeste* had been found in mid-ocean without a single person on board, dead or alive. It was most mysterious. No-one could remember anything like this ever having happened before.

The two men were sitting in the Nelson Touch, a small tavern in the shadow of the famous Rock of Gibraltar. From one side they could see the Rock, which dominated every view of the British strategic base, and from the other side they could see the harbour in which several ships of various sizes were rocking gently in the waves. The British and Dutch had captured the Rock from the Spanish in 1704 during the War of the Spanish Succession, and since the Treaty of Utrecht in 1713 it had remained British.

"How high is the Rock?" Morehouse asked, ordering another drink for himself and Vecchio. "I've been here lots of times and have always forgotten to find out."

"It's about fourteen hundred feet high," Vecchio replied. "It's made of limestone, and during the days of Napoleon, we, that is, the British, carved out huge caves inside it and filled them with cannon. They were then meant to be used against the French, if necessary, but since then life here has generally been quite peaceful."

"Yes, I know that," Morehouse smiled. "And I hope our salvage claim will also be a peaceful operation. Sailing two undermanned ships here, mine, the *Dei Gratia*, and the *Mary Celeste*, wasn't easy I assure you. Especially during the last day or two when we hit some rough weather. None of us had any sleep for a couple of days."

"Well, you look and sound all right now," the British official said.

"Yes, that's because we all collapsed into bed once we reached here," Morehouse explained, "and slept for almost a full day. And now, sir, what can you tell me about our salvage claim, about what we'll have to do? I've never been involved with one before, so this is all new to me."

The tall smooth-faced and bright-eyed Vecchio looked at the bearded and weather-beaten Morehouse and told him that he hoped that the proceedings would go smoothly. "I don't foresee any particular problem here," he said. "Nevertheless, there are certain procedures that have to be gone through, and I hope that Mr Solly Flood, who deals with such matters here, will not make life complicated for you."

"Good, because from the way I see it," Morehouse replied, "we found an abandoned ship at sea, took possession of it since there was no-one aboard and brought her safely into harbour. Should there be any problem with that? This isn't the first time someone has claimed salvage, is it?"

"No, captain, you're right. But there may be a few legal problems to sort out and the whole proceedings may not go as smoothly as you describe."

"Why is that?"

"Because we're talking about quite a lot of money here, captain. Thousands of dollars, and as you know, nobody likes paying out sums like that if they can possibly get out of it. And also" – and here the Vice Admiralty Court official leaned in towards the captain of the *Dei Gratia* and lowered his voice – "I've heard rumours that some people here are talking about this whole affair, you know, the *Mary Celeste* being found in mid-ocean with no-one aboard, as being an insurance fraud."

"*What!*" Morehouse almost shouted. "That was the last thing on my mind when I decided to bring in the *Mary Celeste*. Who's saying that?"

"Well, among other people I have heard, Mr Solly Flood has mentioned it."

"And who is this Mr Solly Flood?" Morehouse asked.

"He's another official who works in the Vice Admiralty Court. I've heard that he is very suspicious about your whole story."

"Why, what's he saying? Does he think that I've made up this whole damn episode?"

Vecchio shook his head and put his finger to his lips. He then told Morehouse that he was not allowed to tell him anything else, but no doubt he, the American sea captain, would know soon enough.

The British marshal was right. Mr Solly Flood *was* determined to make problems over the matter and as soon as Morehouse heard this, he contacted the American consul in Gibraltar, Horatio Jones Sprague.

The American official then invited Captain Morehouse to come and see him. Once there, Sprague asked the captain to take a seat in his book-lined office overlooking the harbour.

The Gibraltar-born official, who looked similar in many ways to Thomas Vecchio, that is, he had the dress and mannerisms of a government official, then ordered his assistant to bring in coffee and cakes and the two men got right down to business.

"Well, it's like this, Captain Morehouse," Sprague began. "I have asked the State Department to see if you can collect whatever is due to you without going through all the rigmarole that the British like to carry out here."

"Why, what do you mean?" Morehouse asked.

"What I'm simply saying is this. These British bureaucrats, that is, those that you are up against, the ones working here in the Vice Admiralty Court, love to tie everything up in red tape and then drag it all out interminably."

"But I've got my own ship here and its cargo to deliver as well as the *Mary Celeste*. And please remember, sir, the *Mary Celeste* has also got a cargo which is supposed to be on its way to Genoa."

"Yes, I know that," the consular official said. "But that doesn't seem to bother the British. Especially Mr Solly Flood. Therefore, I suggest that for the time being, you send a cable to Genoa and tell them that their cargo has been delayed here in Gibraltar."

"I see, and for how long?"

Sprague looked up at the ceiling and then at Morehouse. "I don't know, captain. I don't know. As I've just said, it seems to me that these Brits, and especially this Flood fellow, love to make a mountain out of a molehill. So be warned. Ah, and yes," Sprague added, pulling a document out of the leather pouch lying on the table in front of him, "your salvage claim's official title is 'David Reed Morehouse, Master of the brigantine *Dei Gratia* and for the Owners, Officers and crew of the said brigantine, claiming as Salvors'."

Morehouse took the large piece of paper bearing the seal of the British Vice Admiralty Court at the top, scanned it quickly and handed it back to Sprague.

"Aye, you're right. It does look like this Solly fellow plans to make a mountain out of a molehill. I just hope that this enquiry goes quickly. I've got a cargo to deliver and every day I hang around here in Gibraltar, money is being lost."

A couple of days after this meeting, on 18 December 1872, the salvage hearing began. It took place in the court of Sir James Cochrane, the Nova Scotian-born judge and commissary of the British Vice Admiralty Court of Gibraltar. The somewhat nervous crew members of the *Dei Gratia* were present, and so too was a Mr Henry Peter Pisani, a lawyer who had been retained by Morehouse to represent him and his crew. Morehouse decided not to attend, and when asked why, he justified himself by saying that he had never stepped aboard the *Mary Celeste* until the abandoned ship had reached Gibraltar.

"How long do you think we'll be here?" a nervous Charles Lund whispered to Deveau.

The first mate shrugged his shoulder. "Dunno. I was told that we are due to complete our testifying today. After that, I guess, anything can happen."

"Hmm. I don't like this," Anderson muttered. "I don't trust these Brits. Why, I remember a few years ago when I was in the harbour in Bermuda, some of those British officials—"

"Ssh!" Deveau hissed. "I want to hear what's going on."

At this point, the court proceedings got under way. At first, the crew members of the *Dei Gratia* were asked routine questions that were easy to answer. What were their names? If they had permanent places of abode, where did they live? Did they have any families? How long had they worked as sailors and what was their experience at sea? What were their jobs on the *Dei Gratia*?

But then Oliver Deveau and the other four sailors noticed that, as the questions went on, they became increasingly more pointed and complicated. Especially those asked by the prosecutor, Mr Solly Flood.

"Who is that man?" Lund asked the *Dei Gratia*'s second mate, John Wright, pointing to where the attorney general was sitting. "He seems determined to trip us all up. It's like he's calling us liars, y' know, that we're making up the whole story just so we can collect the salvage money."

Charles Lund was correct. Solly Flood, or as he liked to call himself, Mr Frederick Solly Flood, Advocate and Proctor for the Queen in her Office of Admiralty, was an extremely pedantic seventy-one-year-old lawyer who loved to make sure that in the legal proceedings he dealt with all the i's were dotted and the t's crossed. He had been born Frederick Solly, the son of a London fishmonger. However, in 1820 he had the surname Flood added to his name by 'Royal Licence' after his father died. In this way he set out to prove that he was a descendent of Sir Frederick Flood, a renowned Irish peer, lawyer and politician. The lawyer now facing the crew of the *Dei Gratia* had been educated at Harrow and Cambridge and started practising law in London soon after he graduated in 1828. However, he had lost a fortune in gambling and so had come to Gibraltar in order to recoup his losses for his old age. He did not like living on the Rock and hoped to see out his days on a farm in Ireland. To the impatient crewmen of the *Dei Gratia*, it seemed that Flood was taking out his bitterness on them.

However, it was not just Flood's bitterness that was relevant here, it was also his professional interest in the case. He was sure that something crooked lay behind the whole story. He had never heard of anything like it before.

He found it completely inconceivable that the crew of the *Dei Gratia* had simply come across the abandoned *Mary Celeste* in the middle of the Atlantic Ocean and that her crew had mysteriously disappeared while the ship was basically intact. And not only that, but the captain and crew of the *Dei Gratia* had also found the cargo in good condition. This whole cockamamie story simply did not make any sense to him. The arrogant and pretentious attorney general was convinced that insurance fraud or foul play, piracy or mutiny was behind the mystery, and he, Frederick Solly Flood, Her Majesty's attorney general in Gibraltar, the prosecutor in this case was determined to get to the bottom of it.

The pompous prosecutor stood up and faced the crew of the *Dei Gratia*. "Seeing that Captain David Reed Morehouse has chosen not to be present here today, although I cannot think of a good reason why, I will have to deal with you in his absence. In this way I hope that we will proceed and get to the bottom of this matter."

After each of the crew had stood up and answered the attorney general's questions, they sat down to wait for the next stage in this procedure, a procedure that was new and somewhat bewildering for all of them.

"Now, are you the first mate?" Flood asked Deveau.

Deveau stood up in the dock. "Yes, Your Honour," he said firmly. "First mate Oliver Deveau." He looked at a page of notes he had prepared in advance. "I am chief mate of the vessel, the *Dei Gratia*. I left New York on the fifteenth of November, bound for Gibraltar 'for orders'. My captain was, or rather, still is Captain Morehouse. On the fourth of December, while we were in the mid-Atlantic some six hundred miles off the coast of Portugal, the captain called me and said that there was a strange sailing ship on the windward bow, apparently in distress, which would probably be requiring assistance. That was about one o'clock in the afternoon, sea time. I came up on deck from where I had been checking some things in the hold and saw a vessel through the glass, my telescope, and she appeared to be about four or five miles off."

"I see, Mr Deveau. Now would you kindly tell me, or rather tell the court," Flood continued, his thin voice penetrating the courtroom. "What is your explanation for the disappearance of the crew of the *Mary Celeste*?"

Deveau shrugged. "I can't think of a reason, Your Honour. All I know is that when I went on board I found that the captain and his family, that is, his wife and baby daughter, as well as the crew were nowhere to be found, dead or alive. In addition, there was quite a lot of water in the bilges."

"How much?"

"About three feet, Your Honour."

"I see," Flood said, puffing out his stomach in its pale grey waistcoat before asking his next question. "Mr Deveau, who else went on board with you that first time?"

Deveau looked at the second mate. "Mr Wright, the second mate here was with me, Your Honour. And John

Johnson, here on my left, remained in the small boat that we rowed over in while Mr Wright and I went aboard."

"I see," Flood repeated. "And did you find anything else strange when you first went on board? Anything broken or not in place? Anything not shipshape?"

"Well, Your Honour, after searching through the ship, we found the ship's logbook in the captain's cabin and we saw that the last entry that had been made was on November the twenty-fifth. We thought that that was strange because the date was December the fourth—"

"In other words," Mr Solly Flood interrupted, "the log had not been written up for about ten days?"

"Yes, Your Honour."

"And did you find anything else untoward when you went on board the *Mary Celeste* that first time?"

"Yes, Your Honour," Deveau answered after looking at his fellow crewmen. "We saw that the binnacle was broken. And the wheel had not been lashed down so that the ship was not being controlled, that is, it was just being blown about by the wind."

"And what about the sails and the rigging? Were they also in poor condition, like the binnacle?" Sir James Cochrane, the judge of the British Vice Admiralty Court intervened.

Deveau turned to face his second questioner. "Some of the rigging needed replacing, Your Honour, and so too did several of the sails, especially the topsails."

"Tell me, first mate Oliver Deveau," Flood continued, enjoying being the focus of everyone's attention. "In what condition did you find the cabins, that is, those of the captain and his family, and also those of the crew?"

"They were as you would expect to find them, Your

Honour. The crew's cabins were as crews' cabins usually are, you know, a few clothes and personal possessions lying around, but nothing out of the ordinary. And as for the captain's cabin," Deveau continued, "it was also as expected, neat and tidy except for his daughter's dollies and toys, which were lying on the floor or in her cot. We did not expect anything else, Your Honour, as the captain of the *Mary Celeste*, Captain Briggs, was known to be a respected and professional officer as well as being a good God-fearing man. In other words, Your Honour, everything in the cabins seemed to have been left behind as though everyone on board had suddenly abandoned the ship in a great hurry."

"I see," the attorney general said, somewhat disappointed by the first mate's answer. "Now please give the court some more details of how the conditions were as you expected them to be."

Deveau paused for a few moments, looked down and then replied. "The captain's cabin was shipshape, Your Honour, except that the bed had not been made and the bedding was soaking wet. As I said, there were some of his small daughter's toys scattered on the floor and there was a bag full of dirty clothes in a cupboard. The captain's wife's harmonium was also in the cabin," the first mate added, "and there was a shelf of music books above it as well. But as it has already been said here, it looked as if everyone on board the *Mary Celeste* had abandoned ship in a hurry. But why, I don't know." Deveau shrugged again.

"Now, Mr Deveau," the attorney general continued. "Will you please tell the court about the lifeboats on board the *Mary Celeste*? Were they also in good condition and was there a sufficient number of them on board?"

"That I cannot say, Your Honour. You see, when we went on board we found no lifeboats. There had been one lifeboat but it was no longer in position. We assumed that it had been used by the captain and his family and crew when they abandoned ship, but this was mere speculation."

"And the anchors? Where were they?" Sir James Cochrane intervened again.

"They were where they should be, Your Honour. Securely in position in their rightful place."

"And now, Mr Deveau," Mr Solly Flood continued, anxious to regain control of the proceedings. "I would like to ask you again a few questions about the dates of your voyage, that is, when you were serving on the *Dei Gratia* as first mate and when you first saw the *Mary Celeste*, and about how you communicated between the two ships."

"Yes, Your Honour," a suspicious Deveau answered. "Do you mean after I went on board to bring her into Gibraltar or how the two captains, Briggs and Morehouse communicated with each other?"

"No, Mr Deveau," the pompous admiralty official leered. "I mean, do you know if the two captains, Captain Briggs and your own Captain Morehouse, had met and talked before you left New York?"

Deveau paused and looked at his fellow crewmen in the dock. Then he faced Mr Solly Flood. "I don't know, Your Honour. All I know is that we, as members of the crew of the *Dei Gratia*, had nothing to do with the crewmen of the *Mary Celeste*. And as for the two captains, I guess that it is possible that they may have met each other in New York before we set sail, Your Honour, but I don't really know. Perhaps they met to talk about their forthcoming voyages, but that is all I can say. I am not a close friend of either of them, and neither of them took me into their confidence. And as for the dates of the two ships' voyages, I have already told you earlier this morning."

"So what do you think happened to the captain and crew of the *Mary Celeste*?" Sir James Cochrane asked.

Oliver Deveau stood still for a few moments as he collected his thoughts. "Well, Your Honour," he said at last. "I think it was like this. The men on the Mary Celeste must have noticed that there was quite a lot of water in the bilges and this worried them. As I said earlier, we found the sounding rod lying near the pumps and when we, John Wright and myself, went on board, we found that there was about three and a half feet of bilge water present. Perhaps even more."

"Is that a lot, a dangerous amount?"

Deveau shrugged. "No, Your Honour, it's not very dangerous, but it is more than I would like to see in my ship if I were a captain in the middle of the ocean."

"What about the hatches, Mr Deveau?" Sir James Cochrane asked in a kinder tone than the clearly suspicious Solly Flood. "What were they like? Open? Closed? In position where they should be?"

"The hatches were lying open on the deck near where they should have been, Your Honour," Deveau answered. "Perhaps they were like that in order to allow the fumes of the alcohol in the barrels below to escape."

"Did *you* smell any alcoholic fumes when you first went on board?" Sir James continued.

Deveau shook his head. "No, Your Honour, not in general. But when I went below and stood close to some of the barrels, I could definitely smell alcohol. However, I guess that if there had been other smells in the air, they would have been blown away by the time we went on board. You must remember, sir, going by the lack of further entries in the ship's log, it seems that Captain Briggs and his crew had abandoned the *Mary Celeste* about ten days earlier."

"And you found no signs of violence?"

"That's right, sir. We found nothing like that."

Mr Solly Flood was just about to ask another question when Sir James said, "Right, I think we have heard enough for today. I will adjourn this hearing until this coming Friday." He turned to face the crew of the *Dei Gratia* waiting expectantly in the dock. "And you gentlemen, please make sure that you are all present then. Is that understood?"

"Yes, sir," they replied, and filed out into the setting sun to make their way over to the Nelson Touch tavern.

Chapter 12
The enquiry drags on

"Why do you think that Flood character kept asking you such pernickety tomfool questions?" Charles Lund asked Deveau that evening. The crew of the *Dei Gratia* were sitting in the Nelson Touch having a drink and going over the day's events. "Didn't he believe you?"

"It's not about if he believed me or not, Charlie," Deveau replied, finishing off his tankard of ale, "but, from what he was asking and the way he was doing so, I think he is sure that, before they left New York, Captain Morehouse and Captain Briggs had worked out some way to fool the insurance company and make a lot of money."

"But everyone knows that they wouldn't have done that," Anderson said. "Captain Briggs is a God-fearing family man and Captain Morehouse has also got a good name. I mean, that was why I was pleased when he signed me up. He's a fair bloke, not given to monkey business."

"I agree," second mate Wright added. "That's why I signed up with him as well."

"D'you think we're gonna get our salvage money in the end?" Anderson asked Deveau.

Deveau shrugged. "I don't know, man. From the way Flood is talking and asking questions in that nasty prissy manner of his, it doesn't look like it. We'll just have to wait and see what the next session brings, won't we?"

*

Two days later, Deveau was called to the stand once the court had reconvened in the large hall. Everyone had settled down and Sir John Cochrane had just given the signal to Attorney General Solly Flood that the enquiry could now continue. "Your Honour," Deveau began. "If I may say so, since you mentioned it earlier, I have been thinking about the time when we first boarded the *Mary Celeste*."

"Oh, yes, Mr Deveau," Attorney General Solly Flood said, looking around the courtroom before concentrating his gaze on the first mate. "And when was that?"

"It was at three o'clock in the afternoon on the fourth of December and not the time I said earlier."

"Oh, and I suppose your other answers to my questions were also not exactly true," Flood said, looking around triumphantly.

"No, Your Honour, that is not so," Deveau replied. "Everything else that I said here two days ago is God's own truth."

"Well, I'm glad that the Good Lord is on your side, Mr Deveau, because from what I understand, you are going to need all the help that you can get. Now let's hear from some other members of your crew and see what they have to say. Let's hear if they also have help from above and if their words agree with yours. Yes, celestial help is what you'll all be needing, if your bringing the *Mary Celeste* here fails to result in any salvage reward."

Feeling pleased with his witticism, Flood looked around the court expecting to see a smiling response of approval. However, none was forthcoming. And from the look on the face of Sir James Cochrane, it was clear that he too was not pleased with how Mr Frederick Solly Flood was handling the case. However, despite what Sir James thought of him, the attorney general pressed on and called for second mate John Wright to take the stand. But, before Flood could begin his asking his questions, Sir James Cochrane intervened and told Mr Henry Peter Pisani, the crew's lawyer, to cross-question Wright.

Pisani, a conservatively dressed lawyer in a dark suit who was well-versed in maritime law, stood up and faced the second mate. Pisani gave a slight cough and then asked Wright to give his own detailed description of what had happened and what he had seen when he and Deveau first climbed aboard the *Mary Celeste*.

"It was just as first mate Deveau described it, sir," Wright began, determined to support his fellow crewman. "There was about three and a half feet of water in the bilges and the ship looked as if it had been hastily abandoned."

"What do you mean by that – it looked as if it had been hastily abandoned?"

Wright scratched his head, paused and then began. "Well, sir," he said, thinking back to that weird half hour when he and Deveau had first inspected the silent *Mary Celeste*. "The captain's cabin was all in order, save for a few of his baby daughter's toys lying around and the crew's cabin was also as expected. Y'know, beds half made, a few clothes lying around, a pair of boots on the floor and stuff like that. There was nothing odd, sir, in any of the cabins. Just the usual situation when a ship's crew shares a cabin; not tidy but not very untidy, either, if you know what I mean."

Pisani nodded. "And were there any signs of violence that you noticed when you first went on board?"

"No, sir. None. None at all."

"Nothing broken or smashed? No signs of blood anywhere?"

"No, sir. Nothing like that, apart from the broken binnacle and the torn topsails. I'm telling you that if there had been any signs of blood anywhere I would have remembered them."

Pisani nodded again. "Thank you, Mr Wright, and now I see that Mr Solly Flood wishes to ask you some more questions."

The *Dei Gratia*'s defence lawyer, Pisani, had hardly sat down when the excitable attorney general got to his feet. He began repeating the questions Pisani had asked, hoping to trip the second mate up, and it was clear to everyone present that he was very disappointed when Wright repeated the same answers.

"And are you absolutely sure about the pumps and the bilge water?" Flood insisted.

"Yes, Your Honour. Absolutely."

A disappointed attorney general then told Wright that he could step down and that Charles Lund should take his place. Unfortunately for Flood, Lund's testimony did not contradict anything that Deveau and Wright had said in any serious way. There were a few discrepancies regarding the times of various events, such as when the two ships lost or regained sight of each other in the North Atlantic, but these details were considered insignificant. In order to cover himself,

Lund explained that if his testimony did not exactly match that of the first and second mates, it was because of the stormy weather that they had encountered.

"Your Honour," he said to Sir James Cochrane at the end of his testimony. "When you are halfway up a mast or fixing the rigging in a storm, you aren't thinking about what time of day it is. You are more worried about loose ropes and torn sails and how much water has flooded into your cabin than whether you can see the other ship or not."

Sir James accepted this explanation and motioned for Lund to step down. He then announced that there would be another break in the proceedings and that the court would reconvene on Saturday, 21 December 1872.

When the salvage enquiry started again, Augustus Anderson took the stand. As before, Attorney General Solly Flood was ready for him with a barrage of questions: questions designed to prove how the other crewmen had not told the truth. Or that if they had, it had not been the complete truth.

"As you know, Your Honour," Anderson began, "I was with Mr Deveau when we first climbed up onto the deck of the *Mary Celeste*. I immediately saw that her topsails were torn and useless and that some of her rigging needed to be repaired and, yes, that was true about some of her ratlines as well."

"And what about the cabins, Mr Anderson?"

"They were like the first and second mate described, Your Honour. In a normal condition as expected."

"Are you sure about what you have said?" the attorney general persisted.

"Yes, Your Honour," Anderson replied. "I've got a very

good memory and I wouldn't tell you no lies."

"And what about the ship's compass and binnacle?"

"They were broken as you've been told, Your Honour, and we wasn't able to repair them. We used Mr Deveau's own compass, the one he brought over from the *Dei Gratia* for steering, and it was that what got us here, that is, to Gibraltar."

"Did *you* see the logbook of the *Mary Celeste*?" Flood continued, implying that whatever was in it was a closely guarded secret between the first and second mate.

"Yes, Your Honour, of course I saw it," Anderson replied. "And I agree with everything that Mr Deveau and Mr Wright have said here."

A dissatisfied Solly Flood then asked Anderson to step down and called for John Johnson to take the stand.

"Mr Johnson," the attorney general began. "Did you go on board the *Mary Celeste*?"

"*Niet.*"

"What do you mean – *niet*? What sort of answer is that?"

"I-I sorry, s-sir. I b-born in Russia and I not s-speak English good," Johnson stammered under pressure.

"Well, did you go on board the *Mary Celeste*? Yes or no?" Flood repeated.

"*Niet*, no. I no go on *Mary Celeste*."

The attorney general saw that he would not get much out of the Russian-born sailor and told him to return to where he had been sitting next to Charles Lund.

At this point, Sir James Cochrane who was clearly not pleased with the prosecutor's attitude told him that if he had wanted to examine the logbook of the *Dei Gratia*, he could have done so at any time since the enquiry started.

"How so?" the exasperated Flood asked, angered that the judge and commissary of the Vice Admiralty Court was castigating him in public. "I have asked to see it on more than one occasion and this has been denied me."

"That is not so, sir," Sir James replied. "This logbook has been here in court for the last week or so and you could have examined it whenever you chose to do so."

Hearing this exchange, the crew members of the *Dei Gratia* smiled to each other. This was the first good thing that they had heard since the enquiry began. However, their joy was short-lived when they heard Sir James' next announcement.

"At the end of the three days spent in this court, I see we are no nearer the truth about what happened to the captain and crew of the *Mary Celeste*, to say nothing of the captain's wife and baby daughter. I therefore declare that this ship will not be released, and its cargo will be impounded until we get to the bottom of this matter. In addition, any salvage money, however much it might be, will not be given to the crew of the *Dei Gratia* until more questions have been answered. I will later inform the court when this salvage enquiry will resume. In the meanwhile," he added, addressing the five crew members of the *Dei Gratia*, "please make sure that you do not leave Gibraltar and are ready at a moment's notice to return here. That is all for today."

He banged his gavel and everyone stood up to leave.

*

"These men are lying," Flood fumed to Sir James Cochrane that evening. "Of that I am sure. There is some conspiracy afoot and I mean to get to the bottom of it."

"What do you mean," Sir James replied. "What sort of conspiracy? These men do not seem to be sharp enough to carry out any such plan. As far as I can see, they're just a bunch of simple hard-working sailors."

"*Bah!* to that, is what I say," the prosecutor reacted, banging his fist down on the table in Sir James's office. "They're just part of a well-thought-out plot to defraud the company which insured the *Mary Celeste*. I'm telling you, all this story about a missing crew and finding the ship abandoned in mid-ocean is nothing but a bunch of nonsense! And, yes, why hasn't their captain, appeared in court? Now answer me that, Sir James. To me it all seems a very fishy tale."

"So what are you going to do about it? I mean, about uncovering this conspiracy as you call it?"

"I'm going to call in Mr John Austin—"

"The nautical surveyor who you've used before?"

"Yes, him and also Mr Ricardo Portunato, the diver."

"What for?"

"I'll ask him to examine the hull of the *Mary Celeste* and see if there is any evidence of an accident or foul play of some sort or other."

"And when do you propose to contact these two?"

"Monday morning, Sir James, and of course, the court will cover their expenses."

"Do you really think that all of this is necessary, Mr Flood?"

"Yes, sir. I definitely do. I am convinced that something is or was afoot here and I am determined to find out what it is."

The following morning, the attorney general had his assistant contact the surveyor and the diver and asked them to come to his office that Monday afternoon.

"Gentlemen," Flood began. "I want you to investigate what has happened on board the *Mary Celeste*."

"The ship in the harbour, sir, moored next to the *Dei Gratia*?"

"Yes, Mr Austin. That same one. Now this is what I know or have been told about it…" and the attorney general launched into an impartial description of what he assumed had happened aboard the abandoned brigantine and what he expected the surveyor and the diver to find.

"And both of you, please carry out your tasks as efficiently and as expeditiously as possible," he added. "A lot of money is involved here. Thousands of dollars, in fact. I would be very pleased if you would submit a full and detailed report about what you find within one week. Is that clear?"

John Austin and Ricardo Portunato nodded, and after tying up a few loose administrative ends, the men left the attorney general's office wondering what they would discover. If anything.

It was also at this time, Christmas 1872, that the *Dei Gratia* and her crew left Gibraltar and set sail for Genoa. She was, after all, a merchant ship with a hold full of cargo to deliver, and the longer she waited in Gibraltar, the more money would be lost and penalties for late delivery incurred. Captain Morehouse decided to stay behind in Gibraltar, and Deveau was appointed to command his ship in his place. The crew would later return to Gibraltar in order to hear the verdict concerning their claim for salvage.

When the Honourable Judge James Cochrane heard about this, he recorded his displeasure thus:

The conduct of the salvors in going away, as they have done, has, in my opinion, been most reprehensible and may probably influence the decision as to their claim for remuneration for their services, and it appears very strange that the captain of the Dei Gratia, *who knows little or nothing to help the investigation, should have remained here, whilst the first mate and the crew who boarded the* Mary Celeste *and brought her here should have been allowed to go away as they have done.*

This did not bode well for the salvage claim, but while the judge was recording his opinion, the *Dei Gratia* and her crew were sailing south to deliver the goods in her hold. After all, money was money and business was business.

Chapter 13
Enter Mr Winchester

19th Century map of the Atlantic Ocean

It was a cool blustery day in mid-December in New York when ship owner Mr James Winchester's secretary knocked on the door of his office.

"Yes, Franklin, what is it?" Winchester asked as he pointed to a pile of documents lying on the desk to his right. "Can't you see I'm trying to catch up with all this work before the Christmas vacation?"

"Yes, sir, but I think this is important," and the impulsive secretary took the piece of paper he was clutching and thrust it at his employer. "Sir," he said. "I've just received a cable from Gibraltar. It's about the *Mary Celeste*."

"And about time too," Winchester said, reaching out to take it. "Give it to me and let's see what's happened to her. She should have delivered her cargo by now."

The telegram did not say much. All it said was: 'Brig Mary Celeste found fourth [December] brought to Gibraltar.' After making some enquiries Mr James Henry Winchester learned that a salvage investigation was being held and that he, the majority shareholder of the *Mary Celeste*, should come to Gibraltar as soon as possible.

"*Damn! Damn! Damn!*" Winchester swore once he had read the cable. It had been sent by Horatio Jones Sprague, the American consul in Gibraltar, and he stressed that the quicker Winchester arrived there, the better.

"What's the problem, sir?" the secretary asked. He was not used to hearing his normally mild-mannered employer using such intemperate language.

"They want me to go to Gibraltar immediately, that is, if there's a ship that's available," Winchester replied. "Dammit, and I was planning to spend Christmas and New Year here with my family. I'm probably going to miss out meeting my cousin as well."

"Is it *that* urgent, sir, or could you send someone else? Perhaps I could go instead."

"No, Mr Franklin, it must be me. You see we are talking about possible insurance claims worth thousands of dollars, both for the ship and its cargo. But crossing the Atlantic in mid-winter is not exactly my idea of pleasure, and my wife, who isn't too well at the moment, will be a bag of nerves until I return."

"Yes, sir. I understand. My wife was the same when you sent me to Miami last January, and that is much nearer than Gibraltar."

"Yes, so you understand. Now, be a good man and cancel all my meetings from tomorrow for the next month or so and be ready to take over in the meanwhile."

Franklin smiled to himself. This was the opportunity he had been waiting for. To prove to his boss that he was not just an assistant, but an employee who could be counted on to run things when the boss was away. And to do so well. However, despite his desire to show how invaluable he could be, he said, "Yes, sir. I know I'll be pleased to take your place for a while, but couldn't you solve this problem by telegraph, or by going through the State Department? Isn't that what they are there for?"

"No, Mr Franklin. I can't. I understand what you are saying, but not this time. There's too much money at stake here to leave this to a whole bunch of petty bureaucrats who are more concerned about their own affairs than mine."

Christmas day 1872 found an anxious Mr J.H. Winchester on board the *Abyssinia*. She was a large three-masted passenger and cargo ship whose hold was fully laden with barrels of petroleum and boxes of agricultural machinery. Her destination was Gibraltar and she was sailing east along the same route that the *Mary Celeste* and the *Dei Gratia* had taken two months earlier. Winchester's previous bad mood about his voyage had changed into one of curiosity. Now he was leaning over the rail at the bow end of the ship staring into the grey roiling waves of the North Atlantic wondering what the British wanted from him in Gibraltar. And why in God's name was the British Vice Admiralty Court involved in his affairs? He was an American, after all, and the *Mary Celeste* was an American ship. Her last voyage had had nothing to do with the British at all.

Winchester arrived in Gibraltar on 15 January 1873 after a voyage via Liverpool. As soon as the *Abyssinia* docked, he made his way over to the American consul's harbourside office. After an animated conversation with Mr Sprague, who filled him in with the details about the enquiry – "although it sounds more like a trial to me," Winchester commented – the majority shareowner of the *Mary Celeste* went to book himself into the hotel that the consul had recommended.

"The food and beds there are good," the efficient and dutiful Sprague said, concluding their conversation, "and best of all, it's a very clean and well-run establishment."

The following morning, accompanied by the consul, Winchester entered one of the most imposing buildings on the Rock, the home of the British Vice Admiralty Court. After identifying himself to one of the clerks and filling in a few forms, which Winchester thought were a waste of time, he was told that the enquiry would not reconvene until the twenty-ninth of January.

"Why the delay?" he almost shouted at the clerk. "You sent word, a cable, telling me to come here as quickly as I could. I missed Christmas and New Year with my family and now you are telling me that this damn enquiry – trial more like it – isn't going to start again for another two weeks. Why?"

"Well, it's like this, sir," the bland-faced clerk replied.

"Mr Solly Flood, the attorney general, has asked for further investigations to be made before the enquiry continues and we must make allowances for that."

"But I was given to understand that they would be over by now," Winchester fumed.

"I know that, sir, but Mr Austin, the surveyor, and Mr Portunato, the diver, still need some more time. It seems that the Christmas holidays slowed everything down. You know what it's like, sir. Any excuse not to work hard."

"So what am I supposed to do here for the next two weeks?" Winchester asked, thinking about his business back in New York and having to waste his precious time here on the other side of the Atlantic. "I have a company to run and the alcohol in the hold of the *Mary Celeste* should have been delivered by now."

The clerk shrugged. There was nothing he could add. Muttering something about having to leave the ship owner and the consul to see about another matter, he turned around and walked off down the long corridor as quickly as he could. *These Americans*, he thought. *Always wanting everything done immediately. Pushing, pushing. This is Gibraltar, not New York. And anyway, the Rock is a British outpost, not a part of the United States.*

It was during this period that Sprague wrote to the US Department of State that Mr J.H. Winchester had arrived in Gibraltar,

For the purpose of claiming the Brig and attending to the interests of all those concerned in her case... in the meanwhile nothing is heard of the Mary Celeste, *and in face of the apparent seaworthy conditions of this vessel, it is*

difficult to account for her abandonment, particularly as her Master, who was well-known, bore the highest character for seamanship and correctness... the attorney general seems to take the greatest interest in this case and rather entertains the apprehension of some foul play having occurred... so the matter is wrapped up in mystery.

After cooling his heels in Gibraltar by conducting as much of his business as possible by telegraph and by making a few trips to see the sights on mainland Spain, Winchester found himself in the Vice Admiralty Court early on 29 January 1873. Instead of walking immediately into the enquiry as he expected, he was first asked to sign some documents in which he identified Captain Briggs's signature on the *Mary Celeste*'s bills of lading. After that, an exasperated Mr J.H. Winchester, accompanied by George F. Cornwell, Winchester's attorney in Gibraltar, was escorted into the courtroom. Minutes after he entered, he found himself being closely questioned by Mr Solly Flood.

After Winchester answered the initial questions concerning his identity and how he was connected to the *Mary Celeste*, Flood started to bombard him with a series of technical questions about the abandoned brigantine.

"So you say that you had the *Mary Celeste* refitted before this voyage?" Flood began.

"Yes, Your Honour. About four years ago, that is, quite some time before this last voyage. In 1868 to be exact. After we, that is, my company had bought her, we had another deck added and her length extended to 103 feet. We also increased her weight to 282 tons and we had the hull re-sheathed at the same time, with copper, if you really must know."

"I see and—"

"But excuse me, Your Honour," Winchester interrupted. "How is this relevant to this enquiry?"

"It's for me to ask the questions here, sir," the self-important prosecutor replied and continued. "So she was virtually a new ship when she left New York last November?"

"Yes, Your Honour. You could say that."

"So she was worth a lot of money, a lot more than what she was worth when you first bought her?"

"Yes, Your Honour."

"How much was your *Mary Celeste* worth when she was abandoned, or when the crew of the *Dei Gratia* claimed they found her?"

Winchester paused and began whispering to Cornwell who was seated to his right. A few moments later, reading from a page that his attorney had given him, Winchester said that the *Mary Celeste* had been insured for $14,000 although she was probably worth two thousand dollars more.

"Hmm, that's quite a tidy sum," Flood commented. "And Mr Winchester, how much was the cargo worth, that is, by the London market?"

The ship owner went into another huddle with Cornwell. Then he stood up, straightened himself out and turned back to face the attorney general.

"About $36,000, Your Honour."

"So in other words, Mr Winchester," the prosecutor summarised, "you claim that your ship, the *Mary Celeste* was worth some $14,000 plus another $36,000 in all?"

"Yes, Your Honour."

"That is, about $50,000 altogether?

Winchester, wondering where this line of questioning was leading to, nodded. "Yes, Your Honour"

"I see. And are you the sole owner of the *Mary Celeste*?"

"No, Your Honour. But I am the majority shareholder and that is the reason I am here now instead of any of the other shareholders."

"And was Captain Briggs another shareholder?"

"Yes, Your Honour, he owns or owned a third of the ship's shares. And," Winchester added before the attorney general could interrupt him, "I will take this opportunity to add that he bears or bore a high character, the character of a courageous officer and good seaman who would not, I think, desert his ship except to save his life. I am telling you, Your Honour, that Captain Briggs is, or was known to be a conscientious and reliable captain and a good God-fearing Christian. I will also say the same about the first mate, Mr Richardson, who —"

"Excuse me, Mr Winchester," Flood interrupted. "We are not here to describe Captain Briggs's character or sailing abilities or, indeed, that of his first mate however good they were. We are here to see about the salvage payment that Captain Morehouse has claimed."

"Yes, Your Honour," Winchester muttered, determined not to let himself be riled by the attorney general.

"Now tell me, Mr Winchester, or rather tell this board of enquiry, how do you think that your ship, the *Mary Celeste*, came to be abandoned in the middle of the Atlantic and discovered by Captain Morehouse and the *Dei Gratia*? Were there any sea monsters present? Were there any storms in the area that would have caused the good Captain Briggs to abandon ship?"

"I don't know, Your Honour," Winchester replied. "I don't believe it was a question of sea monsters, but I do know that Captain Briggs was a good and experienced captain. It is hard for me to think that he would have readily abandoned the *Mary Celeste* without a good reason, and especially in a storm, something that happens frequently in the North Atlantic."

"Why so?"

"Your Honour, if you are in the middle of a storm at sea, you are more likely to survive by staying on board a large vessel than by abandoning it for a much smaller lifeboat. And you must remember, Captain Briggs not only had to think about himself and his crew, but also about his wife and baby daughter. I'm positive that he would have had their interests at heart above all else."

As soon as Winchester had said this, he noticed a smile on the face of Mr Cornwell, his attorney, as well as on the face of Sir James Cochrane.

"So, Mr Winchester," the frustrated Flood continued, pedantically repeating the insurance fees for the ship and her cargo, "you cannot say why, or give any substantial reason why your ship, the *Mary Celeste*, which you say was insured for $14,000 plus approximately $36,000 for its cargo, that is about $50,000 in all, came to be found abandoned in the middle of the North Atlantic?"

"No, Your Honour, I cannot."

"Mr Winchester," the attorney general continued, "do you know anything about the *Mary Celeste* being used for smuggling contraband goods from America to Europe?"

"No, Your Honour. I do not. Has any evidence of this been found? Because if so, I find it very difficult, in fact impossible, to believe this charge knowing the reputation of Captain Briggs. In addition, I was with Captain Briggs in New York harbour the day before she sailed and I would have noticed any illegal cargo on board."

"Yes, but—" Flood persisted.

"Nothing, Your Honour," Winchester interrupted. "Nothing. There was absolutely nothing illegal being carried by the *Mary Celeste*."

At this point, Sir James Cochrane leaned over to Mr Solly Flood and whispered in his ear that he should stop this line of questioning as there was no evidence that the *Mary Celeste* had been used to smuggle goods across the Atlantic. The attorney general reluctantly agreed and abruptly changed his tactics.

"Mr Winchester," he said, beaming. "Did you know that arms were carried on your ship, the *Mary Celeste*?"

Winchester went into a quick huddle with his attorney who then turned to face Mr Solly Flood.

"Of course, my client knows that there were some arms aboard," Cornwell replied. "Mr Winchester has just informed me that every merchant ship carries some in case of mutiny or pirates. That's quite standard."

"Ah then," the attorney general gloated. "So you have heard that a bloodstained sword, a sort of cutlass I believe, was found aboard your ship, have you?"

As he said so, a buzz filled the courtroom. Bloodstains and swords. This was exciting. This was new.

"No, Your Honour, I have not heard anything about such a weapon being found on board – with or without bloodstains. If Captain Briggs and perhaps his first and second mates were to carry any weapons, they were more likely to be revolvers, not swords. As I said, I never saw any swords on board when I was there prior to their leaving New York."

"Well, what I have just said is true, Mr Winchester. Such a sword was found in Captain Briggs's cabin," Flood insisted. "And I want to know what it was doing there. I mean, why was there a sword on board, and why was it stained with blood. And yes, whose blood was it?"

Winchester looked astonished, shrugged and asked, "How did you find this weapon? As I have just said, I didn't know anything about it. It must have been Captain Briggs's personal souvenir or something like that. You know, a memento from the Civil War. Anyway, who found it?"

"Well, obviously it wasn't me," Flood replied, for once answering a question. "My court-appointed surveyor, Mr John Austin, found it. And now, sir, I want to know what it was doing there. Perhaps your answer, if indeed you have one, will shed a great deal of light on why the *Mary Celeste* was abandoned in mid-ocean."

"Well, before Mr Winchester answers you, Mr Solly Flood," Sir James said, rising in his chair. "I suggest that we adjourn for the day and continue in two days' time. I would like time for us to consider what we have heard today."

Hearing this, Mr Winchester stood up and looked at Sir James. "Your Honour," he began. "Is that really necessary? I mean, to adjourn this enquiry for a couple of days? You see, I left my home and family as well as my office in New York well over a month ago and I would really like to get to the end of these proceedings and return home as soon as possible."

"Yes, I'm sure you would, sir," Sir James replied. "But

owing to the strange nature of this enquiry, the mysterious abandoning of a ship in the North Atlantic, we must do our best to find out what really happened. Besides, I am sure that another day or so spent in Gibraltar will not seriously affect either your domestic plans or your business affairs. Am I right?"

Winchester nodded. He realised that he had no choice but to agree.

"Well, in that case," Sir James announced from the bench. "We will reconvene here on the day after next at ten o'clock to give us time to examine some of the evidence given here today. After that we will proceed with the relevance of this sword that Mr Austin, the surveyor, found aboard the *Mary Celeste*."

Chapter 14
The sword and the cuts

The morning that Mr Winchester, accompanied by Mr Cornwell, was on his way to the Vice dmiralty Court was very cool, as a stiff breeze was blowing in over the Rock from the Atlantic Ocean. Mr Winchester pulled up his collar and muttered to his attorney that, at least, however cold it was here, it was still warmer than in New York. Cornwell nodded, pulled up his own collar and the two men continued on their way over the cobbled streets. It was not that they were late, but neither of them wanted to be the subject of the attorney general's probable remarks if they were not present when the next session began. Soon after, the two Americans, the ship owner and his lawyer, took their place in the wood-panelled courtroom.

"Now, Mr Winchester," Flood began the enquiry's new session. "I wish to repeat what we said about the sword that was found on board the *Mary Celeste*; the bloodstained sword. Are you absolutely sure that you didn't know that Captain Briggs kept arms on the *Mary Celeste*?"

"No, I didn't know specifically, but as I said here two days ago, I am not surprised to hear that he did so. After all, there have been incidents of piracy in the past, although as far as I know, there haven't been any in the last few years."

"Well, sir," Flood said dramatically. "Your captain, your God-fearing employee as you called him, kept this sword in his cabin." The attorney general leaned over and removed the cloth cover from the long object on the bench in front of him. He swung it around above his head for effect and then laid it down on the bench. "Yes, sir, this is his sword, and now, Mr Winchester, can *you* account for the bloodstains on it?"

The ship owner was silent for a couple of minutes. Then he went into a huddle with Cornwell before saying, "No, Your Honour, I cannot, but I must add that I am not surprised."

"Not surprised, sir?" the astonished attorney general replied. "*Not surprised?*"

"No, Your Honour. I am not at all surprised. As I mentioned the last time we met here, captains and commanders of ships, both military and commercial, have often been known to carry arms. They have done so, and I presume will continue to do so, mainly as a preventative measure in case of pirates or mutiny. Therefore, I say that there is nothing exceptional here about Captain Briggs's having a sword with him on board. In fact, the opposite would be true. However, if I were asked, I would have thought that a revolver would have been more useful."

"But this sword is bloodstained, sir. *Bloodstained!*"

Winchester looked at Cornwell, shrugged and then turned back to face the open-mouthed attorney general.

"You don't care about this?" Flood asked at last. "Or that there were also bloodstains found on the deck?"

"Of course I care, Your Honour," Winchester replied more forcefully than he had intended. "Captain Briggs was one of my best employees as well as being one of the *Mary*

Celeste's fellow shareholders, so of course I am very concerned what happened to him, his family and the crew of this ship. However, I have no explanation for the bloodstains on the sword or on the deck. Perhaps they were the result of a crewman cutting himself while working on board or perhaps these bloodstains came from the cook cutting up some meat or something similar. I don't know." And he shrugged again.

"All right," a disappointed Flood said. "We will leave the question of blood for the present and now, let me ask you about some suspicious cuts that were made in the ship's woodwork. What have you got to say about them?"

"Nothing, Your Honour. This is the first time that I have heard about such cuts. You see, I—"

"Hold it there, Mr Solly Flood," Sir James Cochrane interrupted. "I would like to hear from Captain Shufeldt, a past navy commander and court-appointed official, who, following my earlier instructions, has inspected the *Mary Celeste*. Captain Shufeldt, please tell this enquiry what you think about these cuts."

"Yes, sir." A large weather-beaten naval officer in a dark blue suit and a bright white shirt stood up and moved to the centre of the court to reply. He coughed, cleared his throat and began. "I was asked by this board of enquiry to inspect the state of the *Mary Celeste*, that is, the ship's actual physical state, and it is true that I did find some cuts made in the upper woodwork of the ship. However, I was not too impressed by them. You see, Your Honour, it must be taken into consideration that ships are often subject to rough treatment either by the sea or by the weather or indeed the crewmen on board and also that this ship had apparently been abandoned for whatever reason some ten days beforehand."

"Are you saying, sir," the attorney general asked, "that these cuts do not indicate that anything in particular, anything untoward had taken place? Weren't they the marks and cuts resulting from signs of violence made by a mutinous crew or perhaps pirates?"

"No, Your Honour, they weren't," Shufeldt replied, looking straight at the attorney general. "I am saying that these cuts which you refer to were probably caused by nothing more than splinters from the natural bending of the planks, or a crew member carrying something sharp and inadvertently cutting part of the ship. Accidental damage as it were. Something that often happens to ships at sea, especially when they have been subjected to stormy weather.

"Then later," he calmly continued, "these protruding pieces of wood were possibly broken off by the action of the waves or indeed by the sailors on board to prevent themselves from being wounded by the wooden shards in the future. And in any case, Your Honour, from my long experience as a sea captain I can quite definitely say that these cuts did not cause any real harm to the ship.

"All in all, Your Honour, it is impossible to say exactly how these cuts were made and why. And," he added just as Flood was beginning to stand up to ask another question, "I would also say that no obvious signs of human injury, such as bloodstains and the like, were found in the vicinity of these cuts."

Winchester smiled when Solly Flood showed further signs of disappointment on hearing this expert testimony.

"Are you sure, sir?" the attorney general persisted.

"Yes, Your Honour. New planking in a ship – and I know

that the *Mary Celeste* had been recently refitted before setting off on this last voyage – often suffers from such splintering. It is only after some time at sea and, indeed, the passage of time in general, that the wood settles down as it were and that such splintering ceases to occur."

Seeing that he would get no further help from the expert witness, Flood told Captain Shufeldt that he could step down.

Later that week, Attorney General Solly Flood was to be further disappointed following a private conversation with Thomas J. Vecchio, the marshal of the court.

"Mr Solly Flood," the marshal began. "Did you know that I too ordered a new search of the hold of the *Mary Celeste* to be made?"

"No, sir, I did not. When did this happen and what did you find?"

For an answer, the tall thin-faced, bearded judiciary official passed a foolscap folder to the surprised attorney general. "First read my report and then come to my office tomorrow morning."

The next morning, Flood appeared at the marshal's office, report in hand. "I see, sir," he said, sitting in a padded chair facing Mr Vecchio across his large desk. "You found absolutely no evidence that the crew of the *Mary Celeste* had tampered with the barrels of alcohol that were in the hold."

"That's right, Mr Solly Flood. I found all of them – all seventeen hundred of them, seventeen hundred and one to be exact – to be unopened. I asked my men to open a random fifty of the barrels and they reported that almost all of these barrels were full and that they were, to quote, 'in excellent order'."

"Ah, *almost*, you say," a triumphant Flood said. "That

means that some of the barrels had been tampered with."

"Not so, Mr Flood." Marshal Vecchio smiled. "You see, I asked around and I found out that when alcohol is stored in red oak barrels, which is the situation here with the *Mary Celeste*, it does have the tendency to evaporate, and this is what happened here. Of course, had this alcohol been kept in metal barrels, there would have been no evaporation at all."

"So the crew cannot be charged with tampering or being influenced by alcohol," the disappointed attorney general concluded.

"Exactly, sir. And in any case," Vecchio continued. "The alcohol in these barrels was of the raw sort, the industrial sort, not the sort that one drinks for pleasure."

"What do you mean?"

"I mean, sir, that if anyone were foolish enough to drink this stuff, they would probably lapse into an alcoholic coma and die. This particular alcohol was being transported to Genoa on the *Mary Celeste* in order to fortify Italian wines or to be used for medicines and the like."

"Oh, and I—"

"And in addition, Mr Flood, we have heard it mentioned several times now in this enquiry that Captain Briggs was a religious God-fearing man who would have certainly not allowed any of his crew to become drunk, I mean on regular alcohol such as beer and table wine. In fact, if any of them did become drunk, he'd have probably locked them up."

"Yes, sir," Flood replied quietly. He then looked up at the marshal. "Is that it? May I go now?"

"Yes you may, Mr Flood, but be careful from now on and I'll see you at the enquiry."

The chastened judicial officer left the room. That night in

the solitude of his office, Solly Flood took stock of what had happened so far. None of his theories were making sense. Any ideas that he had had regarding the disappearance of the ten souls on the *Mary Celeste* had fallen apart in the courtroom. Theories about swords, blood, mutiny and piracy had been dismissed by expert witnesses. Ideas about sea monsters had been laughed out of court and now the marshal of the court had dismissed any ideas of the captain or his crew drinking any of the alcohol in the hold. He couldn't even blame the weather as a cause leading to the ship being abandoned. Nothing exceptional had happened in the North Atlantic during their crossing. It was true that, according to the ship's log, they had experienced squalls and storms, but nothing out of the ordinary. A close reading of the ship's log, from when the *Mary Celeste* had left New York at the beginning of November until its last entry some three weeks later, had not shed any light upon the mysterious abandoning of the ship. Solly Flood was baffled. And not only was he baffled, but he had been laughed at in court and even Sir James Cochrane, the court's judge and commissary, had rebuked him in his office during the enquiry's proceedings.

Later, he was to be further disappointed when he read a specially commissioned report prepared by a Dr J. Patron. This court-appointed official stated that the supposed bloodstains found on the *Mary Celeste* were not in fact bloodstains. He had removed the reddish-brown stains found on the foredeck with a chisel and then examined them very thoroughly. After that he had compared them with other bloodlike traces found in the ship's cabins and had come to the conclusion that those on the foredeck were definitely not bloodstains. The red smears found on Captain Briggs's sword, Dr Patron had reported, were due to some sort of rusting. It was well known, he said, that the corrosive salty sea air had a habit of 'attacking' metal objects which were not used every day and that these marks on the blade of the sword – 'a ceremonial sword, I may add' he had written – may have been the result of such an attack.

The attorney general was furious. All his work to get to the bottom of the case and find a guilty party had come to nothing. At the same time, the court had allowed the *Mary Celeste* to be returned to Mr Winchester. This meant that the ship's new crew could now receive their personal belongings, which had been confiscated earlier as possible evidence.

Now, at the beginning of March 1873, some three months after the *Mary Celeste* and the *Dei Gratia* had sailed into the port of Gibraltar, Captain Morehouse aided by his attorney, Mr Henry Pisani, took the stand. Morehouse, who in wishing to support his crew, had decided that he had nothing to lose by testifying. It was also at this point that the enquiry changed its tactics. It moved from investigating what had caused Captain Briggs and his family and crew to abandon the *Mary Celeste* to how much money, if any, the men of the *Dei Gratia* were to be paid. By now, the *Dei Gratia* crew were thoroughly sick of the whole situation. All they wanted to do was leave Gibraltar and get on with their lives. The only thing that kept them going was the thought that they would – "would," insisted Deveau – receive several thousand dollars in salvage money. It was therefore a hopeful group of five men who watched their captain deal with Mr Frederick Solly Flood and the other court officials.

"Captain Morehouse, Captain David Reed Morehouse," the attorney general began in his familiar pompous tone.

"You are I believe the captain of the *Dei Gratia*, the two-masted brigantine which was responsible for bringing the *Mary Celeste* into the harbour here at Gibraltar."

Morehouse, who had been very suspicious about this hearing from the very beginning and in fact still was, nodded. "Yes, that is so, Your Honour."

"And you knew Captain Benjamin Briggs, the captain of the *Mary Celeste*."

Morehouse nodded. "Yes, Your Honour. That is also true."

"And you had a meal with the aforementioned captain on the day or night before the *Mary Celeste* set sail from New York at the beginning of November 1872."

Morehouse nodded again. "Yes, Your Honour. We did indeed meet to have a meal in New York before he set sail. We wanted to talk about our next voyages across the Atlantic and also to discuss some business affairs."

"And did this include talking about which routes you were going to take?"

"Yes, I'm sure it did. It's natural that two sea captains would talk about such matters before a voyage such as this, no?"

The attorney general did not answer but then asked, "And could you have co-ordinated where to meet later in your voyage?"

The answer the attorney general received was a loud mocking guffaw. "Do you know how large the Atlantic Ocean is, Your Honour?" Morehouse asked. "You ask me if we had planned to meet up somewhere in the middle of it and do so without taking into consideration that I left New York ten days after Captain Briggs? That idea, if I may say so,

Your Honour, is positively ridiculous."

Flood looked somewhat shocked at this reply and was about to say something when Morehouse continued, "And by the way, Your Honour, why should I have wanted to co-ordinate such a meeting in mid-ocean, assuming that that was even possible?"

To cover his embarrassment, the red-faced Solly Flood quickly moved on to his next question. "Captain Morehouse," he persisted. "Did these business affairs that you talked about at your last meeting with Captain Briggs involve any questions of money in any shape or form?"

"No, Your Honour. Not at all. That is, we didn't talk about insurance or the values of our respective cargoes. The only monetary matters we talked about was how the rates of shipping insurance had increased recently in general, the state of the weather, our families and about the crews that we had signed up. As you know, Captain Briggs had signed up some foreigners, Germans or Dutchmen, and he had asked me some questions about them. That was all."

"Are you sure, Captain Morehouse, that that was all?"

"What do you mean, Your Honour?"

"I mean that you met with Captain Briggs, not merely to enjoy a good meal and each other's company but that you had used this meeting to plan an insurance fraud," the attorney general persisted.

"*What!* I never…"

Morehouse never completed his sentence as his legal adviser, Mr Pisani, tugged at his sleeve and then whispered to him not to say another word.

"What is this, Henry?" Morehouse whispered back. "Did you hear what that man Flood has just said? He accused me of conspiring to cheat the insurance companies."

"I know, I know," Pisani whispered back. "But don't allow him to rattle you. He has failed completely in this enquiry up to now and so he is trying a new tactic. So take my advice, captain, just be careful what you say, especially with regard to your relationship and conversations with Captain Briggs."

Morehouse nodded and turned to face his accuser, Attorney-General Solly Flood.

"Did Captain Briggs tell you where the *Mary Celeste* was sailing to?"

"Yes, Your Honour. He said she was bound for Genoa."

"And did he tell you what was in her hold?"

"Yes, Your Honour. He told me about the barrels of alcohol."

"Did he inform you how much these barrels were worth – what they were insured for?"

Morehouse looked hard at the attorney general and shrugged. "As I told you a few minutes ago, Captain Briggs said nothing about what his cargo was worth. However, what I do remember," Morehouse continued, "is that he told me that he was taking his wife and daughter with him and that he was leaving his young son, Arthur, who was to continue with his schooling and be in the care of his family in Nova Scotia."

"I see, and you didn't talk about money?"

"Of course we did. As I told you, Your Honour, we talked about our ships and the rates of insurance but as I have just said, only in a general sense and certainly not as you contend, about some non-existent plan to defraud the insurance companies."

Captain Morehouse then stood up as straight as he could

and looked at the attorney general in the eye. "Tell me, Your Honour, which meeting between men in our position doesn't usually include any talk about money? I'm sure that when you meet with your fellow lawyers you talk about—"

"Captain Morehouse," Flood interrupted. "We are not here to talk about my affairs. We are here to try and get to the bottom of what really happened to the *Mary Celeste* – why was she abandoned in mid-ocean and what is going to happen now as a result."

The captain of the *Dei Gratia* looked down for a moment like a chastened schoolboy and then looked straight at the attorney general.

"Your Honour, all I can remember is that at the meal in question, the last time I saw my friend Captain Briggs, we talked about everything that was relevant to us at the time: the meal, our families, sailing, money and cargoes. That is all."

"I see," Flood said changing his line of questioning at last. "Captain Morehouse, did you yourself go aboard the *Mary Celeste*?"

"No, Your Honour, I did not."

"So how do you know what happened on this ship?"

"My crewmen told me and I believe what they said. I know Mr Deveau and Mr Wright to be excellent and reliable sailors with many years of experience between them."

"Captain Morehouse, can you tell this enquiry about the state of the *Mary Celeste*? I assume you saw her from your ship even if you didn't board her?"

"That's right, Your Honour. I saw that her sails and rigging were in need of repair, especially her topsails. In addition, I noted that the staysails, the topgallant and the flying and royal jib sails were not unfurled as I would have expected them to be in the circumstances."

"What do you mean by that, captain?"

"With the winds as they were I would have expected all of those sails to have been unfurled. I also saw that the foresail and the upper foresail were absent."

"Meaning?"

"What I have just said, Your Honour. Absent, missing, not there. I assumed that they had been blown away in a storm or something like that."

"So your men, the ones who brought her in to port here, would have had to replace them?"

"Yes, Your Honour."

"Now, tell me, captain, how far had the *Mary Celeste* sailed under those circumstances, from the time of the last entry in her log until you came across her?"

Morehouse shrugged. "How should I know? Probably some four hundred miles, I guess."

"Do you mean to tell this enquiry, captain, that the *Mary Celeste*, this abandoned ship, sailed about four hundred miles with no crew on board?"

"Yes, Your Honour, it does seem like that."

"And is that possible?"

"I believe so, Your Honour. I'm only telling you what I saw and heard."

"Even with her sails and rigging in need of repair?" Flood persisted.

Morehouse shrugged. "Even so, Your Honour. You must remember that the *Mary Celeste* was carrying a full set of sails and that the strong westerly winds would have taken her on a prevailing westerly course towards Europe."

Just as the attorney general was about to ask another question about this unmanned voyage, he felt a tap on his right shoulder and saw Sir James stand up.

"It's getting late in the day. I think we should adjourn until tomorrow and then we'll all be feeling more rested to deal with this fascinating question: how the *Mary Celeste* sailed so far without any crew on board. Good day."

And with that, yet another exhausting and frustrating day for the captain and crew of the *Dei Gratia* and also for Mr Solly Flood came to an end.

Chapter 15
The verdict

19th Century courtroom

"When's this bloody enquiry gonna end?" an annoyed Charles Lund asked his fellow crewmen as they sat around a square table in the corner that night in what had become their home from home in the Nelson Touch. "We've been stuck here on the Rock for nearly three months now and I'm telling you that *I have had enough*!"

"So have we all, Charlie, so have we all," Oliver Deveau

sighed. "And all those tomfool questions that this Flood character kept asking Captain Morehouse. How should he know how many miles the *Mary Celeste* had sailed and that kind of thing? He's a sea captain, not a damned mathematician or explorer."

"Aye," Wright added. "And the way he kept saying that he and Captain Briggs had planned the whole thing in order to trick the insurance companies out of a fortune. I'm telling you, if this pompous Solly Flood knew Captain Briggs personally, he would never have asked such stupid questions."

"That's true," Lund said, standing up to order another tankard of ale. "But I think we should ask Mr Pisani to say some more on our behalf. Y'know, he should tell Flood that we are honest sailors who have had enough and want to get on with our lives. I for one want to go home and see my family. I've never been away from them before for as long as this."

"Me too," Deveau and Anderson both said just as Captain Morehouse entered the tavern and made his way over to where his crew were sitting in the far corner.

"Have you got any more news for us, captain?" Wright asked. "You said you and Mr Pisani were going to try and bring all this to an end."

"Yes, Mr Wright," Morehouse replied, "but first I need a tankard of ale. It's thirsty work talking to all those court officials."

Deveau stood up and walked over to the bar. He ordered two more tankards, one for his captain and the other for himself. Then after he and Captain Morehouse had started on their ale, the captain faced his expectant crew.

"Well, men, if we're lucky, and I'm not promising anything, mind you, this whole business may be over tomorrow. I've had a long chat with Mr Pisani and he says that he's going to talk to Sir James, Mr Vecchio and Mr Solly Flood."

"Huh! Fat good that will do, talking to that damned Flood character," Lund said. "He's determined to prove that we're all criminals and either murdered Captain Briggs and his lot or that we're out to cheat the insurance people."

"No, no, Charlie, maybe not this time," Morehouse said, holding up his hand. "Despite what's happened in court these last few days, Mr Pisani sounded quite optimistic."

"Well, that's more than I feel," Lund said.

"Me too," Anderson added.

"Well," Morehouse said. "Mr Pisani told me that he had heard from two of the clerks that Mr Vecchio and Sir James have also had enough of Mr Solly Flood's questions and insinuations and that they also want this enquiry to come to an end. In fact, Pisani said that one of the clerks had said to him that the court considered it had wasted enough time on this particular enquiry and that it had other things to do."

"So what does that mean, captain?" Deveau asked. "They're about to settle the amount we're going to get from the salvage soon?"

"Yes, Mr Deveau, I believe so. Mr Pisani told me that we should all appear in court early tomorrow morning and, if we're lucky, we may be able to go home, or wherever we want to go, by the end of this week."

"Hallelujah," the normally quiet John Johnson said in his Russian-accented English. "Hallelujah."

*

The next day, 14 March 1873, the crew and captain of the *Dei Gratia* assembled in the front of the Vice Admiralty courtroom to finally hear the results of their salvage claim. They had been kept waiting in Gibraltar for three months and were impatient to find out how much money they would be awarded and if they could now continue with their maritime careers and live their normal lives again. Mr Winchester, even though he had been there for a shorter period, was equally impatient to hear what would happen now.

As they sat expectantly waiting, the fat attorney general, Frederick Solly Flood, Sir James Cochrane and Thomas J. Vecchio entered the courtroom and the three men took their places on the bench beneath the coats of arms of Queen Victoria and the British Admiralty. As the powerful Mediterranean spring sunshine shone through the large courtroom, Attorney General Mr Solly Flood stood up to repeat his reading of the reports that he had received from the court-appointed surveyor, John Austin, and the diver, Ricardo Portunato. He wanted to reinforce how correct this enquiry had been and why it had taken so long.

"I will not read this whole report," Flood announced as he held the thirty-page document in his hands. "Just the relevant parts that are germane to this enquiry. After all, this investigation has gone on long enough," he added as if he had had nothing to do with drawing the whole procedure out since the past December.

"Now, Mr Austin who, as I have mentioned in the past, spent five hours on board the *Mary Celeste*, examining every square inch, from bow to stern, port to starboard, the upper decks, the lower decks and the hold. In his report he recorded that he found some strange unexplainable marks – some cuts – on the upper parts of the hull which he associated with some sort of shipboard violence. He was not able to prove what had caused these cuts or if they had been the results of mutiny, piracy or just the normal wear and tear that ships, especially sea-going ships like the *Mary Celeste*, are subject to. All he could say was that these cuts, some six or seven feet long, had been made recently by something sharp during the *Mary Celeste*'s last voyage. In addition," Flood added, "Mr Austin is absolutely sure that these cuts, which as I've said appeared along the length of both sides of the hull, were man-made. Their length and similarity in style are proof that they were not the result of any sort of accident or natural phenomenon such as planks bending and splintering, claims that have been made earlier during this enquiry. Mr Austin also claimed that the rigging of the *Mary Celeste* was not as the crew, especially Messers Deveau, Anderson and Lund have claimed, to be in need of any repair and that seawater had not caused any real damage in the hold or the galley or indeed in the bilges."

At this point, the attorney general paused, looked around the courtroom and then, clearly relishing his role as the centre of attention, looked directly at the owner and the men of the *Dei Gratia* before continuing, "I would also like to repeat that my surveyor, Mr John Austin, noted that he found a sword in Captain Briggs's cabin, a sword which appeared to be bloodstained. However, it also looked as if someone had made an effort to remove these bloodstains but had not succeeded in doing so. This sword, a ceremonial sword which had a narrow blade and was decorated, as was its scabbard, may have been used to murder one or more persons, though this last point cannot be proved. I use the word 'may' because these bloodstains may not be bloodstains at all, but, as it has also been claimed during this enquiry, these stains may in fact be a form of rust caused by the salty sea air on unprotected metal."

As Captain Morehouse heard the attorney general dredging up the story of the sword again, he realised that he and his crew's hopes of obtaining much or any money as the result of their salvage claim were receding even further.

"In addition," Flood continued, "both Mr Austin and Mr Portunato, a diver whom I commissioned to examine the hull of the ship in question, the *Mary Celeste*, stated in their reports that the ship's hull was in a good condition and did not provide any reason for Captain Briggs, his family and crew to abandon their ship. They also said that any foul weather that the *Mary Celeste* may have encountered had not been extreme enough to force the men to abandon ship." And with those words, the self-satisfied attorney general laid his reports on the bench in front of him and sat down. The smile on his face showed that he felt he had dealt this case – which to his mind included a hidden insurance fraud – a heavy blow.

Now it was Sir James Cochrane's turn to take centre stage. He stood up, looked around the courtroom and then at the expectant faces of Captain Morehouse and his crew.

"Now that we have heard this final report, it is up to me to move on to the question of how much money in terms of a salvage claim should be paid to Captain Morehouse and the crew of the *Dei Gratia*."

As he said this, all the six men sat up, stretched their backs and looked hopefully up at the judge and commissary of the

Vice Admiralty Court. After all, this was what they had been waiting to hear for the past three months. This was what had caused Captain Morehouse to allow three of his men to go over to the *Mary Celeste* in mid-ocean resulting in his own ship and the abandoned brigantine both being severely undermanned for the last six hundred miles of their voyage. Would any of this be taken into account, and would the attorney general Mr Solly Flood's ongoing deluge of insinuations of bad seamanship, foul play and lies play a major part in determining how much the men of the *Dei Gratia* would receive?

"Gentlemen," Sir James began. "This enquiry has decided after much deliberation and also consideration of the reports made by the court-appointed surveyor, Mr John Austin, and the diver, Mr Ricardo Portunato, that the sum of the salvage money to be paid to Captain Morehouse and his crew shall be..." and here he consulted a piece of paper in his hand. "The sum shall come to £1,700, that is, about 8,300in American dollars and—"

"*What! Is that all?* Is that what we risked our lives for? $8,000! Is that all?" gasped Anderson. And before anyone could say anything more, Sir James looked down at the page before him and continued, "This sum is based on the fact that the value of the *Mary Celeste* and her cargo of seventeen hundred barrels of alcohol was worth about $50,000—"

"*But, sir, that's impossible!*" Mr Pisani stood up to interrupt. "Even when the *Mary Celeste*, which had formerly been known as the *Amazon*, was sold two years ago in a wrecked condition to Mr Winchester and his company, she was worth much more than that."

"Mr Pisani," Sir James said, looking hard at Captain

Morehouse's lawyer. "You are talking out of turn. You will have an opportunity to raise your objections later."

"But, sir," Pisani persisted. "This miserable sum doesn't take into account that Mr Winchester had invested $16,000 in having the Mary Celeste refitted from prow to stern prior to this last voyage. This £1,700" – a sum he said slowly and deliberately – "is laughable. It's paltry and it's a figure that we cannot possibly accept. In addition—"

"Mr Pisani," Sir James interrupted loudly. "I have warned you about speaking out of turn. Your continuing to do so may well be interpreted as contempt of court."

"That may be so, sir," Henry Pisani replied, "but you have awarded Captain Morehouse and his crew the wretched sum of £1,700. From my experience," the inflamed lawyer hurried on before he could be stopped, "these men should have received at least twice that amount, that is, closer to £4,000."

"Mr Pisani," Sir James warned, but the lawyer could not be stopped.

"By awarding these men, sir, such a miserable sum, you are implying that they acted badly in some way or other and that they are responsible for some form of illegal act, an act which I say *did not happen*!"

"Mr Pisani," Sir James said when it was clear that the lawyer had finished. "I have not said all that I wish to about this claim. There is more."

Again, Mr Winchester, Captain Morehouse and his crew sat up straight to hear what else Sir James had to say. Perhaps he had a legal way of sweetening the bitter pill they had just been forced to swallow.

"This court of enquiry, again after much thought," Sir James said, "has decided that you, that is, the captain and crew of the *Dei Gratia*, should also pay for this investigation that—"

"*What!*" Anderson burst out. "*We have to pay for all this?*"

Sir James continued as if he had not heard. "You shall pay the costs for this investigation, this enquiry, since it has been deemed that you, through your behaviour on the *Mary Celeste* and later in this courtroom, have been held responsible for this enquiry taking place here in the first place."

Soon after this last statement, the enquiry was declared to be over. In a stunned state, Captain Morehouse and his men, together with Mr Winchester and Mr Pisani, dejectedly left the Vice Admiralty building and walked over to the Nelson Touch. There, sitting in their regular places at the far end near the window overlooking the harbour, they discussed their situation.

"Mr Pisani," Captain Morehouse began. "Isn't there anything that we can do? Can't we submit an appeal of any sort?"

"I don't think so, sir," Pisani replied. "I will look into it, but I must say that judging by the tone of the court, I doubt that even if we do submit an appeal, it will make any difference. In fact, if you ask me, it may even worsen the situation."

"How so?" Deveau asked. "It can't get much worse than it is now."

"It can," the lawyer said. "You see, if Flood and Sir James and the others have their way, you might not even receive the £1,700."

Captain Morehouse's and his crew's moods were not

improved the next day when they read the following in the *Gibraltar Chronicle & Commercial Intelligencer*:

The Judge thought it right to express the disapprobation of the Court as to the conduct of the Master of the Dei Gratia *in allowing the first mate, Oliver Deveau, to go away with the ship which had rendered necessary the analysis of the supposed spots or stains of blood found on the deck of the* Mary Celeste *and on the sword.*

"But I thought that in the end they decided that those marks weren't bloodstains after all," Anderson fumed.

Pisani shrugged. "My friend, I don't think that's going to make much difference now. We are just going to have to learn to live with the court's decision."

"But I don't want to," Deveau said. "I was counting on that money for my family. Now what will I have to show my wife when I get home after such a long absence? A mere handful of dollars?"

The others, including Captain Morehouse, nodded and muttered in agreement, while at the same time they realised that there was not much that they could do about it.

"Aye," Anderson added. "And we also have to pay the court costs. I guess that that's not going to leave us with anything in the end. That accursed Flood fellow really had it in for us, didn't he?"

The rest of the glum group of sailors around the table nodded as they considered what to do next.

"Right," Lund muttered. "And after working like crazy with hardly any sleep that week we were on board her. I'm telling you, guys, I've never worked so hard on a ship in all my life. No, I never have."

"Well, men," Morehouse said, looking at his angry and disappointed crew. "There are two bright spots of light at the end of this dark tunnel. The first is that we were not found guilty of trying to defraud the insurance company, and the second is, now that this is all over, we are free to take our cargo on to Genoa."

"Aye," Deveau added. "And I suppose we should be pleased that we were carrying a cargo of alcohol and not something that would have spoiled after sitting in the hold for these past four months."

And so it happened. At the end of March 1873, with the permission of the authorities in Gibraltar, the *Mary Celeste* finally sailed into the harbour at Genoa and finally unloaded her cargo of seventeen hundred and one barrels of industrial alcohol. Nine of the barrels were found to be empty and no-one could satisfactorily explain this. The only explanation that anyone could come up with was that the alcohol in them must have evaporated in the meanwhile.

"Still, that's not a major loss," Morehouse said to the crew the night they checked into a small hotel near the harbour. "I was expecting worse. I suppose that the wood of those nine barrels must have been a bit thinner or more porous than the others. Remember, those barrels had been sitting in the hold for four months."

"So will we be able to sail home now, captain?" Lund asked.

"Yes, but not before we have the hull examined. I don't want to cross the Atlantic in a leaking sieve."

"But, captain," Wright said. "The court-appointed diver has already done that recently, no?"

"I know that, Mr Wright, but I would still prefer to have the hull examined once again just to be on the safe side."

The hull of the *Mary Celeste* was then thoroughly inspected a few days later and Mr Winchester then set out to find a new cargo and a new captain to take back to New York. He knew that he had lost hundreds if not thousands of dollars while the *Mary Celeste* was riding to anchor at Gibraltar and now he was planning to cut his losses. However, he soon discovered that he had another problem – the four-month long enquiry and all the publicity it had generated in the local and international press had given his ship a bad name.

"Why won't anybody use it now?" Winchester complained to an Italian port official over a glass of Chianti at the end of May. "It was the crew who disappeared, not the ship or the cargo. Actually, apart from a few cuts and the torn topsails, she wasn't in such a bad state when Captain Morehouse's men boarded her."

"I know what you are saying, *il mio capitano*," Signore Lorenzo commiserated. "But you must remember, sailors are very, er how do you say? Very superstitious people. Your good ship has acquired a bad name – a very bad name, in fact. Me, if I were a sailor today, I think I would be feared to sail back to America on her. *Si, si*, I would not want to sail in her at all."

Signore Lorenzo's fears were echoed by many of the sailors in Genoa. The story of what had happened to the *Mary Celeste* quickly spread around the taverns and hostels surrounding the port and as Captain Morehouse's crew had all returned to the *Dei Gratia*, Mr Winchester, as the owner of the *Mary Celeste*, found it much harder to engage a new crew than he thought it would be.

Although he did his best to allay any possible new crew member's fears, Winchester, together with the new captain he had signed on, George W. Blatchford, still took three weeks before he could muster sufficient men. Once he had done so, he sailed back to New York still hoping to recoup his losses. However, as a result of all of the negative publicity, both in the port and in the papers, in the end the *Mary Celeste* was to return to America with an empty hold. Not only were few men prepared to sail on her, but no merchant wanted to trust his cargo in her hold. Winchester had already lost money on a deal shipping fruit from Sicily to New York and he did not want his ship to hang around pointlessly in Genoa any longer.

Finally, in August 1873, the *Mary Celeste* set off for her homeward voyage back to the east coast of the United States. This time her destination was Boston, not New York. As Captain Blatchford and his somewhat fearful crew looked out west over the choppy waves of the North Atlantic, they wondered what if anything would happen to them – would they too mysteriously disappear? And what kind of reception would be awaiting them several thousand miles away on the east coast of the United States?

Chapter 16
The *Mary Celeste* sails again

To the great surprise of the crew of the *Mary Celeste*, no-one made any fuss as she sailed quietly into Boston harbour on 1 September 1873. Two weeks later she left Boston and returned to New York, arriving there on the nineteenth of September, nearly eleven months after she had set out on her last and mysterious voyage. The sailors, harbour officials and workers in the harbour seemed more concerned with talk of the country's current financial situation and whether a depression was imminent. It was soon after the *Mary Celeste* had been securely attached to a couple of black iron bollards on the harbour wall that Captain Blatchford walked over to meet the ship owner in his office. He was looking forward to the ship's next voyage.

"There won't be one, captain," Winchester told him as soon as the bearded mariner had settled himself down and faced his employer across a busy-looking desk.

"What do you mean, sir?" the surprised Blatchford asked. "There won't be one? As you know, the ship is in good condition and we had her checked out most thoroughly before we left Genoa."

"I know all that, captain, but no-one wishes to charter her. It looks like what happened to her has scared everyone off."

"But if you don't mind my saying so, Mr Winchester, that's crazy."

Winchester shrugged. "I know that, but there's not much we can do about it, is there? Public opinion is public opinion and gossip is gossip."

"Wait," Blatchford said snapping his fingers. "How about if you change her name? Say from the *Mary Celeste* to, oh I don't know, the name of some American flower or mountain or even the name of a town or president, y'know, the *Black-eyed Susan* or *Cincinnati* or even the *President Monroe*?"

"Yes, I'd thought of that," Winchester answered. "But the *Mary Celeste* is already her second name. When she was built she was called the *Amazon*. If she has another name change it will make people even more suspicious. No, captain, I think that for the time being, she'll have to remain the *Mary Celeste*."

"So, sir, if you don't want to change her name, how about changing the ship itself?"

"What do you mean?"

"How about adding another mast or making her a bit longer or adding another deck or half-deck, sir? You know, something that will make her look different from the present *Mary Celeste*. Then you could call her the *Mary Celeste II*. Here, I'll show you." And Captain Blatchford took a large piece of paper from a pile on his employer's desk and drew an accurate sketch of the *Mary Celeste* before adding another mast and sails, as well as an extra half-deck by the ship's stern.

Winchester took hold of Blatchford's sketch, studied it carefully and shook his head. "It's a good idea, captain, but to make changes like those, even if they did mean that we'd be able to carry more cargo in the future, would cost a fortune. A fortune that unfortunately my company does not have at the moment." And he put the sketch back down on the desk.

Blatchford shrugged. "Well, if that's what you want, so be it. You're her owner and you've got the right to do with her whatever you want. But personally, sir, I think you're making a big mistake, but we'll see."

Winchester nodded and began going through a few documents on his desk.

"So what are you going to do? Sell her?" Blatchford asked next. "Will anyone want to buy her now knowing what they know?"

Winchester nodded. "Yes, captain, I hope there is someone out there wanting to buy her. I'll probably have to sell her at a loss, but I don't think that I've got any alternative. I'll pay you what I owe you and recommend you to anyone who wishes to employ you. I can't be fairer than that, now can I?"

"No, sir, I suppose not."

A few days later, seeing that no-one in Boston wanted to buy his ship, Winchester rounded up a crew for a short one-time voyage and had them sail the *Mary Celeste* back to Boston.

"Maybe we'll have more luck there this time," he said to his wife that night. "If not, we'll just have to try again in New York, after all, this city is much bigger than Boston and there's always a demand for ships in good condition, even if they are not new."

At the end of the month, after an unsuccessful stay in Boston, the *Mary Celeste* was back in New York. That night when she was tied up at her moorings, Winchester told his wife that although several people had come to look at the ship in Boston, no-one would put any money on the table.

"I suppose they came more out of curiosity," she said. "They just used the idea of buying her as an excuse to go on board and see what all the fuss was about. As you told me yesterday, these people came to see the ship expecting to see a ghost or two, or even the bloodstains that were reported in the papers, and then said no anyway." She placed another portion of meat dumplings on her husband's plate.

"I'm afraid that you're right, my dear," Winchester replied. "We'll just have to hope. That's all."

In the meanwhile, all sorts of rumours about what had happened to the *Mary Celeste*'s captain, family and crew continued to circulate in the local and national press. Some of these stories referred to the rough weather out in the Atlantic while others printed graphic reports about sea monsters and disappearing islands. Yet other papers published sensational, dramatic and bloody accounts of pirates, mutiny and mutilation.

"Just listen to this, my dear," Winchester said one evening as he sat down in his drawing room after his evening meal, reading from the *New York Herald*.

This newspaper, as well as Mr J.H. Winchester of the ship-broking company of the same name in New York, has now learned some new additional facts about what happened to Winchester's ship, the Mary Celeste. *It seems that under suspicious circumstances the crew mutinied and overpowered the ship's officers, mutilated them and in the end took them as prisoners or threw them overboard. This will explain the bloodstains found on board when the men of the* Dei Gratia *boarded her in the middle of the North Atlantic.*

"What a lot of rubbish!" Mrs Winchester said. "You haven't learned anything of the sort. You yourself told me that there was no evidence of any violence on board and that the enquiry in Gibraltar eventually even agreed with that."

"I know, my love, but listen to what else the report says." Winchester continued reading.

The mutiny probably happened during the night when most of the officers were sleeping. It seems to be a repeat occurrence of that well-known mutiny in which Captain Bligh was attacked by his rebellious crew on the Bounty *in the South Pacific, which happened just over one hundred years ago. Proof of this latest mutiny on the* Mary Celeste *may be found on the bloodstained sword that was produced as evidence in court. However, unfortunately we still do not know exactly what the fate was of the ship's captain, Benjamin S. Briggs, and of his wife, Sarah Elizabeth, and his two-year-old daughter, Sophia Matilda. No bodies have been found either in the ship or washed ashore, and so their fate remains a mystery, even several months after this mutiny took place.*

These speculative reports about what had happened to Captain Briggs, his family, crew and the *Mary Celeste* had a bad influence. Month followed month and Winchester could not find anyone to buy his ship. He became so pessimistic that he instead decided to use her again. He took on John Q.

Pratt as her new captain and in October 1873 the *Mary Celeste* sailed off to Kingston in the Caribbean. Nothing extraordinary happened during this voyage and after she returned to New York, Winchester finally succeeded in selling her to another shipping company.

"How much do you want for her?" the agent for Cartwright and Harrison asked. "I mean taking her past history and reputation into account."

"That shouldn't be relevant," Winchester replied. "You're wanting to buy a ship – a ship that's in good condition, if I may add – not a piece of history."

"You may be right there, Mr Winchester, but we'll be wanting to find crews for her and you know what these sailors are like. Suspicious as all hell."

That night after Winchester had signed the necessary papers with Cartwright and Harrison, he told his wife that he had lost over $8,000 on the *Mary Celeste*. "And I was so hopeful, so optimistic when I bought her. Captain Briggs was a fine fellow and I was sure that he, myself and the *Mary Celeste* were on to a good thing. Now look at me. Thousands of dollars poorer and one less ship on the company's books."

"Fear not, James," his wife said, walking over to give her husband a hug. "I'm sure with your brains and business know-how, you'll be all right. As you've told me more than once, every commercial venture has its ups and downs."

"Yes, I suppose you're right, my love, but I still can't help thinking about what could have happened and what will happen to the *Mary Celeste* in the future. I wonder if her new owners will have any more luck with her than I did."

James H. Winchester was right to wonder about what would happen to the *Mary Celeste*. In the same way she had lost money for him, so she did for her new owners.

"Did you hear what happened with your old ship, the *Mary Celeste*?" a business friend asked Winchester one day. They were sitting in the ship owner's office chatting about an old deal, and this prompted Winchester's friend to bring up the now famous ghost ship. "She was sailing on one of her usual runs to South America, when her cargo, a whole load of timber, was washed overboard in a storm. Somewhere off the coast of Brazil, I heard."

"That's terrible. Someone can't have lashed that load tight enough on deck. Now if that was me…"

"And that's not all, James," his gossipy friend added. "On another voyage, from here to Mauritius in the Indian Ocean, she ran into a fantastic storm off the Cape of Good Hope. Many of the horses that she was transporting on board died and my friend Mr Cartwright told me that he had lost a fortune as a result."

"Well, was Cartwright at least able to make up for it on the homeward voyage?"

"No, James. In a way that one was even worse. Although the captain, Captain Tuthill, eventually found a cargo to bring back from Calcutta, he himself died and never made it back here. It seems that he became so ill that the ship stopped at the island of St Helena and put him off there to recover but he never did. He died there three weeks later."

"Hmm, him and Napoleon, eh?"

"Aye, but do you know what that means, James? It means that three captains have died on your old ship."

"Three? Who?"

"Well, there was the first one, a Captain McLellan, who died when the *Mary Celeste* was first called the *Amazon*, then there was your friend, Captain Briggs…"

"And now you say that there was this Captain Tuthill fellow," Winchester added. "But we're not altogether sure what really happened to Captain Briggs. I mean, there's a small chance that he may still be alive somewhere, although personally, I doubt it."

"Aye, that's true, and all those deaths happened within the space of less than fifteen years. I must say, James, your old *Mary Celeste* does seem to be a cursed ship. Normally," his friend continued, "I'm not a superstitious man – you know, all that stuff about walking under ladders, crossing your fingers – but I'm telling you, my friend, you won't ever catch me stepping on board that *Mary Celeste*. Oh, no, man. Not for all the tea in China. If she were mine, I'd sell her off as quickly as I could, or at least I'd change her name."

However, despite this last unfortunate voyage, Cartwright and Harrison did not get rid of the *Mary Celeste* immediately or even change her name. They kept operating her until February 1880 before selling her at last; a sale which caused them to lose several thousand dollars.

"It's the only way to cut our losses," Cartwright said to Harrison the night after selling the ship off to a Mr Wesley Gove in New York. "Good luck to him is all that I can say."

Harrison also raised his glass. "You're right, my friend. Let's hope that that Mr Gove will make more money out of her than we ever did. That ship was damned from the start. That's all I can say. By the way, do you know the name of her new captain?"

"Yes, he's called Fleming. Captain Thomas L. Fleming."

"Well, let's raise a toast to the new captain of the *Mary Celeste* and wish him and his crew all the best of luck. I'm sure that they're going to need it."

Chapter 17
The final voyage of the *Mary Celeste*

19th Century engraving of the Mary Celeste

Sailing under Captain Fleming, the *Mary Celeste* did nothing to cause any new or sensational stories to become associated with her. For the next four years she fulfilled her role as a merchant brigantine sailing ship until, in 1884, Wesley Gove sold her to a consortium of shippers in Boston. This group included a man called Captain Gilman C. Parker who had decided to make a tidy profit out of the *Mary Celeste*.

"You know the history of this ship?" one of Parker's friends asked him one morning as they were looking at their new brigantine.

"Of course I do," Parker replied. "It's that crazy story about how her crew disappeared twelve years ago in the middle of the Atlantic and were never seen again."

"That's right, Gil, but..."

Parker shrugged and smiled. "But who cares, man? That's history. No-one cares about that old story today. She's just another merchant ship sailing the ocean. That's all. Our job is to make money out of her – a lot of money. So come, let's see how we can do so."

"All right, so how are you planning to make this fortune?"

"Huh, that's easy. We'll fill her up with a cargo worth nothing, old clothes and other junk, insure her for a lot more than the cargo is really worth and..."

"... sink her and claim the insurance."

Parker slapped his friend on the back. "Exactly, my friend. Exactly."

"But won't anybody find out? I mean, you're not the first person to think of that trick. Don't you think that the insurance companies are on to it?"

"I know that, man," Parker grinned. "That may be so, my friend, but who's gonna argue with me and the boys when that old ship is at the bottom of the ocean? How are they gonna prove what I have done?"

And so Gilman C. Parker put his plan into action. At the end of 1884 he had the *Mary Celeste* loaded with boxes of old clothes, rubber boots and butter, together with cases of rotten fish and bottles of weak ale. He then informed the ship's insurers that the ship would be carrying goods worth $30,000. On 16 December 1884 the *Mary Celeste* left Boston harbour as she had done so many times over the past ten years and set off south in the direction of Port-au-Prince, Haiti.

"This ol' tub is in terrible condition," Ernest Berthold, the helmsman, said to Parker one morning as they were sailing south of the coast of Florida. "Are you sure she'll make it? I'm surprised she's got this far."

"Well, if she doesn't, we'll still be all right," Parker replied.

"Why, what d'you mean, captain?"

"Fear not, Berthold. You'll find out soon enough."

And so the twenty-three-year-old *Mary Celeste* kept sailing south as well as she was able to. Her ragged sails caught as much wind as they could, and her rotten rigging did its best to fulfil the task for which it was made.

Standing next to Berthold was Jacob English. "D'you honestly think she'll make it?" he whispered to the helmsman once he saw that that Parker had gone below. "It's hard to imagine that this old tub was once the fine ship that we saw in that picture in the paper last week. The mysterious *Mary Celeste*. Now look at her. To tell you the truth, mate, I only signed up for the money and now I'm wondering if that was a good idea. I'm really beginning to regret it. What about you?"

Berthold nodded. "I agree with you, but it's too late now. We're here till the end."

"Yeah? Whose end? This ship, ours or both?"

Berthold clapped English on the back. "Don't be such a pessimist, my friend. I'm sure the captain knows what he's doing. Do you think he wants to commit suicide in the middle of the ocean?"

Just then, Captain Parker rejoined the two men by the wheel. "Keep her on a southerly route, Berthold. I'll tell you when to change course."

"Yes, captain," Berthold replied. "But, sir, won't we be hitting the Rochelois Bank reef soon? I saw that you had marked it out on one of the charts below."

"Fear not, Berthold, I'll tell you what to do when we get near the reef. But if you want, you can have English or Joe Howe take over from you."

"No, no, captain. I'll be all right for another hour or two," Berthold replied as he held the wheel and waited for further instructions. He did not want to be shown up as some sort of coward or a sailor who in times of stress could not be counted upon. He was well aware of the fact that a sailor's good reputation on board, as well as within the closed maritime community of the north-east American coast, was invaluable.

Around midday on 3 January 1885, while Berthold was at the wheel, he suddenly realised that the rocky coral reef off the coast of Haiti known as the Rochelois Bank was looming up fast in front of the *Mary Celeste*.

"Run and tell the captain that we've got trouble ahead," he shouted to English. "Tell him to come up on deck. *Now!*"

Parker was by his side within a couple of minutes.

"What's the problem, man," he asked casually.

"Look ahead, captain," Berthold replied, pointing to an ever-growing smudge on the water. "There's a reef over there and we'll be on it very soon."

"Fear not, man, you'll be all right," Parker said as he fumbled to light his pipe in the wind. "Just you stay on the course I told you."

"But captain, we—"

"Listen man, just you keep to the course I gave you and let me worry about everything else. D'you hear me?"

"Yes, captain," Berthold muttered and gripped the wheel as the dark smudge began to take on the shape of a distinctly rocky outline. "But I still think that…"

Berthold was not able to complete his thoughts as suddenly he felt a sharp juddering as the copper plated hull of the *Mary Celeste* jammed onto the hidden outer extremes of the Rochelois Bank and came to a noisy metallic stop.

"*What the hell?*" he shouted as he was thrown away from the wheel and slid along the now sloping deck. "We've hit the bank, the reef!"

Holding on to a side rail and pulling himself upright, he saw Captain Parker do the same, as he realised that the captain did not look as shocked as he was.

"What's the matter, captain?" Berthold asked. "You're smiling. You're not hurt."

"I know, I know," Parker said dismissively. "I'm all right. See, not a scratch. I was expecting that."

"What do you mean, expecting that?" crewman Joseph Howe asked as he rubbed the side of his head. He looked at his bloodied hand, which he had just pulled down from his face, and realised that his right cheek was bleeding.

"I was aiming to sink this old tub all the while," Parker explained as Jacob English limped over to join the small group around the wheel. "Are you all right, Jake?"

"Yes, captain," English replied rubbing his leg. "I think I twisted it a bit when I fell."

"But can you still walk?"

English nodded. "Yes, cap'n. I think so, although it's killing me like hell." And he winced as he rubbed his leg again.

"What are we going to do now we're stuck on this damned reef?" Berthold asked.

"No problem," Parker smiled. "We'll launch the lifeboats and make our way to the mainland."

"That's it?" a shocked Howe asked. "Just like that? Sail away and leave all our gear and the cargo behind?"

"No, man," Parker replied. "You'll all take your own gear with you and—"

"But why did you tell me to head for the reef?" Berthold demanded. "You knew we'd get stuck on it. And what about the cargo? It must be worth thousands of dollars."

Captain Parker tapped the side of his nose. "Insurance, man. Insurance."

"What d'you mean, insurance? Are you trying to fiddle the insurance companies?"

Parker nodded.

"Because if so, I don't want anything to do with it," Berthold said. "I've got a clean record, I have, and I don't want to go to no jail. Besides, I've got a wife and little 'uns to look after."

"Me too," Howe and English added.

"Fear not, men," Parker smiled as he calmly tried to relight his pipe. "We'll all get into the lifeboats and head for Port-au-Prince or Miragoâne. Whichever is the nearest. And, don't forget to take as much liquor out of the hold as you can. We can sell it once we get ashore. I mean," he said as he looked at the incredulous faces of his crew, "we might as well try and make as much as possible out of this, no?"

And that is what happened. Captain Parker and the *Mary Celeste*'s seven-man crew packed their personal gear into the two lifeboats, together with as much liquor as they could fit on board. Then without as much as a backward glance at the *Mary Celeste*, now perched on the top of the rocky reef and gently swaying in the swirling sea, they rowed the twenty-five miles to the Haitian mainland. There, in the port of Miragoâne, Captain Parker informed Mr Mitchell, the American consul's agent, what had happened.

"Well, it was like this," Parker began, doing his best to look sufficiently distressed at having lost his ship. "We had an accident and we ran aground on a reef, y'know, the coral reef, the Rochelois Bank."

"You mean that long reef off Gonâve Island?"

Parker nodded and looked down sorrowfully at the floor.

"But how could you have done that?" Mitchell asked. "It's a long reef, well-marked on all the charts. Your helmsman must have been blind or drunk not to see it."

Parker shrugged. "I cannot answer you that, sir. I wasn't standing next to him when it happened. I assure you, sir, that if I had been, this terrible accident would not have occurred."

"But…"

Parker continued, making sure that he seemed both sad and angry at losing his ship. "One minute we were sailing along as smoothly as possible and then suddenly we were stuck up there on the reef. High and dry. Just like that." And he snapped his long fingers. "I tried to see if there was a way of getting her off the reef, but when I understood that there was no way to do so, I ordered the men to take their personal belongings, pack them into the lifeboats and then row for the mainland. Luckily the sea was calm so we had no further problems."

"So, Captain Parker, what do you plan to do now?"

"I'll just have to sell her off at a loss, I suppose. That is, the ship and her cargo. The men are all in a hurry to go home and I suppose that's all I can do."

Fortunately for Parker, Mitchell believed his story. He paid the devious and lying captain $500 for the *Mary Celeste* and her cargo and then sailed out to inspect the ship and her rotting contents. By the time he had stepped onto the doomed ship's foredeck, Parker and his crew were sailing as passengers on another ship bound for the United States.

That night, as Parker and the rest of his crew were sitting in the bar drinking, they sailed past the Bahamas on their way north to New York.

"Well men, we've done it." Parker grinned. "We'll land in New York, I'll fill in the insurance claim forms and then we'll have a few more thousand dollars in our pockets. So now, let's drink to that."

They all raised their glasses, each man with his own vision of what they would do with their newfound riches. New houses, a good life with the ladies, or perhaps settling down on dry land for a change.

But it was not to be.

At the same time that the crew of the *Mary Celeste* were thinking about how to spend their ill-gotten gains, Mitchell was sharing his office with Kingman N. Putnam, a marine surveyor who had recently arrived in Haiti from New York.

"What's the reason you're here this time?" Mitchell asked as he slid a glass of whiskey over to the surveyor.

"I've come to investigate what happened to the *Mary L.*

Phipps, you know, that schooner that went down recently."

"You mean that you suspect some sort of insurance fraud?"

Putnam nodded.

"Well," Mitchell continued. "It's a good thing that you are here now, because I want to report another one." And the American consul's agent went on to tell the surveyor about how he had rashly bought the *Mary Celeste* and her cargo – "Unfortunately without checking her out first." He suggested to Putnam that once he had finished with the *Mary L. Phipps*, he should look into what had really happened to the *Mary Celeste*.

Putnam took up Mitchell's suggestion, and later he sailed over to the stranded *Mary Celeste* and carried out a personal inspection of the ship and her hold. He recorded that the over-insured cargo, which had allegedly contained expensive cutlery and footwear, really consisted of old clothes, cheap rubber boots, quantities of diluted alcohol and rotten fish, as well as some sort of unidentifiable material which had been registered as butter. After giving a copy of his report to Mitchell, the surveyor sailed back to New York to inform the authorities about Captain Gilman C. Parker's activities. These of course would include insurance fraud and barratry – the deliberate act of damaging a ship for financial gain. There in his New York office Putnam reminded the various officials he spoke to that barratry was a crime that carried the death penalty.

On 20 April 1885, three months after Parker had run the *Mary Celeste* aground on Rochelois Bank, he and the crew were arrested and found themselves standing in the dock in a Boston court.

"You are accused of being involved in a strategy," Attorney George P. Sanger proclaimed, reading out the charge sheet, "of barratry, of wilfully and corruptly conspiring and combining to cast away and destroy the said vessel, the *Mary Celeste*, with intent then and there to injure, that is to say, to defraud any person or corporation who might there afterwards underwrite any policy of insurance on the goods on board. Have you anything to say before I continue?"

Parker looked down at the wooden floor and muttered, "No, Your Honour." The rest of the crew just shook their heads.

The attorney continued, "It is very possible that although this is legally a capital offence, if you and your crew are found guilty of the aforementioned crimes, that is, committing insurance fraud and barratry, you will instead be asked to pay a fine of $10,000—"

"Each?" Parker interrupted.

"Yes, each and every one of you," Attorney Sanger replied sternly, looking at all of the crew in turn. "And in addition, you will then be sent to prison for ten years for conspiracy. Do you understand?"

Parker looked down at the wooden floor, now fully understanding that his plan to make 'a fast buck' was going to prove very expensive. The crew standing next to him also looked down dejectedly. Each one of them was thinking about their grim own fate, a future which looked to include paying off a huge fine as well as a decade in prison. It would also mean that their lives at sea were over.

In the days that followed, the name of the *Mary Celeste* hit the headlines again as the jury debated the case session after session. At last, on 15 August 1885, the jury were asked if they had agreed on a verdict.

"No, Your Honour," the foreman, William H. Fay, announced to Judge Carpenter. "We have debated and discussed this case long and hard and no matter how we try, we cannot come up with a verdict that we all agree upon."

The result was that the judge worked out an agreement in which the defendants withdrew their insurance claims but had to repay any monies that they had received.

"And as for the charge of barratry, Captain Parker," the judge stated. "I will defer this for the time being, but rest assured, you have not been found innocent of this heinous crime. It is possible that I will order you to be arrested again in the future for this and then stand trial."

Parker shook his head in disbelief. He was sure that he was about to be found guilty of one of the worst crimes in the book of maritime law.

"In the meanwhile," Judge Carpenter said, gathering up the files and documents on the bench in front of him. "You are free to go, but I'm warning you, do be careful. I may yet have need to call you back here."

But Captain Gilman C. Parker did not have much time to be careful. Three months later, in the winter of 1885, he died in poverty, his reputation as tattered as the worn-out sails on the *Mary Celeste*. His name and deeds had gone before him and no-one would employ him, let alone be caught talking to him. Local gossip claimed that the shame of what he had done together with his ever-worsening poverty and depression were responsible for his unexpected death.

In addition, one of the shipping merchants who had had some doubtful dealings with Parker with regard to loading the *Mary Celeste* with the worthless cargo on her fateful voyage to Haiti, committed suicide.

Her final voyage over, the *Mary Celeste*, the iconic ghost ship, the ship that would be forever linked with a missing crew, theories of sea-monster attacks, bloodthirsty pirates and numerous conspiracy theories had claimed her last two victims.

Other ghost ships

The *Mary Celeste* was probably the most iconic ghost ship of the nineteenth century. Despite her fame, however, she was definitely not the only vessel to have aroused such curiosity and publicity. Far from it. Wikipedia lists seventeen other ghost ships which are categorised as belonging to 'Folklore, Legends and Mythology', while six others are listed as 'Unsubstantiated' and a further twenty-eight ghost ships are defined by Wikipedia as 'Historically Attested'. The *Mary Celeste* is in this last category.

The most famous legendary ghost ship is probably the *Flying Dutchman* (*De Vliegende Hollander* in Dutch). The myth about this sailing ship started in the seventeenth century when the Netherlands was a major maritime country. According to this myth, while sailing around the Cape of Good Hope, the ship was caught in a very bad storm. In order to save himself and his crew, the captain, Willem (or Hendrik) van der Decken, made a pact with the Devil. Although they were then saved, this ship was condemned to sail forever without arriving in any port. If, however, she were sighted by another vessel, her crew would send messages to people who were already dead. According to superstitious sailors, spotting the *Flying Dutchman* at sea, often off South Africa's Cape of Good Hope, meant that their own ship would soon encounter a disaster. There were reports of her being seen at sea during the nineteenth and twentieth centuries: reports that claimed that this mysterious ship was lit up in a ghostly fashion.

The first printed version of this myth appeared in 1790 when John Macdonald described the *Flying Dutchman* in his book, *Travels in various parts of Europe, Asia and Africa during a series of thirty years and upwards*. Other written reports followed in 1795 and 1803. Another person who claimed that he had encountered this ghost ship was the future King George V and his older brother, Prince Albert Victor. While serving in the navy, on 11 July 1881, George recorded that 'the *Flying Dutchman* had crossed our bows'.

The *Flying Dutchman* has also been used for more than two hundred years as a motif in literature. In 1798, Samuel Taylor Coleridge referred to a ghost ship (but not specifically this one) in his classic poem *The Rime of the Ancient Mariner*, while in 1813, Sir Walter Scott referred to the *Flying Dutchman* as a pirate ship in *Rokeby; A poem*. He wrote that seeing this ship 'is considered by the mariners as the worst of all possible omens'.

Other writers such as John Boyle O'Reilly (1867), J. Slauerhoff (1928) and Brian Jacques (2001) wrote about this legendary ghost ship. In 1951, six years after atomic bombs had been dropped on Hiroshima and Nagasaki in the Second World War, Ward Moore took the *Flying Dutchman* story and converted the ship into an airplane. He wrote that this cursed airplane was destined to keep flying forever without landing until the world ended in a nuclear war.

Here are seven real, brief stories about ghost ships that have been deemed 'Historically Attested' by Wikipedia from their list of twenty-eight such stories. Like the mystery of the Mary Celeste, *all of the following details about these ghost ships from the twentieth and twenty-first centuries have been recorded in some way or other in newspapers, films and photographs. In contrast to the story of the* Flying Dutchman, *they cannot be considered as mythical or even as just figments of the imagination.*

Carroll A. Deering – January 1921

The Carroll A. Deering

For a less dramatic but more realistic variation of the *Mary Celeste*, in January 1921 the *Carroll A. Deering*, a five-masted schooner, ran aground on the shores of North Carolina, USA with no crew on board. She had been built in 1919, and in July 1920 had set sail from Puerto Rico for

Newport News to pick up a cargo of coal. She was to take it to Rio de Janeiro but during this part of the voyage her captain, Captain Merritt, fell seriously ill. (Echoes of the early history of the *Mary Celeste*?) The *Carroll A. Deering* changed course and took the sick man and his son, who acted as first mate, to Lewes, Delaware. The replacement captain was called Willis B. Wormell and the new first mate was called Charles B. McLellan. (Another echo of the *Mary Celeste* when this ship, then known as the *Amazon*, was commanded by a Robert McLellan who became seriously ill, was taken ashore and died.)

The *Carroll A. Deering* eventually sailed from Rio on 2 December 1920 and continued to Barbados where McLellan became drunk and complained to another captain that he was unable to discipline the crew without Captain Wormell interfering. McLellan was heard to threaten the captain and was later jailed. Wormell bailed him out and the voyage continued.

On 28 January 1921, the ship was sighted off the coast of North Carolina by a lightship captained by Captain Jacobson. He reported that a sailor with a foreign accent had told him, by using a megaphone, that the *Carroll A. Deering* had lost its anchors in a storm off Cape Fear. However, owing to a breakdown in radio communication, this situation could not be reported to its owners. Jacobson also noticed that the crew of the *Carroll A. Deering* appeared to be 'milling around' on the quarterdeck, a place where they were usually forbidden to be. The next day, another ship spotted the doomed ship aiming for the Diamond Shoals where it would surely be wrecked. (Echoes of the last voyage of the *Mary Celeste* and Rochelois Bank reef?) This other ship did not try to warn the schooner of trouble ahead as they could not see anyone on board.

Three days later, the *Carroll A. Deering* was spotted stuck on the Diamond Shoals, but due to bad weather, other ships could not come to her rescue. She remained high and dry for several more days and when she was finally boarded on 4 February 1921, her would-be rescuers found that she had been abandoned. Like the *Mary Celeste*, her binnacle, the receptacle for the ship's compass, had been destroyed and her steering wheel had been broken. In addition, the ship's log, two lifeboats and the crew's personal gear had disappeared, while the navigation equipment was also missing or had been damaged. The coastguard ship *Manning* tried to salvage the *Carroll A. Deering* but was not able to do so. In the end, one month later on 4 March 1921, the wrecked ship was blown up so that it would not become a danger to other ships in the vicinity.

The American government investigated this incident and claimed that there had been some strong hurricanes in the area. They also suggested that a mutiny or an act of piracy had taken place and closed the case in late 1922 without coming to an official and definitive conclusion.

Another conclusion invokes the maritime influence of the infamous Bermuda Triangle. It was also reported that when the coastguard boarded the *Carroll A. Deering* they found two distress signals lodged high in the ship's rigging. The investigators claim that the crew of the schooner had gone to the rescue of another ship, the steamer *Hewitt*, which was known to be in trouble in the area. As the *Hewitt* later sank with all hands, it may not only have included the crew of the unfortunate steamer, but also that of the *Carroll A. Deering*.

SS Baychimo – October 1931

SS Baychimo

Ten years after the *Carroll A. Deering* had been blown up, the world was faced with another ghost ship story. This time the vessel was SS *Baychimo*, a 1,322-ton cargo ship which had been built in Gothenburg, Sweden in 1914. Like the *Mary Celeste*, which had originally been called the *Amazon*, this Swedish cargo steamer first sailed under the name of *Ångermanelfven*, a name inspired by a Swedish river. She was used to ply the route between Sweden and Hamburg and completed at least nine voyages before the First World War broke out in 1914. After the war, she was handed over to the Allies as part of the German reparations in lieu of British shipping losses caused by the Kaiser's navy. She was renamed SS *Baychimo* and based in Ardrossan, Scotland, and was now owned by the Hudson's Bay Company.

She continued her uneventful career until October 1931 when she became trapped in pack ice off the west coast of

Canada near Vancouver. Seeing that a terrible blizzard was imminent, Captain Sydney Cornwell sent his crew ashore over the Alaskan ice to the northern village of Barrow, a kilometre away, for shelter. There they sat out the hurricane and then rushed back to their ship thinking that their bad luck was over. However, this was not to be. After a few hours of steaming through the frozen seas, the *Baychimo* became stuck again in the worsening pack ice. However, the crew did not seem too distressed about this, as they even played football on the ice to relieve their boredom.

Then one week later, the huge ice floe which was holding the ship in position broke away from the main pack ice and started floating towards land. Captain Cornwell had no control over his ship and he was worried that this movement would cause the ice to crush his vessel and its cargo of rum. (Echoes of the cargo of industrial alcohol in the hold of the *Mary Celeste*.) Refusing to abandon ship and perhaps make for land over the ice, Cornwell radioed for help.

On 10 October 1931, the *Associated Press* reported, 'Practically all hopes have been given up of the *Baychimo* getting out of the ice… Some passengers have been taken off by dog team to Wainwright and are to spend the winter there, while others are to fly to Nome.' Five days later the *Associated Press* wrote that 'Three Northern Air Transport planes are taking off for the *Baychimo*, icebound near Wainwright, today to bring out 12 to 15 passengers… They are taking a ton of supplies from here for the crew of the *Baychimo*, which will winter at the boat.' The remaining crew then built a wooden cabin near the frozen ship in order to keep an eye on her and to be able to live out the winter in more comfortable quarters, especially as it would have been impossible for them to heat the inside of the *Baychimo*.

Then on the twenty-fourth of November a huge blizzard struck the area and when it was over Captain Cornwell and his crew went to see what had happened to their ship. Imagine their surprise when they could not find it. It had completely vanished. The men decided that the *Baychimo* had sunk and that that was the end of their Swedish steam cargo ship. Except that it was not. Several days later they were told by an Inuit seal hunter that he had seen their ship some forty-five miles away at the foot of Skull Cliff near Barrow. Cornwell and his men made their way to the ship, decided that she was in no condition to survive the Arctic winter and took all the pelts in the hold in order to sell them. These they had transported south by air and then decided to abandon the now useless *Baychimo*.

It was at this point that this ship began her life as a ghost ship. Instead of being crushed by the ice and sinking below the frozen wastes of the Beaufort Sea as expected, the empty ship began to be seen regularly and even boarded by different people. She was spotted twice in 1932, at least three hundred miles from where she had originally been abandoned. In March 1933 a group of Inuit boarded her and then had to remain in her for ten days as a blizzard prevented them from leaving. Five months later, the Hudson's Bay Company planned to salvage her but this came to naught as she was too far out to sea. The *Baychimo* was boarded again in July 1934 by a group of explorers and one year later she was spotted sailing unmanned off the Alaskan coast. Another attempt was made to salvage her in November 1939 by Captain Polson, but this had to be abandoned as the winter pack ice began threatening the safety of this crew.

She was then sighted several times between 1939 and 1962, and the last recorded sighting of this now famous ghost ship was in 1969 when she was found stuck in the pack ice by a group of Inuit men. This was a similar situation to that of some thirty-eight years earlier when Captain Cornwell had abandoned her stuck in the ice of the Beaufort Sea. The *Baychimo* has not been seen since 1969 and it is not known whether she is still floating around off the Alaskan coast or has finally gone down to Davy Jones's locker.

MV Joyita – October 1955

MV *Joyita*

From the frozen wastes of the Arctic Circle, we now move to the warm seas of the South Pacific. Here, among the exotic islands of Samoa, Tuvalu and Tokelau, everyone on board the seventy-ton ship, *Joyita*, the 'Little Jewel', had disappeared, causing this ship to be known later as the '*Mary*

Celeste of the South Pacific'.

Her story is as follows: she was originally built as a wooden luxury yacht in Los Angeles in 1931 and named after Jewel Carmen, the wife of film director Roland West. During the Second World War, after the Japanese attack on Pearl Harbour, she was requisitioned by the United States Navy, converted into a patrol boat and named YP-108. One year later she ran aground and was severely damaged. She was repaired and after the war was sold off as war surplus equipment. She changed ownership three times between 1948 and 1955, her last owner being Dr Katharine Luomala, a professor at the University of Hawaii. She chartered the *Joyita* to her friend Captain 'Dusty' Miller, a British sailor living in Samoa. He planned to use the ship as a trading, fishing and occasional passenger vessel in the South Pacific.

It was 3 October 1955 that her story as a ghost ship began. On that day she sailed out of Apia harbour, Samoa bound for the Tokelau Islands to the north. The distance was two hundred and seventy miles and the voyage should have taken up to two days' sailing. She was carrying a crew of seventeen including Captain Miller, as well as nine passengers in addition to two children and a doctor. Only one of her two engines was working, and she had experienced problems with the clutch of her port engine just before this voyage. In addition she was carrying medical supplies, food, some timber and eighty empty 45-gallon oil drums in the hold.

Five weeks later Captain Douglas of the merchant ship *Tuvala* spotted the *Joyita*. She was over six hundred miles west of her planned route and was partly submerged and listing heavily. When he sent some of his men aboard, they could find none of the passengers or crew, dead or alive. In addition they discovered that four tons of her cargo were missing and that the radio, because it was damaged, had a range of only two miles and was tuned to broadcasting the international distress signal.

They found that there was still fuel in the *Joyita*'s tanks, and it was reckoned, from the amount that had been used, that whatever had caused everyone to abandon ship had happened some fifty miles away from their destination, Tokelau Island. This meant that the *Joyita* had sailed altogether about two hundred and twenty miles.

In addition, the starboard engine was covered with several mattresses and the *Joyita* had been running only one engine, as the port engine's clutch was still in pieces. Between the engines, an auxiliary pump, which had not been connected, was fixed to a piece of wood between the two engines. Investigating below decks, Captain Douglas's men found that there was probably too much water in her bilges (similar to that of the *Mary Celeste*'s), and that the lower decks were flooded. This was probably due to a fault in the ship's cooling system, i.e. some corroded pipes had been leaking. To complicate matters, the bilge pumps had become clogged with marine rubbish, making them to be almost useless.

On the upper deck, the ship's dinghy and three life-rafts were missing, and passenger Doctor Parson's bag was found to contain a scalpel and a stethoscope together with four long bloodstained bandages. It was also discovered that all of the electric clocks on board had stopped at 10.25 a.m. but the switches for the navigation and cabin lights were still on. As with the *Mary Celeste* and the *Carroll A. Deering*, some of the navigational instruments were missing or broken. Captain 'Dusty' Miller's firearms had also vanished.

The official board of enquiry reported all of this in February 1956 and noted that the *Joyita* was in a poor state of repair. This part of the enquiry was easy to carry out. However, it was not able to explain what had happened to everyone on board and also noted that it was 'inexplicable on the evidence submitted at the inquiry' what had happened to the twenty-six people who had sailed out from Apia harbour four months earlier.

In addition to the mechanical problems mentioned above, the later investigation reported that although the *Joyita* should have been perfectly buoyant with her cork-lined holds and cargo of empty oil drums, the subdivisions and watertight bulkheads were missing. This meant that any water below decks would have flooded the engine rendering it useless.

The enquiry concluded that Captain Miller was responsible for sailing a ship in such poor condition, especially as he had the use of only one engine. He was also blamed for setting out to sea with a damaged radio and for having an expired licence to carry passengers.

Once the enquiry was over, the *Joyita* was auctioned off the following year by her owner, Dr Katharine Luomala, for nearly two and a half thousand pounds and refitted and overhauled. But then there was a legal problem concerning the transfer of registry from the USA to Britain without permission. After this had been cleared up, the *Joyita*'s bad luck continued. In January 1957 she ran aground in the Koro Sea east of Fiji and had to be repaired once again. She resumed sailing in October 1958 but ran aground once more in November 1959 north of Fiji. This time she was able to float off the reef during a high tide, but then it was discovered that her pumps had been incorrectly fitted and she was abandoned on land by her owners. Any useful equipment was taken off and the remaining hulk of the *Joyita* was sold to Major Cassling-Cottle who planned to turn the wreck into a tourist site. This never happened as the ship was stripped by other people and, by the late 1970s, there was very little left of her.

The question now is what caused the *Joyita* to be abandoned in mid-ocean despite the fact that, although her engine room was flooded, her hull was in good condition, and what happened to those on board? As with the *Mary Celeste*, several theories involving human and supernatural factors have been put forward to explain the crew and passengers' disappearance.

Some claim that Captain Miller had died or been severely injured – evidence: the bloody bandages found in the doctor's bag – and this had caused everyone else on board to panic, take the life-rafts and try and make for the nearest land. While this may sound rational, it does not explain the missing cargo, unless this was stolen in the meanwhile.

Another theory is that Captain Miller had had a falling out with Chuck Simpson, his first mate, and that in the resulting fight, one or both of them had been injured or fallen overboard. As a result, panic spread to the remaining twenty-four people on board, who then abandoned ship.

Other sources, such as the *Times and Herald* (Fiji) *The Daily Telegraph* (London) blamed the Japanese. It should be noted that this incident occurred only ten years after the Second World War and that there was still much anti-Japanese feeling in the area of the South Pacific. This was due to the Japanese fishing fleets, which were poaching in local waters, as well as people remembering enemy Japanese wartime activities in this area. The Fiji newspaper claimed it had an 'impeccable source' which alleged that the *Joyita* 'had observed something the Japanese did not want them to see', while *The Daily Telegraph* blamed Japanese forces still active in the area. These anti-Japanese theories were 'proved' when knives marked 'Made in Japan' were found on board. However, it was later shown that these knives were old and rusty and had possibly been left behind several years earlier when the *Joyita* had been a fishing boat.

One theory for the disappearance of the *Joyita*'s passengers and crew was that they had been kidnapped by a Russian submarine. The Australian newspaper, *The Argus*, appeared with banner headlines claiming, 'Red Sub Hits *Joyita*' on 2 February 1956. This was a vague possibility seeing that this had happened during the Cold War.

Other theories claimed that a mutiny had taken place as a result of the *Joyita*'s burst pipes, which flooded the engine room and caused other critical damage. The advocates of the mutiny theory claim that the mattresses covering the starboard engine, the only one that was working, were there to protect the switchboard from being damaged by spray or to minimise the leaks as much as possible.

Altercations broke out between Captain Miller and his crew, who demanded that he return to Samoa. He refused and a violent mutiny took place. The captain was injured and this, the pro-mutiny claimants say, was the reason for bloodstained bandages being found later in the doctor's bag. As a result, first mate Simpson became the new captain and he decided that everyone on board, including the injured Captain Miller, should abandon ship and take the logbook, food and navigational equipment with them. Those who oppose this theory, state that Simpson, as an experienced sailor, would not abandon a larger if somewhat damaged ship in mid-ocean. However, Robin Maugham, a British author who investigated this story and wrote *The Joyita Mystery* in 1962, claimed that Simpson *et al.* had abandoned her as they had sighted a nearby island. Maugham claimed that they never reached the island but drowned on the way due to strong winds and rough seas.

Another theory states that, like the *Mary Celeste*'s final captain, Captain Miller, who had many debts, deliberately damaged the *Joyita* in an effort to illegally obtain a large amount of money through a false insurance claim. However, this theory, to use a nautical term, does not hold water for two reasons. He had made no attempt to scuttle the ship, as the ship's seacocks were found to be closed like they should have been, and also Miller needed the *Joyita* for future runs in the South Pacific.

High Aim 6 – October 2003

Another ghost ship found in the South Pacific was the *High Aim 6*. She was a Taiwanese fishing boat found drifting off the north-west Australian coast on 8 January 2003, two months after she had left the port of Liuchiu, Taiwan. Like the *Mary Celeste*, there was no-one on board when she was sighted. She was also found to be carrying enough food and fuel, and the crew's personal property was undisturbed. In addition, the ship was in good condition and there were no signs that a violent struggle had taken place. As the *High Aim 6* was flying under an Indonesian flag and manned by Indonesians, that country's police began to investigate this mystery.

At first they thought that the ship had been carrying illegal immigrants in the hold, but this theory was disproved when the hold was discovered to be full of rotting fish. Eventually the Indonesian authorities located an Indonesian member of the crew. He admitted that Captain Tai-cheng and the engineer, Lin Chung-li, had been murdered on 8 December 2002 although the reasons for this were never made clear. After this mutinous action, the remaining sailors abandoned ship and sailed back to their homeland presumably in the ship's lifeboat(s). No other crewmen were ever found despite a very wide-ranging search.

The *High Aim 6* was transferred to the Australian Fisheries Management Authority who towed her to Broome on the north coast of Western Australia. A serious forensic examination followed and in the end it was concluded that a mutiny had indeed taken place. The above authority planned to sink her offshore as a habitat for fish but in the meanwhile she became a local tourist attraction for about a year. In October 2004 she was dismantled and buried in a local landfill.

Jian Seng – Spring 2006

Another ghost ship found off the north coast of Australia was the *Jian Seng*. Unlike the other ghost ships mentioned here, there is no information about where she had sailed from or which her home port was. The *Jian Seng* was spotted and photographed by an Australian Coastwatch airplane in March 2006 drifting in the Gulf of Carpentaria. The photos were studied by Australian Customs and a patrol boat, the *Storm*

Bay, was sent to see what had happened. Again, like the *Mary Celeste*, they did not find anybody on board and there were no signs that any violent action had taken place. In addition, there were no official identifying marks to be seen; in fact it looked as though these had been deliberately removed. The hold contained a large quantity of rice and the Australian authorities assumed that the *Jian Seng* had been used as a supply ship for other fishing boats in the area. Her engine was inoperable, and it was thought that she had gone adrift after her tow rope had broken. Since much of her equipment had been removed, the Australian authorities concluded that she may have been on her way to be scrapped when something mysterious happened.

After observing the *Jian Seng* for a few days, the captain of the *Storm Bay* recommended that the abandoned ship be towed to the nearest harbour. As a result, the *Jian Seng* was taken to Weipa, Cape York, Queensland and, seeing that nobody submitted a claim for her, she was scuttled on 21 April 2006, one month after she had originally been sighted from the air.

This whole story caused a backlash in the Australian government when Senator Ludwig attacked the country's customs authorities. He claimed that they had been much too slow in locating this ship, especially as ships like her had been known to be involved in illegal drug smuggling and transporting illegal immigrants.

Bel Amica – August 2006

This was yet another ghost ship found floating in the sea, with no crew on board and with all her identification marks removed. The sixty-six-foot-long *Bel Amica* was discovered off the coast of Sardinia at Punta Volpe – 'Millionaires' playground' – in the Mediterranean Sea on 24 August 2006. When the local coastguard climbed aboard and then towed her to the port of Olbia to be examined, they found that, as with the *Mary Celeste*, there was also a half-eaten meal which had been left behind. They also found French maps of North Africa, some clothes and the only possible clues to her past, a flag of Luxembourg and a plaque of some sort bearing the name, *Bel Amica*.

The authorities could not find any evidence of this ship being registered anywhere. Shortly after the mysterious ship was found, the owner of the *Bel Amica* was discovered. His name was Franc Rouayrux from Luxembourg. He could not satisfactorily explain why he had left his ship anchored off the Sardinian coast, except that he had to leave her to return home urgently in connection with some unexplained emergency. The Italian press did not buy this story and suggested that Rouayrux had abandoned his ship as a way of evading Italian taxes. None of the ship's crewmen were ever located and the *Bel Amica* has since entered the long list of ghost ships.

Kaz II – April 2007

The *Kaz II* is the smallest ghost ship that appears in this section of this book and like the *Joyita*, the *High Aim 6* and the *Jian Seng*, its story happened in the northern seas surrounding Australia. Since this £60,000 white-painted catamaran was less than ten metres long, she was called a 'ghost yacht'. The disappearance of her crew from a boat in good condition has been compared to that of the *Mary Celeste*.

The *Kaz II* was sold to and captained by Derek Batten from Perth, Western Australia, an amateur sailor with a certain amount of small boat experience. He had already sailed on the *Kaz II* in the area of the Great Barrier Reef and had taken a sailing course in the past. His fellow crewmen were his neighbours, the Tunstead brothers, Peter and James. The aim of this particular voyage was to sail around the northern coast of Australia, from Townsville, Queensland to (probably) Fremantle, Western Australia, via the Gulf of Carpentaria, the Timor Sea and the Indian and Pacific Oceans.

The three men, described in the local press as 'typical Aussie blokes' left Airlie Beach on 15 April 2007 near Whitsunday Island, Queensland. Three days later, a helicopter sighted them drifting about one hundred miles north-east of Townsville. What caused suspicion was that none of the sailing trio was seen to be on deck and her leading triangular sail was severely ripped.

When the Australian authorities boarded her two days later, there was no crew to welcome them aboard even though the catamaran was in good condition, food was on the table (like the *Mary Celeste*) and all the boat's navigational, emergency and communication equipment was also in working order.. A half-empty cup of coffee and a laptop were found on a table, a newspaper was on the floor and some clothes were piled up on a bench. It was assumed that the crew had not voluntarily abandoned ship as there was one small boat on the deck and the anchor was up. However, a lifeboat was missing, although it was unclear whether there had been a second one on board at the beginning.

The *Kaz II* was towed into Townsville harbour and the Queensland police began their investigation on the twenty-first of April. The police found no signs of violence and everything was in its normal place and 'shipshape'. A firearm and some ammunition were found under 'Captain' Batten's bed in a locked box but these had not been used recently. Unlike any other investigations into ghost ships, the crew left behind a video that they had taken just before they all went missing.

It showed that, although they were sailing through rough seas and talking about "threatening skies", none of them was wearing a life jacket. Peter Batten was steering but the engine was not running. A long rope was seen hanging off the back of the boat and they had not pulled the fenders (protective devices to stop the boat from bumping into other boats in the harbour) onto the deck.

Various authorities, including the Townsville coastguard and the navy, began a search and rescue operation for the crew on the eighteenth of April. This included the use of two commercial ships, nine airplanes and two helicopters. They did not find them and the whole operation was called off after a week's intensive work. Once the *Kaz II* had been towed back to Townsville, the police went aboard to examine her and concluded that foul play or an attempted insurance scam could be ruled out.

Four months later, on 4 August 2008, the Townsville Coroner's Court initiated an inquest. It was led by Michael Barnes who concluded that 'an unfortunate series of events' had befallen the three men. He suggested that one of them had fallen overboard trying to unravel a fishing line which had got caught up in the yacht's port side rudder or propeller and that the second man had also fallen into the sea while trying to rescue him. Barnes also claimed that the remaining third man had been accidentally knocked overboard by the boat's boom when trying to turn the *Kaz II* around so that he could rescue his two crew mates. Since the men were in the water (presumably without life jackets), the catamaran had continued sailing, leaving them behind to drown.

Coroner Barnes concluded that he 'cannot be so definitive about the circumstances under which the deaths occurred', and added, "Once the three men were in the water there was very little chance they could get back on the boat. It would be beyond their reach in seconds. From that point, the end would have been swift. None of them was a good swimmer, the seas were choppy, they would have become exhausted and sunk beneath the waves. Although I cannot exclude the possibility of a shark attacking them, drowning is a far more likely cause of death."

As with many of the other ghost ship stories recorded here and elsewhere, there were several theories about what caused the disappearance of Derek Batten and his two friends. One theory to explain the mystery of the *Kaz II* is that a freak wave washed one or more of them overboard and that the remaining person(s) drowned trying to rescue him/them. A second theory says that the catamaran had struck a sandbar near George Point and the three men all jumped overboard to free her. As they were doing so, a strong gust of wind blew and released their boat from the sandbar, leaving them behind to drown or be eaten by sharks in mid-ocean.

North Korean ghost ships

Perhaps the most recent ghost ships to be encountered are those belonging to North Korean fishermen that have washed ashore on the west coast of Japan. This is a regular occurrence and is a result of the Koreans sailing far out to sea in order to catch fish, squid and king crabs in the Sea of Japan. These fishing boats are too small to be so far out at sea and the crews probably died from hunger, exhaustion and exposure, which left the unmanned fishing boats to eventually wash up on the Japanese shores. Another reason for these ghost ships is that several of them have been used by North Koreans wishing to flee their oppressive regime. They set out for South Korea and owing to high winds and rough seas and their lack of experience at sea, they get washed overboard and/or drown on their escape to freedom. These empty boats then eventually wind up on South Korean and Japanese beaches. Wikipedia quotes that in 1987 eleven fortunate defectors reached Japan and four more did so in 2006. Five years later, nine more defectors crossed the Sea of Japan and arrived in Japan instead of in South Korea as they had originally intended.

The *Mary Celeste* in print and in literature

It did not take long for the story of the *Mary Celeste* to appear in print. Even before she had sailed out of New York harbour on her fateful voyage, the *New Bedford Evening Standard* was printing articles about three lost merchant ships, the *Cairo*, the *Guatemala* and the *Umpire*. Then on 21 December 1872 as part of the newspaper's regular 'Marine Intelligence' column, it published the following notice:

Brig Mary Celeste, *from New York Nov 17 for Genoa, is reported by cable as having been picked up as derelict and towed into Gibraltar 16th inst. She was commanded by Capt. Benjamin Briggs, of Marion, who had his wife and child with him, and much anxiety is felt for their safety.*

Soon after this report appeared, other imaginative reporters and writers jumped on the bandwagon to describe what had really happened in the North Atlantic. Some of these reports were nothing but short articles full of fanciful lies, printed as a way of writing *something* even though they did not know the truth. On 24 February 1873, even while the enquiry was being held in Gibraltar, *The Boston Post* published an article, 'A Brig's Officers Believed to Have

Been Murdered at Sea', stating that murder and mayhem had taken place on board. It said:

It is now believed that the fine brig Mary Celeste, *of about 236 tons, commanded by Capt. Benjamin Briggs of Marion, Mass, was seized by pirates in the latter part of November and that, after murdering the Captain, his wife, child, and officers, the vessel was abandoned near the Western Islands where the miscreants are supposed to have landed... The* Mary Celeste *was fallen in with by the British brig* Dei Gratia, *Capt. Morehouse, who left New York about the middle of November,* [found] *the hull of the Celeste in good condition and safely towed* [her] *into Gibraltar...*

The general opinion is that there has been foul play on board, with a sharp cut on the wood, indicate force or violence having been used... as spots of blood on the blade of a sword in the cabin, and on the rails

This was followed on the next day by an even more sensational report in the *New York Herald*, which repeated much of what the *The Boston Post* had printed the day before and added:

many things were found in the confusion on the vessel (including ladies' apparel). This circumstance has aided to the suspicion of some outrage on the part of the crew. They were mostly foreigners, and in case of mutiny by breaking into the cargo the men might have become inflamed by liquor to the commission of murder.

Note the references to 'ladies' apparel', a salacious detail which adds to this report's sensational aspect but nothing else, and to the crew being 'mostly foreigners' which was true. However, this last point implies that good North American sailors would not have behaved as hinted, especially by becoming 'inflamed by liquor'. It is true that there was liquor on board – seventeen hundred and one barrels of it – but the *Herald* conveniently forgot to note that it was of the industrial type and not drinkable and that Captain Briggs, a devout Christian, would never have allowed his crew to do so in any case.

Then a few days later, on 3 March 1873 while the enquiry was still being held in Gibraltar, *The Boston Post* published a small notice which referred to the supposed bloodstains – 'damning spots' – which had been found on Captain Briggs's ceremonial cutlass.

In addition, the *New York Sun* published yet another inaccurate story saying that it had heard that due to a past change of ownership, when J.H. Winchester had bought the *Mary Celeste*, then called the *Amazon*, from Richard W. Haines, she 'had been improperly cleared and sailed under false colors'. This whole story, the newspaper claimed, was a clever insurance scam and that although she was originally valued at $2,600, Winchester had insured her for $16,000. 'This discrepancy', it added, 'furnishes a clue upon which the insurance companies will probably act.' This, the *New York Sun* noted, was probably in order to boost their readership. And if such a style of reporting were not enough, it had also printed dramatic stories relating to the missing crew and more details about piracy and mutiny.

On 11 March 1873, the *Bath Daily Times* reinforced other

newspapers' claims that the ship owner, J.H. Winchester, had found proof that the crew of the *Mary Celeste* had staged a mutiny. Without quoting any sources, this Maine newspaper wrote, '[we] have now received additional information leaving little doubt that the crew mutilated and overpowered the officers, killing them or taking them prisoners.'

Not to be outdone by any rival newspaper, the *New York Sun* published on the following day a report headed: 'The Abandoned Ship – No Mutiny, but a Scheme to Defraud the Insurance Companies'. Among other juicy and inaccurate details, the report went on to say that there were:

several suspicious circumstances [which] *show that more selfish motives than the revolting of the sailors and the slaying of their officers might have prompted the abandonment of the vessel... the* Mary Celeste *had been improperly cleared and sailed under false colors... It was charged that the deception was resorted to for the purpose of getting her registered as an American vessel* [and had] *formerly sailed under the British flag, better known as the* Amazon.

In 1870 she took her present name, and was afterward registered as American built. Deputy Surveyor Bell discovered the deception a few months ago, and took measures to seize the brig on her next arrival in port. Contrary to expectations, she failed to arrive here [New York]...

Subsequently the brig reappeared in Boston... and was appraised at $2,600... when she sailed hence on her last voyage she was insured at the rate of $16,000, or $13,400 *over the Boston appraisement. This discrepancy furnishes a clue upon which the insurance companies will probably act*

J.H. Winchester immediately responded to this defamatory report and followed it with a true record of how he came to be the legitimate ship owner of the *Mary Celeste*.

But the *New York Sun* just would not let go. In a scurrilous reply to Winchester's report, this newspaper responded two weeks later with another article headlined, 'Was the *Mary Celeste* Deserted by her Officers and Crew to Obtain Salvage?' Calling the *Dei Gratia* the *Moorehead*, the newspaper claimed that the men of the *Mary Celeste* had deliberately abandoned her in order to claim salvage to the tune of $98,785!

In addition to this outrageous fabrication, the sensation seeking newspaper also claimed that:

A reward for any knowledge of the crew was offered on Tuesday (25 March) by the Secretary of the Treasury, who states that the deck of the vessel was covered with blood stains.

This last 'fact' like many other 'facts' in this report was completely untrue, as William Richardson, the Secretary of the Treasury, did not offer any reward.

In the meanwhile, other newspapers, both in America and Europe also continued in this imaginative vein reporting that the *Mary Celeste* had been seized by pirates. On 15 March 1873, the day following the end of the enquiry, the *Gibraltar Chronicle & Commercial Intelligencer* also referred to 'the supposed spots or stains of blood found on the deck of the

Mary Celeste and on the sword'.

Perhaps a better-known story regarding the fate of the *Mary Celeste* was that written by a twenty-five-year-old doctor and then unknown writer of detective stories, called Arthur Conan Doyle. His story, written in the first person by J. Habakuk Jephson, an alleged survivor of the *Marie Celeste*, (note the spelling of *Marie*), was published anonymously in *The Cornhill Magazine*, January 1884.

Much of it was based on what was known at the time about the *Mary Celeste*, but Doyle changed various details such as the names of the crew and captain while he also added the names of several imaginary passengers. Since his story was so widely read, the name of the original *Mary Celeste* is now generally thought to be spelt as the *Marie Celeste*.

In 'J. Habakuk Jephson's Statement', the sickly and charming Jephson, armed with a small 'lucky' carved black stone, sets out from Lisbon on his way to Boston. As the captain sees that he is short-handed in Lisbon, in addition to taking on Jephson, he also takes on four black sailors, one of whom is called Goring.

After six days out at sea, the captain's wife and baby disappear and on the following day, the captain is found dead. It is supposed that he committed suicide due to the loss of his family. Then several strange things happen on board and Jephson becomes suspicious of Goring. In the meanwhile, the black sailors become very interested in Jephson's lucky charm.

More violence occurs when they approach Africa instead of Portugal as several of the black crewmen attack Jephson. They tie him up after killing Harton, an accountant and passenger. When the *Marie Celeste* reaches the shore, the black crewmen, together with some other Black Africans, kill the rest of the crew, spare Jephson because of his lucky stone and send the unmanned *Marie Celeste* to drift out to sea. Here she is later found sailing uncontrolled by the *Dei Gratia*, whose name in this story remains the same.

The rest of this story has nothing to do with the *Mary/Marie Celeste*. It concentrates on Jephson's adventures in a temple and how Goring eventually saves Jephson's life despite his original plan to kill him.

Conan Doyle's story was first published anonymously, but since it was written in the first person as an explanation of what had happened to the *Mary Celeste*, several people and newspapers thought that this was a genuine report. As a result, the *Boston Herald* reprinted it saying that the mysterious disappearance of Captain Briggs *et al.* was now solved.

An interesting spin-off of Doyle's story appeared one hundred and thirty years later. In 2014, Valerie Martin, an American novelist, published *The Ghost of the Mary Celeste*. In this historical novel, using the story of the *Mary Celeste* as a background, a rational-minded journalist, Phoebe Grant, sets out to expose a spiritualist medium, Violet Petra, from Philadelphia, as a fraud. The novel also includes Conan Doyle as a struggling author and Captain Briggs and his family who had already suffered several tragedies in the past. As the novel's blurb says, 'These stories converge in unexpected ways as the mystery of the ghost ship deepens. But will the sea yield its secrets, and to whom?'

Another story about the *Mary Celeste* in first person 'I was there' mode, was written by Jacob Hammell (sometimes spelt Hamel). His apparent deathbed confession as told to another sailor, Carl Johanson, appeared in the *Portland Daily Press* (6 November 1897). Under the following long headline, Hammell claimed that he had survived a traumatic event on board the *Mary Celeste*:

A Tale of the Sea – The Disappearance of the Crew of the Marie Celeste [note the spelling] *– a Dying Sailor's Story of an Ocean Mystery – It Recalls a Famous case and Introduces Into Its History Three Murders – It Reads Like the Delusion of a Wandering Mind and That Is Very Likely what it Is*

Hammell claimed that he had killed the rest of the crew, that is, those who had not already died of smallpox over the previous two weeks. Hammell then returned to the *Dei Gratia* and reported that there was nobody on board the ghost ship. Later, when more of Captain Morehouse's men came aboard the *Mary Celeste*, Hammell distracted them while he searched for and found a tin box containing over $8,000 which he kept while leaving some gold and a five-pound note behind. Hammell's final dirty trick was that he 'let go one boat, with the plug out, while the men were away'.

In his book *The Mysterious Case of the Mary Celeste*, Graham Faiella comments that this was not a good story as it did not account for what happened to the money and the gold and that his ending – 'That's all the story you need to know' – was completely unconvincing.

On 17 September 1904, the *Chambers' Edinburgh Journal*, a popular magazine which featured articles mainly about poetry, science and the arts, published John Laurence Hornibrook's account of what had really happened on board the *Mary Celeste*. This report was written in the style of a novel and contained many critical inaccuracies. In describing the lifeboat on board, Hornibrook noted that it was slung on the ship's davits instead of being stored on the deck, while he more than doubled the size of the crew to include 'seventeen hands'. These, he said, were 'composed chiefly of Americans, Danes, and Norwegians' which meant that all told, twenty people went missing on that fateful November day.

Hornibrook rightfully dismissed theories about piracy, desertion or the ship being on the verge of foundering in mid-ocean – 'for not a single [life]boat was missing'. He also dismissed theories about rough seas sweeping everyone overboard or an attack of collective madness that had made them all 'voluntarily cast themselves into the sea'. Hornibrook also claimed that there had not been a homicidal maniac on board who had killed everyone sailing on that ghost ship.

After stating what had not happened, Hornibrook decided to tell his readers what had really happened in the seas of the North Atlantic. He said that a huge octopus or devil-fish – a giant squid – had first attacked the helmsman. He had yelled out for help, a sound that brought his fellow crewmen to defend him from the marine monster's tentacles. However, this was to no avail as the octopus (or squid) then caught hold of the rest of the crew and threw them overboard. This had happened so quickly that no marks were left behind as evidence. The only sign that was found, Hornibrook said, were the deep cuts made in the ship's woodwork, cuts that proved that a sailor had attempted to use an axe or large knife in order to chop off one of the monster's tentacles.

Hornibrook concluded his article: 'If, however, this

theory be not accepted, it must be left to the reader's imagination to furnish a better one.'

In contrast to Jacob Hammell's fictitious story, John Ball Osborne, a Yale University graduate and officer in the US Foreign Service, published in an article in the *Sunday Magazine*, (20 May 1906) his own version of this enigmatic story called the *Mystery of the 'Mary Celeste'* in 1906. As a state department official, he had come across some documents which had belonged to Horatio Jones Sprague, the American officer who had played a key part in the Gibraltar enquiry over thirty years earlier.

Osborne clearly felt that he had to set the record straight:

[The case] *has attracted the attention of fiction writers, both American and English,* [which] *has appeared to me so extraordinary, by reason of the apparently unfathomable mystery surrounding it, that I here present the facts as gleaned from the official archives*

Graham Faiella writes that Osborne 'laid out the facts of the affair as punctiliously as a consular official might do'. Osborne made very few factual mistakes and while writing his report, he also castigated Hornibrook for his version in which a giant octopus was responsible for the missing crew. Osborne also added that Conan Doyle's story, 'J. Habakuk Jephson's Statement' was 'not based upon even a flimsy tissue of fact'.

But this telling of the truth did not kill off all the fictitious stories. Four months later, on 16 September 1906, *The Washington Post* published its fourth story in its series, 'Tragedies of the Sea: The Mystery of the *Mary Celeste*'.

Accompanied by a dramatic picture of the merchant brigantine at sea with all her sails billowing in the wind, this article was packed full of mistakes and inaccuracies. These included that the cargo was 'petrol and alcohol' instead of just industrial alcohol; the *Dei Gratia* was captained by 'Moorhouse' and not Morehouse; the lifeboats were hanging on the stern davits and not kept on deck; as well as several mistakes regarding the ship's positions through its references to latitude and longitude. These last mistakes meant that according to *The Washington Post*, the *Mary Celeste* had drifted a mere thirty-five miles from its last recorded position in the ship's log when it was found instead of the nearly four hundred miles which was really the case.

This report, though, did tend to agree that Captain Briggs had deliberately abandoned ship in order to allow the accumulation of alcoholic fumes to escape from the hold. However, it suggested that when everyone was in the lifeboat, they were then all swamped by the ocean waves and drowned as a result.

Another exciting and imaginative newspaper report referring to the disappearance of the Briggs family and crew of the *Mary Celeste* appeared as a scoop in the London *Daily Express*. On 24 September 1924, this newspaper headlined an article:

GREAT SEA MYSTERY CLEARED UP.
What happened to the *Mary Celeste*.
Derelict Gold: Crew's Escape with Stolen £3,500.

The *Daily Express* then reported that they had found a retired seventy-year-old Royal Navy sea captain, Captain R.

Lucy, who claimed that he was the only person who knew how the *Mary Celeste* had been abandoned. He said that he had learned the facts when he had served as a mate on the *Island Princess* in the South Seas. He had been sworn to secrecy by a man named Triggs (which coincidentally rhymes with Captain Briggs) whom he had met in a Melbourne hotel.

Triggs claimed that he was on board the *Mary Celeste* when they came across a rusting steamer in mid-ocean. He and five others had climbed on board the 'derelict' ship as he called her. Her name had been washed away by the sea and the only detail they could learn was that she had been registered in London. On board they found a safe which they opened: a safe which contained £3,500 in gold and silver.

They then launched three boats to carry this back to the *Mary Celeste*, but before doing so, Captain Briggs ordered the ship's carpenter to open one of the sea-cocks and sink the steamer so that she would not be a hazard for shipping in that part of the sea. When it came to dividing up the loot, based on maritime tradition, Captain Briggs took one third, the first mate received £600, the second mate, £400 and Triggs, the bos'n, became £300 richer. The rest of the crew divided up the remaining £1,000 equally among themselves.

In the end, they painted fake names onto their three lifeboats, and loaded with their newfound riches, food and water, sailed for Cadiz. There they reported the loss of an imaginary schooner, saying that she had hit a submerged wreck. This story was widely believed even though, as Macdonald Hastings asks in his book *Mary Celeste: A Centenary Record* (1972), 'Why should Captain Briggs decide to abandon his ship, of which he was part-owner, for a sum of money far less than his own ship was worth to him, even if her cargo was rubbish, which it wasn't.'

From these sensational descriptions about what had happened on board Captain Briggs's ship, it was a natural step for the writers of stories about the *Mary Celeste* to jump from completely inaccurate newspaper reports to thrilling and completely fictitious reports about this ship.

One of the first was *A Great Sea Mystery: The True Story of the 'Mary Celeste'* by Major John Gilbert Lockhart. In this book, which was first published in 1927, Lockhart repeated what he had written in 1924 in a collection of short sea stories, that, for some unknown reason, Captain Briggs had gone mad 'and with the assistance of two apprentices, first bound and then butchered the greater part of his crew, two men, both badly injured managing to escape from him and hide in the hold'.

He justified this by saying that he had found clues 'which had generally escaped notice'. These clues included Mrs Briggs's harmonium (a musical instrument generally used for religious purposes) and also several of her husband's 'books of a religious character'. This suggested to Lockhart that someone on board (probably the captain of the *Mary Celeste*) had been 'suddenly attacked by a terrible fit of homicidal religious mania'. This had caused him to murder his wife and child and the crew. After seeing the 'gruesome task' he had just carried out, he killed himself.

However, Lockhart also conceded that his theory 'was open to much fair criticism. But again, we can only guess' adding that his 'solution' was 'merely conjecture', of which little more could be said, although there was not a lot of positive evidence in its support...

However, Major Lockhart had not finished with the *Mary Celeste* in the above book. He continued writing about this maritime mystery and later 'by way of amends' changed his story and wrote that the version put forward by Dr Oliver Cobb – that the crew had voluntarily abandoned her, fearing an explosion caused by a build-up of the alcoholic fumes in the hold – was 'the true story'.

He continued writing about the *Mary Celeste* until the 1950s and added that the ship's sails were not correctly set; that Captain Morehouse also climbed on board the *Mary Celeste* to investigate; and that a German tanker was also in the area when the *Dei Gratia* came across her sister ship in the middle of the North Atlantic.

Another new twist to the tale of the *Mary Celeste* and what happened to her appeared in June 1925 when *Chambers's Journal of Popular Literature, Science and Arts* published an article, "The Truth about the 'Mary Celeste': A Survivor's Tale." Surely with a title like that, the public would at last really know what had happened out there among the stormy waves of the North Atlantic over fifty years earlier. This was written by a reporter called Lee Kaye who claimed that the source of his report was John Pemberton, the cook on board the *Mary Celeste*. Pemberton told Kaye that Captain Briggs had been in league with Captain Morehouse and that the two men had carried out an insurance scam.

Furthermore, Kaye also claimed that although Mrs Briggs was on board the *Mary Celeste*, their daughter was not. This less than truthful journalist wrote that one day when they were trying to ride out an Atlantic storm, the melodeon-style piano which Mrs Briggs was playing, suddenly moved and rammed into her causing her severe injuries. She died the next day. Her husband flew into a rage and accused Hullock, the first mate whom he hated for having wanted to marry Mrs Briggs before he did, of causing his (Briggs's) wife to die. Briggs believed that the crew was on Hullock's side, and the general atmosphere on board was poisonous. Then, following a brawl, another sailor fell overboard while two others deserted in one of the *Mary Celeste*'s lifeboats. By the time the *Dei Gratia* had caught up with the *Mary Celeste*, Kaye stated that the only person left on board was the cook, John Pemberton. Then in order to increase his own share of the future salvage money, Captain Morehouse told the enquiry in Gibraltar that he had found nobody on board the *Mary Celeste* when he decided to bring her into Gibraltar.

Many people believed this version of the story especially as it contained a love story and because, as Kaye claimed, Pemberton was still alive. All that was needed to prove what had really happened on that fateful voyage was to find the ship's cook and hear from him. This never happened.

Then three years later, Laurence J. Keating, an impoverished Irish journalist from Liverpool, devoted one sixth of his book, i.e. forty pages, to quote this story in one of the most imaginative accounts ever of what had happened on the *Mary Celeste* in November 1872. However, all this was one gigantic hoax. Because Laurence J. Keating was in fact Lee Kaye, and his (Keating's) book, despite its bombastic title, *The Great* 'Mary Celeste' *Hoax: A Famous Sea Mystery Exposed* (1929), did absolutely nothing to expose the truth and was in itself a major literary hoax.

When Keating's book first appeared, *The New York Times*' reviewer (18 August 1929) was equally unimpressed by this authoritative looking 240-page tome. He headlined his article:

Mystery Still Shrouds the Strange Ship 'Mary Celeste' Mr Keating Tries to Prove the Affair was a Hoax, But Merely Succeeds in Re-opening the Case.

In his book Keating claimed to have spoken to survivors and quoted several documents relating to the ship and its disappearance. He justified the style of his narration by writing:

If some parts of our narration may seem a little coloured, it is hoped that readers will be ready to extend the pardon which it is the custom to give the writer who endeavours to interest the people whom he addresses

Keating must have been partly successful, because on 15 May 1929, the *Yorkshire Post and Leeds Intelligencer* noted that this book was 'by no means an improbable story – indeed it is more probable than any other of the various explanations put forward during the past 50 years'.

This Yorkshire newspaper must have been impressed by Keating's book and bought the whole story of John Pemberton, the cook. Keating ended his *magnum opus* with the following words:

He [Pemberton] *manned the galley during three voyages to Brazil, and also during the strange and celebrated passage which started from New York on 7th November 1872, and ended with the brig becoming a 'derelict,' shaping a course for the Spanish coast, the passage, that is to say, which provided the world with the 'Classic Mystery of the* Mary Celeste,*' and which has been* **fully and accurately described in our pages.** [My emphasis]

However, Charles Edey Fay, the Vice-President of the Atlantic Mutual Insurance Company of New York, who was also a writer and extremely interested in this 'Classic Mystery', wrote in his own book, *Mary Celeste: The Odyssey of an Abandoned Ship* (1942):

The character of the Keating narrative may be briefly epitomized as follows:

Here lies a book, of which it may be said
It hoaxed the living and defamed the dead.

This was not Fay's only connection to the *Mary Celeste*. It was his company which had insured her 'freight on charter' back in November 1872. Then seventy years later, he wrote the most accurate and factual description of this mystery, as he said, 'to state in orderly fashion the salient facts of the story'. Using a partial transcript of the Gibraltar enquiry's proceedings, he included details about the ship's crew, the voyage and the enquiry in Gibraltar, and he even wrote about the past history of the *Mary Celeste*. To do so, Fay used all the sources that he could, from his own research to including an incomplete copy of the records of the Gibraltar enquiry – incomplete because it did not include Captain Morehouse's and J.H. Winchester's testimonies. (These surfaced only later in the 1940s and 1950s.) As Graham Faiella notes in *The Mysterious Case of the Mary Celeste*, Fay's book 'remains even to this day a beacon of factual clarity: a benchmark source of reference to which later *Mary Celeste* writers owe a debt of gratitude'. As can be seen from his comments above about Keating and his book, Fay expressed his feelings of disgust when he considered that Keating had defamed the unfortunate but respectable crew who had sailed from New York on that iconic voyage.

For some reason, Fay's book was published as a limited edition by the Peabody Essex Museum (now the Peabody Museum) in Salem, Massachusetts, and only one thousand copies were printed. Later, in 1988, Dover Books of New York republished the book with certain changes from the original. Fay also wrote two articles on this topic which appeared in the August and September 1950 editions of the British magazine, *Sea Breezes*.

Fay was also trying to dismiss the latest theory that the ten souls aboard had disappeared as a result of a violent mutiny. One report in the *New York Sun*, (8 March 1873) headlined 'A Mystery From The Sea', even claimed that:

It is inferred that the crew mutinied and overpowered the officers, killing them or taking them prisoners. They were probably surprised, and quietly gagged and bound. A sword was found that seemed to have been stained with blood, and the fore-topgallant sail was cut with some sharp instrument, perhaps in a struggle with the man on the lookout, as they must have been near land.

All of this was completely against the evidence that Captain R.W. Shufeldt had given in court at the Gibraltar enquiry on 6 February 1873 after he had made his professional inspection of the *Mary Celeste*. He agreed that there were signs of some damage due to the North Atlantic weather but not enough to cause everyone on board to abandon her. As he said, "I am of the opinion that she was abandoned by the master and crew in a moment of panic and for no sufficient reason."

Charles Edey Fay's opinion was echoed over forty years later in 1972 when Macdonald Hastings, a BBC broadcaster and respected journalist, wrote in *Mary Celeste: A Centenary Record*, 'Nothing in this [book] has the least resemblance to truth. Yet it is absurd but true that many believed that this was the answer [to this mystery].' While fifty years later, Graham Faiella in his own detailed and factual book, *The Mysterious Case of the Mary Celeste: 150 Years of Myth and Mystique* (2022), commented on Kaye/Keating's tome, 'No other book or author encompasses the range of *Mary Celeste* accounts, records, cock-and-bull tales and other stories about her mystery.'

And what about Keating's major but secret source, the ship's cook, John Pemberton? Over the years, various researchers and journalists kept prodding Keating to produce his source in order to interview him, but the Liverpool journalist insisted on keeping them at bay. In the end, when a persistent Captain Elwell tried his luck, he was informed that Pemberton had conveniently died. This story, written by 'our special correspondent', then appeared in the London *Evening Standard*; it was actually written by Keating himself. He included a photograph of Pemberton, but later enquiries showed that this was really a photograph of Keating's own father!

In an effort to make Keating's story appear genuine, the *The Strand Magazine* published some very life-like looking illustrations about what had happened. One of these was of Briggs's daughter walking out on the bowsprit and another showed the crewmen falling into the sea from the temporary platform made for Briggs's daughter after Captain Briggs had allegedly gone mad.

But Laurence J. Keating was not the only one during this period to spin tall tales about the *Mary Celeste*. Eight years after his printed hoax had been published, Arthur Cocker, a man who claimed to be the captain of *Humber Lady*, a barge based in Hull on the Yorkshire coast, maintained that like Jacob Hammell, he too was 'the only man who [had] any first-hand connection with the mystery' of the famous ghost ship. In the *Hull Daily Mail* (17 May 1937) Cocker reported that he was a cabin boy on a grain trader at the time and that when he went on board the *Marie Celeste* (his spelling), 'the only sign of foul play was a bloodstained hatchet buried deep in the mainmast'. Cocker said that he had claimed salvage money but this had been refused. To add a veneer of verisimilitude to his story, Cocker added:

I have, however, documents and notebooks taken from the captain's cabin of the Marie Celeste *which have never been seen. The revelations they contain will, in my opinion, throw an entirely new light on the mystery.*

Needless to add, these 'documents and notebooks' were not seen then and have not been seen since, either.

In 1942, the same year that Charles Edey Fay's book appeared, George Sand Bryan published *Mystery Ship: The* Mary Celeste *in Fancy and in Fact*. Like Fay's book, this hefty publication (317 pages in the 1944 edition) concentrated on the facts and stated that Dr Oliver Cobb's theory (the abandoning of the *Mary Celeste* out of fear of an explosion caused by her cargo of alcohol) was very possible.

The reviewer in *The New York Times* (26 April 1942) commented positively on Bryan's book and wrote:

Mr Bryan has a good time, and gives a good time to his readers, in recounting wild tales, from semi-fiction to would-be hoax, which have gathered around the Mary Celeste. *But when he looks at serious conjectures he considers them seriously.*

Another writer who wrote seriously on this topic was crime and mystery author Rupert Furneaux (1908–1981). His book, *What Happened on the Mary Celeste* (1964), is a factual account and tends to support Dr Oliver Cobb's theory. Graham Faiella noted that not only did Furneaux demythicise this maritime mystery but also added a few words about the missing captain, family and crew as well:

So we destroy our gods. But, in mourning their passing, let us spare a thought for the poor people of the Mary Celeste *at the awful moment of realization, when they saw their staunch ship draw away leaving them tossing on the open sea.*

One hundred years after the *Mary Celeste* had been abandoned for no obvious reason, Macdonald Hastings, (1909–1982), author of thirty books, journalist and BBC warcorrespondent, wrote *Mary Celeste: A Centenary Record* (1972).

This book differed from many of the others referred to in this chapter in that, in addition to the book's regular text, Hastings included some imagined conversations that the attorney general, Mr Solly Flood, allegedly had at the Gibraltar enquiry. Hastings also included several similar conversations between Captains Briggs and Morehouse and first mate, Oliver Deveau, together with the imaginary figures of John Pemberton and first mate, Toby Hullock, the 'Bully of Baltimore'. In addition, Hastings included another imaginary conversation between Captain Briggs and Abel Fosdyk, a character and alleged survivor of Briggs's crew who will be dealt with more fully later.

One of the positions that Hastings had had during his career was that of editor of the *The Strand Magazine* 1945–1950. While he was there, he found that the magazine had, in 1913, published a story entitled, 'The Amazing Solution of the Mystery of the *Marie Celeste*'. (Note the incorrect spelling of 'Mary'.) The story went on to say that the eminently respectable Howard Linford MA of Magdalen College, Oxford and the headmaster of Peterborough Lodge had discovered a manuscript belonging to Abel Fosdyk, an ageing school servant. Linford, a teacher of English and mathematics, claimed that Fosdyk, a survivor from the *Mary Celeste*, wrote that he had been aboard the ship during its stormy Atlantic voyage.

In his version of what happened on the *Mary Celeste*, Fosdyk claimed that Captain Briggs's two-year-old daughter was really an eight-year-old tomboy of a girl. In addition, when one of the crew fell overboard, Briggs, at the wheel, told another sailor to jump into the sea to rescue him. The sailor refused and Briggs mocked him for being a coward.

Then after the captain had been told that his seasick wife wanted to speak to him below, the sailor took over the wheel. At this point Fosdyk joined the sailor at the wheel and then Briggs reappeared and slapped his daughter for disobeying him by behaving irresponsibly on deck. Fosdyk was then ordered to build a wooden cage so that Briggs's daughter – here called Baby – could watch the sea without falling in.

But this was not the end of the incident about the sailor's alleged cowardice. Back up on deck, Briggs, despite his wife's pleas not to do so, climbed down a rope into the sea to show that a man could swim in the sea. Following more pleas from Mrs Briggs, two more sailors joined their captain in the sea to make sure he was safe. All went well until a shark attacked one of the sailors as the rest of the crew watched from the deck. Their combined weight on one side of the deck caused the vessel to tilt over and the rest of the crew, except Fosdyk, all fell into the sea and were drowned or eaten by the shark. Fosdyk later claimed that his own life was saved because he had clung to the quarterdeck and was later washed ashore off the African coast.

Fosdyk's story, as retold in the form of a film or play script by Macdonald Hastings, sounded credible if somewhat dramatic. He said it was a good story, told by an old seaman. It supported the theory about the strange cuts found in the wood of the *Mary Celeste*'s bows and it also explained the mythical half-eaten meal allegedly found on board the abandoned ship. However, Linford's story about Fosdyk did not explain how two-year-old Sophia Matilda Briggs had now become an eight-year-old girl. Neither did he explain how any the names he mentioned appeared in the ship's official records crew were English when in fact four of them were German. Linford also made two major mistakes about the *Mary Celeste* itself: he said that she weighed 600 tons when in fact she weighed just over 282 tons and that there was no special deck built on board.

When these errors were mentioned later, Howard Linford said that they must have been due to Fosdyk's memory possibly betraying him, since he was telling his story some twenty years after the events had occurred. Linford also justified himself in the *The Strand Magazine* saying, 'I would like to emphasise the fact that I do not vouch for the truth of anything narrated.' Macdonald Hastings was less forgiving. He wrote, 'I find it surprising that a man of his sort [Linford] could have invented his tale… It is surprising what men will presume, even scholars, for a handful of sovereigns.'

In 2004, Brian Hicks, a Tennessee journalist, published *Ghost Ship: The Mysterious True Story of the* Mary Celeste *and her Missing Crew*. This is a good factual account of this mystery. In addition to writing about the ship and the voyage, he includes chapters on what happened to the *Mary Celeste* when she eventually returned to America: the various hoaxes that were carried out involving this ship as well as other ghost ship stories. In chapter twelve, 'Without a Soul', Hicks' speculations about what happened in the North Atlantic in November 1872, tend to agree with Dr Oliver Cobb's theory that the fear of alcoholic fumes caused Captain Briggs to abandon ship for a short while he then 'watched helplessly as the Ghost Ship sailed away without a soul on board'.

This, however, was not the last modern word about this intriguing maritime mystery. In 2006, Paul Begg, a world authority on Jack the Ripper, published *Mary Celeste: The Greatest Mystery of the Sea*. In his 322-page book, he analyses this mystery together with a serious critique of 'J. Habakuk Jephson's Statement'. Begg also investigates the Briggs family and the ship itself, as well as writing about all the people who were involved in this well-known story. In addition, he also includes a full verbatim script of the Gibraltar enquiry. However, despite his detailed analytical report, Begg reaches no final conclusion as to what had really happened to Captain Briggs *et al.* However he closes his book with the following surprising sentence: 'If it wasn't a waterspout, what could it have been?'

Theories for disappearance – Human

American seamen under attack by pirates

Perhaps the most frequently asked question about the *Mary Celeste* and her crew's mysterious disappearance, together with her crew, is "What really happened?" The answers to this question range from a shrug of the shoulders and a muttered, "Don't know," to blaming various natural phenomena such as giant squids, waterspouts and seaquakes. People have also claimed that there was a mutiny by the crew or an attack by pirates, or that there were problems stemming from fumes rising up from the ship's cargo of industrial alcohol. Even secret islands rising out of the Atlantic Ocean, icebergs, UFOs, the Bermuda Triangle, and compass and navigational problems which caused the ship to get lost and collide with an iceberg have been considered as ways to try and explain this one-hundred-and-fifty-year-old mystery.

Then once this question is answered, it is inevitably followed by, "Why?" Then other questions are asked. "Was this disappearance of the crew organised in order to con the insurance company?" "Did the crew abandon ship because of navigational failures?" "Were they scared that the water swilling about in the bilge would sink the ship?" "What do you know about the captain and his crew?" "Were they never seen again – anywhere?" and more.

The following pages will attempt to put forward some of the most popular theories and answers to these questions and explain why they are credible or not.

Pirates and mutiny

Some people have put forward the idea that Riffian or Berber pirates operating out of Morocco and north-west Africa captured the ship and either forced the unfortunate crew to walk the plank or simply killed them and threw their bodies into the sea. After all, piracy on the high seas has been around for hundreds of years and still exists today. Witness the multi-million-dollar pirate 'industry' operating out of Somalia and the Indian Ocean. If these T-shirted pirates, with their fast speed boats and sub-machine guns, AK-47s and RPGs, can continue the centuries-old tradition of piracy in the twenty-first century, why can't classic pirates be blamed for targeting a simple sailing ship such as the *Mary Celeste* in November 1872?

On 24 February 1873, *The Boston Post* printed an article (see its opening paragraph below) which claimed that the *Mary Celeste* was believed to have been boarded by pirates. The newspaper claimed that they had murdered the captain, his family and crew and then abandoned her 'near the Western Isles'. The article embellished this report by sensationally referring to various items of 'ladies' apparel' which were found on board. It also noted that 'spots of blood on the blade of a sword in the cabin' were found, as the writer tried to reinforce his story by saying that murder and mayhem had led to the disappearance of the *Mary Celeste*'s crew.

A Brig's Officers Believed to Have Been Murdered at Sea.
From the Boston Post. Feb. 24.

It is now believed that the fine brig Mary Celeste, of about 236 tons, commanded by Capt. Benjamin Briggs, of Marion, Mass., was seized by pirates in the latter part of November, and that, after murdering the Captain, his wife, child, and officers, the vessel was abandoned near the Western Islands, where the miscreants are supposed to have landed. The brig left New-York on the 17th of November for Genoa, with a cargo of alcohol, and is said to have had a crew consisting mostly of foreigners. The theory now is, that some of the men probably obtained access to the cargo, and were thus stimulated to the desperate deed.

The Mary Celeste was fallen in with by the British brig Dei Gratia, Capt. Morehouse, who left New-York about the middle of November. The hull of the Celeste was found in good condition, and safely towed into Gibraltar, where she has since remained. The confusion in which many things were found on board, (including ladies' apparel, &c.,) led, with other circumstances, to suspicion of wrong and outrage, which has by no means died out. One of the latest letters from Gibraltar received in Boston says: The Vice-Admiralty Court sat yesterday, and will sit again to-morrow. The cargo of the brig has been claimed, and to-morrow the vessel will be claimed.

The general opinion is that there has been foul play on board, as spots of blood on the blade of a sword, in the cabin, and on the rails, with a sharp cut on the wood, indicate force or violence having been used, but how or by whom is the question. Soon after the vessel was picked up, it was considered possible that a collision might have taken place. Had this been the case, and the brig's officers and crew saved, they would have been landed long ere this. We trust that if any of New-England's shipmasters can give any information or hint of strange boats or seamen landing at any of the islands during the past ninety days, that they will see the importance thereof.

This article was followed the next day by the *New York Herald*'s which repeated the earlier claims of 'foul play' and bloody swords. The *Herald* also added that the crew were mainly 'foreigners' who had also broken into the cargo of barrels of alcohol, which had caused them to 'have become inflamed by liquor to the commission of murder'.

Later that week, on 28 February 1873, a rival New York newspaper published a dramatic article which also claimed that the *Mary Celeste* had been seized by pirates. The article went on to say that Captain Briggs and his 'delicate wife' had been forced to walk the plank and that any valuables on board had been stolen. In addition, the cargo of alcohol was mentioned and the crew were now referred to as 'mutineers'. As Brian Hicks in his excellent book, *Ghost Ship*, points out, the newspaper article was full of factual mistakes; for example, it claimed that the 'ship's cabins were completely ransacked' and that there had been a 'fierce struggle for control of the ship'.

This was not the first time that piracy was mentioned as a way of explaining the crew's mysterious disappearance but this theory holds no water – even bilge water – at all. First of all, there were no signs of a struggle on board and secondly, various valuable items, such as Sarah Briggs's jewellery as well as the personal possessions belonging to Captain Briggs and his crew, were found to be in place when Deveau and Wright made their first exploratory search on board. The alleged blood on the sword – a decorated ceremonial cutlass belonging to Captain Briggs – was found still in its scabbard in the captain's cabin At the hearing, Dr J. Patron, appearing as an expert witness, said that the reddish-brown stains 'about a millimetre tick and half an inch in diameter' on the sword were not blood but 'a yellow and imperfectly crystallised substance' and did not represent anything at all like blood.

This statement further disproved any theories about the appearance of pirates and their take-over of the ship. In addition, all the items on board that could have been thrown around or smashed in a pirate capture or mutiny, such as furniture, the ship's instruments (apart from the binnacle) and other equipment, were not displaced or damaged in any way. If the *Mary Celeste* had been the scene of a violent fight between the crew and mutineers and/or pirates, they must have been the most considerate lawbreakers ever as they had cleaned and tidied the ship up before abandoning her!

Finally, as Brian Hicks has pointed out, there were only a few confirmed reports of piracy in the North Atlantic as late as the 1870s. There were hardly any cases of it off the infamous Barbary Coast, but there were occasional incidents of Riffian piracy in the seas off Gibraltar. It may also be relevant to consider the fact that when Captain Briggs did abandon his ship, he was still in the middle of the Atlantic Ocean – well over six hundred miles off the coast of Portugal – an area too far from the Portuguese coast for pirate activity.

Yet another 'human' theory claims that the crew of the *Dei Gratia* murdered the crew of the *Mary Celeste* in order to obtain the salvage money and then threw their bodies overboard. However, as previously mentioned, there were no signs of a fight of any sort found on board, and if there had been, Captain Morehouse's crew certainly cleaned up the scene of their crime extremely thoroughly.

Mutinies such as the one described above were rare but they did still occur. In 1842, a mutiny had been planned and discovered on board the overcrowded US Navy training ship, *Somers*, and three of the ringleaders were hanged from the yardarms, as Captain Mackenzie wished that the rest of the crew would see 'justice' being carried out. Perhaps another more publicised mutiny had occurred three years earlier. This happened in 1839 when the fifty-three slaves on the Spanish schooner, *Le Amistad*, managed to free themselves and overpower the crew. They killed the captain and several crew members but then the ship was taken over by a US Navy brig and the slaves were taken to New York. They were released as free men after a trial and this 'mutiny' became an important incident in the fight between the Abolitionists and their opponents in the lead up to the American Civil War, 1861–65.

Bearing the above in mind, the authorities in Gibraltar were very pleased at one point during the official enquiry to decide that a mutiny had indeed taken place on board the *Mary Celeste*. To support this theory, the fact that an alleged bloodstained sword was found by the *Dei Gratia* crew when they first explored the abandoned vessel was used as proof. The ship's first mate, Oliver Deveau, is quoted in the Gibraltar enquiry report:

I also observed in this cabin a Sword in its scabbard which the Marshal informed me he had noticed when he came on board for the purpose of arresting the vessel. It had not [been] *affected by water but on drawing out the blade it appeared to me as if it had been smeared with blood and afterwards wiped.*

Aha! Blood and violence! The long, pointed sword was in its gold scabbard and was probably used, if at all, for ceremonial purposes only. In addition, as stated earlier, the alleged bloodstains were found to be some form of rust caused by the damp atmosphere acting on the sword's metal blade.

Insurance fraud

A completely different theory linking the disappearance of Captain Briggs and his family and the crew, which also involved breaking the law, was insurance fraud. After the passing of the Merchant Shipping Act in 1876, cargo ships had to display the Plimsoll line to show how heavily laden they were. Before this date, unscrupulous ship owners would overload their ships on purpose to cause them to sink and thereby collect a deliberately inflated amount of maritime insurance.

Some people have claimed that the disappearance of Captain Briggs's family and crew was connected to such a scam, but this has been difficult to prove. Although the promise of large sums of money can turn heads, Captain Briggs, known to be a God-fearing, honest man who frequently read his Bible, would not have been a partner to such a criminal activity. According to his contemporaries it would have been completely out of character for him to have been involved in such an alleged insurance fraud. Although several people have claimed that Captains Briggs and Morehouse had cooked up a scheme to defraud the Atlantic Mutual and the four other insurance companies which had jointly insured the *Mary Celeste* and her cargo, Brian Hicks writes that these two captains 'would not have devised such an attention-drawing mystery'. In other words, if they were going to pull off such a financial trick, it would have been done as quietly as possible, without the rest of the world looking over their shoulders.

Those who believe in this insurance scam theory claim that a secret deal was made between Captains Briggs and Morehouse. They say that these two captains conspired on the night before the *Mary Celeste* sailed to defraud the ship's insurance company. The ship was insured for $14,000 (about $385,000 today) which was actually $2,000 less than the ship was worth, while its cargo was valued at well over twice that sum. Even J.H. Winchester, the majority shareholder of the *Mary Celeste* asked at the Gibraltar enquiry, "And now we would ask if an attempt has been made to defraud the underwriters?"

As Brian Hicks writes, this theory about defrauding the insurance companies 'collapses around questions of motive and execution'. He says that if Briggs and Morehouse had planned such a scam, they would not have organised it so that it would receive so much publicity. They would have included details such as a note in the ship's logbook or somewhere else on board. Also, if Briggs were planning to carry out such an illegal act, why did he take his wife and baby daughter with him? Were they there merely to serve as a 'cover' – just to show how innocent he was of such a criminal act? And if he were going to do so, why did he leave his young son, Arthur, behind in America?

In addition, those who believe in this insurance scam conspiracy theory have to take into account the following. It is known that Captain Morehouse set sail some six days after the *Mary Celeste* had left the shores of New York. What were his chances of making a rendezvous at sea in the middle of the possibly stormy North Atlantic one week later? We are talking about an age when ships used charts, sextants and octants for their navigation, which were much cruder technologically than today's gyro and magnetic compasses, GPS, autopilots and speed logs to name just some of the instruments that ships use today. In other words, for Captains Briggs and Morehouse to plan and actually meet up in the middle of the sea at a certain point and at a specific time in order to carry out a 'dirty deed' would have been virtually impossible.

If we are to reject the above theory that Captains Briggs and Morehouse had carried out an insurance fraud, then is it possible to believe in the following theories which were advocated by Captain Briggs's cousin Oliver Cobb or by the captain's younger brother, James?

Captain Briggs' cousin, Oliver Cobb's, theory

Dr Oliver Cobb from Massachusetts, who took on the role of family biographer, proposed the following idea regarding the disappearance of his family and crew on the *Mary Celeste*. In 1940, the eighty-two-year-old Cobb published his long-held theory in *Yachting* magazine, which was supported by Charles Edey Fay (more later), an executive who worked at Atlantic Mutual, one of the *Mary Celeste*'s insurers. Cobb wrote that his cousin and the crew had deliberately abandoned the ship because they had heard rumblings in the hold, noises caused by a build-up of pressure from alcoholic fumes which had escaped from the hundreds of barrels of industrial alcohol. He explained that the barrels of alcohol had been loaded in November and that the ship 'having crossed the Gulf Stream and now being in comparatively warm weather, there may have been some leakage and gas may have accumulated in the hold'. Cobb claimed that Captain Briggs was overly cautious for two reasons: he had his wife and two-year-old daughter on board and also, because he had never carried alcohol before, he was concerned about what might happen if the increasing pressure became critically dangerous.

As a result, Briggs ordered everyone to abandon ship. 'But in their haste', Cobb wrote, 'they neglected to attach a line to the vessel by which they could be towed. That was a mistake, but an understandable one.' As a result, the captain and crew, now alone in the North Atlantic, died of starvation or their lifeboat capsized in the rough sea.

In his detailed book, *Ghost Ship*, Brian Hicks writes that Oliver Cobb 'made one noticeable change to his theory. He now suspected that Briggs had taken the mainsail halyard as a towline for the lifeboat' but this had snapped leaving the captain *et al.* alone in the Atlantic where they all died.

In his book *Mary Celeste: A Centenary Record* (1972) published one hundred years after the crew had disappeared, Macdonald Hastings questions Oliver Cobb's theory and asks whether Captain Briggs, an experienced sailor, would have given such a panicked order to abandon ship. Hastings says, 'If the *Mary Celeste* had blown her timbers, she would still have been a better bet for survival than the ship's [life] boat.' However, he added, if Briggs had abandoned ship, then he had 'behaved like a fool; worse, a frightened one'.

In 1886, J.H. Winchester, the major owner of the *Mary*

Celeste, claimed in a similar theory to that of Oliver Cobb's, that the red oak barrels holding the alcohol in the hold were extremely porous and that the escaping alcoholic fumes together with the foul air in the hold had generated an explosive gas. This had blown off the cover of the fore-hatch on the top deck. This had panicked Captain Briggs who had ordered his wife, daughter and crew to abandon ship and see what would happen from a safe distance. Brian Freemantle in *The Mary Celeste*, who quotes the above situation, does not mention if the captain thought to attach a tow rope to his ship or not. All he says is that the winds 'filled her topsail when, like a frightened deer, away she went, leaving her crew behind'.

Captain Henry O. Appleby, a friend of J.H. Winchester and the man who loaned the ship owner the bail money in Cadiz to retrieve his ship, said that such an explosion had happened to him in the past. This had occurred when he was on his own ship *Daisy Boynton*, while he was carrying a cargo of alcohol on his way to Bilbao, in northern Spain.

N. Putnam, a New York insurance expert who had previously dealt with other maritime mysteries and who was involved with the finances of the final voyage of the *Mary Celeste* in 1885, said that the rope from the *Mary Celeste* to the lifeboat had been cut, not untied. As Dr Oliver Cobb claimed, this proved that Captain Briggs had ordered his crew to abandon ship in a hurry. This was the result of having heard rumblings and small explosions in the hold, a natural sound when dealing with escaping gases in an enclosed space. Several of these ominous noises had been recorded in the ship's log and Putnam suggested that on the day in question a careless sailor had caused the escaping gases to explode when he had gone down to the hold while smoking his pipe.

Captain Briggs's brother James's theory

This theory contrasted with another one put forward by yet another member of the family, James C. Briggs, Captain Benjamin Briggs's brother. James Briggs suggested that his brother had abandoned the *Mary Celeste* because they were sailing too close to the rocky shores of Santa Maria, the southernmost island of the Azores archipelago in the North Atlantic.

This last-mentioned theory was supported by Captain Ansel Weeks, Jnr, a near neighbour who lived about one mile away from the Briggs family in Marion, Massachusetts. He wrote in the *Journal of Commerce* that no mutiny or insurance fraud had taken place and that there were no visible signs of piracy on board. Weeks claimed that even though Captain Briggs was well informed about the area surrounding the Azores, he ordered everyone to abandon ship and thereby avoid being on board the *Mary Celeste* when it inevitably would be smashed up on the rocks. Weeks justified this by stating that Captain Briggs 'may have been deceived by appearances (a surf never showing its worst from offshore) and may have been swamped in trying to reach the port on the south of the island, and of course all on board would have perished'.

The weak point of this theory is that when the crew of the *Dei Gratia* came upon the strangely moving *Mary Celeste*, she bore no signs of distress, apart from a couple of unexplained cuts in the upper woodwork, nor had she been sailing anywhere near any dangerously rocky shorelines.

The burning ship theory

This theory for the disappearance of Captain Briggs *et al.* was put forward by a Canadian writer, Frederick William Wallace. In his book *In the Wake of the Wind Ships* and in an interview he gave to *The Montreal Star* (25 February 1925), Wallace dismissed theories about giant octopuses and said that 'matters that appear mystifying to landsmen are usually commonplace and probable to a sailor'.

He went on to say that 'the menace which caused Briggs to abandon ship came from without [i.e. not within the *Mary Celeste* itself] the ship, and it came suddenly, and without warning'.

This 'menace' was caused by another sailing ship loaded with coal and dynamite. According to Wallace, this second ship drew up close to the *Mary Celeste* in a calm sea when a fire caused by spontaneous combustion broke out on the second ship. The crew of the burning ship panicked, launched a lifeboat and rowed over to the *Mary Celeste*, whose crew in turn took to their own lifeboat. Wallace then said that the now unmanned *Mary Celeste* drifted away leaving all her personnel in the middle of the sea. He then added more fascinating details about men falling overboard and the presence of sharks. This meant that when the *Mary Celeste* was eventually found by Captain Morehouse, all of her crew, Captain Briggs and his family were no longer in the land of the living.

The solution at last?

In May 2006, Adrian Lee published an article in the British newspaper, the *Daily Express*, to say that he had finally solved the mystery concerning the *Mary Celeste*. According to this article, Dr Andrea Sella, an inorganic chemist at University College, London, had conducted an experiment using butane gas to simulate the alcoholic gas which had been leaking out of the brigantine's cargo of seventeen hundred and one wooden barrels of industrial alcohol.

Instead of using real barrels, Dr Sella used cartons or cubes of paper. He placed these in an enclosed space to simulate the hold of the *Mary Celeste* and ignited the butane gas. This resulted in huge but controlled explosion which caused a wave of flame. The surprising outcome was that the paper cubes did not burn and neither were they blackened or scorched. Dr Sella explained this as being the result of a 'pressure-type wave of explosion' which was spectacular, but behind this wave of flame he said that there was an area of 'relatively cool air'. He stated that this laboratory-controlled experiment created a simulation of the situation where either two metal-banded loose barrels in the hold of the *Mary Celeste* had rubbed together to create a spark or a careless pipe-smoking sailor had caused a spark when he opened the ship's hatch in order to ventilate the hold. This would have been done to let the alcoholic fumes that had been building up during the voyage from New York to escape into the atmosphere.

Dr Sella summed up the dramatic results of his experiment saying, 'The explosion would have been enough to blow open the hatches and would have been completely terrifying for everyone on board… It is the most compelling explanation. Of all those suggested, it fits the facts best and explains why they [Captain Briggs, family and crew] were so keen to get off the ship.'

Theories for disappearance – Natural and supernatural

And now for the theories regarding the hand of Mother Nature.

In contrast to the theories referring to human avarice, violence and criminality that caused the captain, family and crew of the *Mary Celeste* to disappear, other theories are based on various natural phenomena. Among others, these include sea monsters, disappearing islands, mermaids and the Bermuda Triangle.

Giant sea monsters

One of the theories attributed to nature is that the ten souls on the *Mary Celeste* were picked off, one by one, by a giant squid lurking in the depths of the North Atlantic Ocean. These creatures, which are not just figments of the imagination of superstitious sailors or Hollywood film producers, really do exist. Giant squids (*Architeuthis dux*) swim around in the deep ocean and have been estimated to grow from thirty-three to forty-three feet in length from the tops of their heads to the tips of their tentacles. They live in all the world's oceans and are found in the North Atlantic especially around the Azores. Evidence of their existence has been discovered, in the form of circular scars from the suckers on their tentacles, on the heads of sperm whales that they have attacked.

Giant squids, as monsters of the deep, are sometimes associated with the legendary krakens – giant octopuses – which originally appeared in Scandinavian folklore. Descriptions of these creatures were featured in a Norwegian manuscript by King Sverre in c.1180. Through these dramatic illustrations, krakens entered public consciousness especially that of superstitious sailors and anyone else concerned with finding an explanation for anything deadly that happened at sea. These krakens were supposed to be so large – as large as a small island –that they could easily sink a ship. In the thirteenth century text *Saga of Örvar-Oddr*, the two maritime monsters Lyngbakr and Hafgufa were said to be the strongest sea monsters of all and had the ability to drag every other sea monster, and presumably every ship, 'under their shadow'.

Later, in the eighteenth and nineteenth centuries, there

were records which showed that various vessels had encountered such monsters of the deep. In 1861, the crew of the French warship the *Alecton* claimed that they had seen a huge tentacled monster in the vicinity of the Canary Islands. The captain noted that it 'seems to measure fifteen to eighteen feet up to its head, in the shape of a parrot's beak, surrounded by eight arms five to six feet long.' After a three-hour battle, his crew then caught this monster in a net and tried to haul it on board. However, at this point, the rope snapped and the monster escaped. The only evidence they had to prove their story was the tip of the monster's tail which had been entangled in their rope.

Giant squids also appeared in two famous books that were published soon before the *Mary Celeste* started off on her fateful voyage. In 1851, Herman Melville wrote about them in his classic novel *Moby Dick*, and three years before Captain Briggs had cast off at New York, Jules Verne had described giant squids in *Twenty Thousand Leagues Under the Sea*. However, despite beliefs in giant squids and other monsters of the deep which went back for centuries, there were no visible signs of any struggles by man or beast found on board the *Mary Celeste* when Oliver Deveau and John Wright first climbed aboard and searched the ship to see what had caused the brigantine's crew to abandon the vessel in mid-ocean.

Vanishing islands

Another natural theory to explain the disappearance of the crew of the *Mary Celeste* was that they had landed on a secret and/or vanishing island. This theory, which sounds somewhat farfetched, may be reinforced by the following events which happened to another seafarer, Dod Osborne, some sixty years later.

In April 1936, Dod Osborne (born George Black Osborne in 1902), together with his younger brother, James, and a crew of four, sailed from Grimsby, Lincolnshire, in the fifty-ton trawler *Girl Pat*. This was supposed to be a regular trawling trip in the North Sea. However, soon after leaving port, Osborne told the crew that they would be sailing further south than usual and nothing more was heard from them until they informed the ship's owners that they had arrived at Corcubión, a small port in north-west Spain. There, Osborne said that they were planning to buy some fresh supplies and carry out some repairs. Then there were reports that the *Girl Pat* had been seen near Dakar, West Africa, and later near the Salvation Islands off the northern coast of French Guiana, South America.

Later there were reports that the ship had been wrecked in the Bahamas and everyone on board had drowned. However, this was not true as the *Girl Pat* was later pursued and captured by the police of British Guiana's Georgetown. Osborne and his crew were arrested for stealing the ship and returned to England. There, despite the fact that they were seen as heroes for having crossed the Atlantic in a small trawler using only a school atlas for navigation, they were tried and sentenced to eighteen months in prison.

The reason that this voyage is perhaps relevant to that of the *Mary Celeste* is that while the *Girl Pat* was sailing off the West African coast, it ran aground in mid-ocean. The ship started listing badly and soon the crew saw that they were sitting on a sandy island in the middle of the eastern Pacific

Ocean. Later, Osborne said that it 'seemed as if a giant hand had grasped the bottom of the boat and lifted her firmly, but very carefully out of the water. She felt as if she had been placed tenderly on a cushion'.

The island, whose coast totalled about one mile and which stood three feet above the water, seemed to be one of several that Osborne and his crew observed rising and falling in the area. After a day, Osborne's island sank below the waves and the crew sailed off. These so-called islands or sandbanks were known as the Phantom Islands and French scientists claimed that they were caused by underground rivers and tectonic movements. Other vanishing islands exist off the western coast of the USA, north of Seattle, and also in the Philippines.

Using this knowledge, several people, including Captain Osborne, have claimed that the *Mary Celeste*, which was found in a seaworthy condition but without its crew, had encountered a similar phenomenon and that the crew had abandoned her as a result. In 1937, in an article for *Life* magazine Osborne said, 'The rest is easy to imagine: the captain and his wife and child and the crew crowding into the lifeboat and rowed away from the island, as my men wanted me to do… Their chances of survival in the desert in 1872 were much smaller than ours would have been in 1936.'

Mermaids

Some of the better-known creatures of the deep which have allegedly lured ships and their crews to a watery death are mermaids. These supernatural beings, which are usually portrayed as having the top half of a seductive-looking female and the tail of a fish, have been known to man for over seven thousand years. In *Merpeople: A Human History*, Vaughn Scribner writes that the Akkadians worshipped them around c.2350-2200 BCE and that the ancient Babylonians depicted them as well. In later history we read that the Greeks had Scylla, a mythical female creature that had twelve feet and six heads, but today our images of mermaids are actually based on medieval Christian paintings and stone carvings in churches and cathedrals. Scribner claims that such depictions of women were yet another way 'to denigrate them as dangerous facets of humanity that might lure men to their death'. Another example of mermaids being sighted came on 9 January 1493: while sailing in the Caribbean near today's Dominican Republic, Christopher Columbus claimed that he had seen three of them.

The Victorians were fascinated by these creatures and an American sea captain, Samuel Barrett Edes, bought one for about $6,000 that had supposedly been killed near Fiji in the South Pacific. It was later sold to the American showman P.T. Barnum who exhibited it in London (1822), Boston and New York but it was later destroyed when his museum burned down in 1868.

The Bermuda Triangle

While the above theory is a possibility, there are people who believe in the factually impossible idea that the Bermuda Triangle (an area of the western Atlantic bounded by Bermuda, Florida and Puerto Rico) may have fatally sucked the *Mary Celeste* under the waves. However, those who support this theory completely ignore the facts that this allegedly treacherous area lies 2,800 miles (4,500 km) to the west of where the *Mary Celeste* was first spotted by Captain Morehouse and his crew, and that the ship was never actually sucked under the waves but remained sailing above the sea to be discovered by the *Dei Gratia*.

UFOs

Another radical theory to explain the disappearance of the crew of the *Mary Celeste* was put forward in 1955 by Morris Ketchum Jessup (1900–1959), an author and astronomer from Michigan. In his book *The Case for the UFO* (Arco, London, 1957), this well-known ufologist devotes a chapter to aliens from flying saucers who kidnap sailors and lost ships. He attempted to prove his theory by saying that the upper rigging and compass of the *Mary Celeste* had been damaged by these aliens when it was spotted by Captain Morehouse and his crew. Jessup also noted that there were no signs of violence on board, a fact that for him proved that the aliens had quickly overcome Captain Briggs *et al.* before taking them away into the unknown. Jessup did not say why the aliens had chosen the *Mary Celeste*, but attempted to justify his theory by adding, 'There is always the possibility that the open seas provide an easy catching place.'

Waterspouts

Waterspout near Cap de Formentor, Mallorca

In 1966, over one hundred years after the crew of the *Dei Gratia* spotted the *Mary Celeste*, Gershom Bradford, a retired American naval lieutenant and senior nautical scientist with the US Navy Hydrographic Office, claimed that a waterspout had forced Captain Briggs to abandon ship. Based on past examples, Bradford explained how such waterspouts activate winds which can rip sails and flood ships, and that this would account for the torn sails and soaked bedding found on the *Mary Celeste*. When Bradford was asked why Captain Briggs had abandoned his larger ship for a lifeboat in the middle of the Atlantic, he speculated that this had not happened immediately but only after the crew had discovered that the waterspout had flooded the hold. Believing that his ship would soon sink, Captain Briggs then ordered everyone to abandon her. Once they saw that their ship was not sinking, they tried to catch up with the *Mary Celeste*. Unfortunately, they failed and were ultimately lost at sea, perhaps as Bradford suggested, in another gale.

While the crew of the *Dei Gratia* were being interrogated in Gibraltar, the first mate, Oliver Deveau, suggested that Captain Briggs had abandoned ship after taking a faulty reading of the depth of the water in the bilge of the *Mary Celeste*. This could be the result of a waterspout causing a low atmospheric pressure, which in turn may have caused the reading of the depth of the bilge water to be dangerously high. Such a situation may have caused Captain Briggs to assume that his ship had taken on too much water to be pumped out and that the *Mary Celeste* was in danger of sinking.

While the above theory sounds credible, waterspouts,

even though they appear to be a threat, are often small and weak and usually occur in tropical and sub-tropical seas as opposed to the cold waters of the North Atlantic. With reference to Bradford's theory, in *Ghost Ship*, Brian Hicks writes that the ex-naval officer 'had no proof of waterspouts in the Atlantic on that day'. However, he concedes that this theory is more likely 'than sea monsters, the [Bermuda] Triangle and little green men'.

A 'seaquake'

In contrast to an above-the-waves waterspout, could a seaquake – a below-the-waves earthquake on the sea-bed – have caused enough turbulence on the ocean's surface to loosen some of the cargo on the *Mary Celeste* causing inflammable fumes in the hold to be released? This potentially dangerous situation may have caused Captain Briggs to order his ship to be abandoned and take to the lifeboat. However, when the cargo in the hold of the *Mary Celeste* was later examined in Gibraltar, it was found to be in almost perfect condition.

This Author's Opinion

After sifting through much of the evidence, I have come to the conclusion that what happened to the ten unfortunate souls who were on board this iconic ghost ship is similar to what Dr Oliver Cobb told *The Boston Post* in 1926, that is, 'Undoubtedly the crew of the *Mary Celeste* abandoned their vessel because they feared an explosion.' Cobb added that the crew may have heard noises coming from the hold; noises that he had been informed were often associated with wooden barrels containing alcohol. Captain Briggs who had never carried alcohol in the past was naturally nervous about this especially as he had his wife and two-year-old daughter on board with him.

Cobb expanded his theory to say that the large quantity of fumes in the hold caused the ship's forward hatch to fly into the air and land upside down on the deck. This so unnerved everybody on board that in their panic, they abandoned ship, leaving everything as it was with the intention of returning to the ship later. Cobb thought that they had panicked so much that they had not even lashed down the wheel. He said, 'In their haste, they neglected to attach a line to the vessel by which they could be towed. That was a mistake, but an understandable one.'

Since the *Mary Celeste* was powered by the North

Atlantic winds blowing uninterrupted over an open ocean, the ship continued sailing much faster in an uncontrollable fashion than the captain and crew in the lifeboat could possibly row and keep up with. This meant that within a very short time, the gap between the brigantine and the lifeboat grew and the desparate and unfortunate Captain Briggs *et al.* had no chance of catching up with her. The result was that they all perished in the lifeboat for one of two reasons: either because they were too exhausted to continue rowing as they had not taken any or enough food with them or because the rough seas of the North Atlantic had swamped them causing them to drown in mid-ocean. Since this grim state of affairs happened well over six hundred miles off the coast of Portugal, their bodies were never washed ashore. As a result no clear evidence of what could have happened was ever found.

In 1940, fourteen years after Oliver Cobb's interview in *The Boston Post*, this eighty-two-year-old cousin of Captain Briggs's, published his confirmation of the above in *Yachting* magazine. This time he added another possibly critical point. He, the family biographer, said that the alcohol, which was loaded aboard on a cold November day in New York, may have leaked and evaporated as alcoholic fumes in the warmer climate when the ship began to approach western Europe. This is possible and credible, as the American consul in Genoa confirmed that somewhere between leaving New York and the point where the *Dei Gratia* came across the *Mary Celeste* near the Azores, nine of the seventeen hundred and one barrels had somehow opened. This meant that 450 gallons of industrial alcohol were then swilling around and evaporating in the bilge water in the bottom of her hold or inside the hull, filling her with these potentially dangerous fumes.

Charles Edey Fay, the executive who worked with the Atlantic Mutual Company which had insured the *Mary Celeste* and who had written his detailed report *Mary Celeste: The Odyssey of an Abandoned Ship*, in 1942, endorsed Cobb's theory of what Brian Hicks in *Ghost Ship: The Mysterious True Story of the* Mary Celeste *and Her Missing Crew* called a 'pressure-cooker cargo'. This became the most accepted theory to explain why this most famous of ghost ships was found in a reasonable condition wallowing aimlessly in the sea but still sailing in the Atlantic driven along by the wind in a westerly direction but with absolutely no-one on board. Evidence of this rushed act of abandoning the ship in a hurry may be understood by the fact that Mrs Briggs's jewellery was left behind in her cabin. It is also reinforced when no signs of violence were found on board, which tends to disprove any other theories regarding piracy and mutiny.

However, if you still do not agree with the above as the explanation to this baffling mystery, a mystery that has engrossed the world for the past one hundred and fifty years, then perhaps the writer in *The Nautical Gazette* (1 May 1920) was right when he wrote:

As to what happened to the crew of the Mary Celeste, *one guess is just as good as another. For the truth is now probably in the sole keeping of the Recording Angel.*

Author's Note

The basic facts in this novel are true. There were two merchant ships, the *Mary Celeste* and the *Dei Gratia* captained respectively by Benjamin Spooner Briggs and David Reed Morehouse. Similarly, the names of the first and second mates and the rest of the crewmen mentioned in this book are also correct. It is also on record that Captain Briggs's wife, Sarah Elizabeth, and his two-year-old daughter, Sophia Matilda, also sailed on the *Mary Celeste* on this fateful voyage across the Atlantic. Briggs and his wife decided not to take their seven-year-old son, Arthur, with them as they did not want him to miss out on his schooling back home.

The dates mentioned here are also accurate. The Mary Celeste was scheduled to leave New York on 5 November 1872. However, a late start caused by stormy weather meant that she finally set out on her iconic voyage for Genoa, Italy two days later on 7 November 1872. The *Dei Gratia* also set out for Gibraltar eight days later on the fifteenth of November and her crew first saw the abandoned *Mary Celeste* some six hundred miles west of Portugal on 4 December 1872. The final log entry made by Captain Briggs on the *Mary Celeste* was made on the twenty-fifth of November. It noted that his ship was six miles away from the island of Santa Maria, one of the Portuguese Azores Islands, some one thousand miles west of the Portuguese coast. This meant that the *Mary Celeste* had sailed four hundred miles, probably without a crew, in ten days. The factual data – length, width, tonnage etc. – about the *Mary Celeste* and the *Dei Gratia* are accurate and are on public record. In addition, according to the internet, the wreck of the Mary Celeste has been located off the coast of Haiti and since 2001 has been historically authenticated.

Similarly, the names of the officials involved and the dates in connection with the salvage hearing held at Gibraltar after the *Mary Celeste* and *Dei Gratia* had arrived there are accurate. Frederick Solly Flood served as the chief official at the hearing and Horatio Jones Sprague was the American consul in Gibraltar. The official enquiry about what had happened to the *Mary Celeste* and how much salvage money was to be paid to Captain Morehouse and his crew began on Wednesday 18 December 1872 and dragged on until mid-March 1873. The result was that Captain Morehouse *et al.* received far less money than they had expected. Some four months after the *Mary Celeste* first sailed into Gibraltar, she left Europe to return to North America to become one of the most famous ships in the history of the sea.

I have used artistic licence to turn this true story of the sea into a novel by adding details which include various possible conversations held between such key players as Captains Briggs and Morehouse. I have also done the same for similar style conversations between Briggs and James H. Winchester, the owner of the *Mary Celeste*. I have also added some other background details which refer to the crews of both the *Mary Celeste* and the *Dei Gratia* and also about the

American and Vice Admiralty legal officials in Gibraltar.

Finally, please note that there are a few differences in the sums mentioned with reference to the insurance costs and values of the *Mary Celeste* and her cargo. These discrepancies are not due to my poor research or editing skills, but rather reflect the different sums quoted by the various newspapers and other publications at the time.

I would also like to take this opportunity to thank my editor, Gary Dalkin, who has edited ten of my other books and also Kirsty Parkinson who, together with Gary, turned a somewhat ungrammatical text into a readable and hopefully exciting novel. I would also like to thank Kirsty Jackson, Victoria Richards, Becca Stevenson, Shannon Bourne and all the team at Cranthorpe Millner, Publishers, for all their work and support.

A Personal Request from the Author

First of all, I would like to thank you for buying my latest book published by Cranthorpe Millner, *Mary Celeste: The Greatest Maritime Mystery Ever*.

This book was very interesting to write and to undertake the necessary research. I hope that you get as much out of it as I put into it. My other books published by Cranthorpe Millner include:

Villains of Yore
Colonel Blood: Soldier, Robber and Trickster
Kill the King: And Other Conspiracies
Wicked Women of Yore: Were They Really Wicked?

In the meanwhile, if you enjoyed reading about the *Mary Celeste*, I would be very pleased if you would write a positive review and send it to Amazon and the other various online book sites. In addition, I also appreciate receiving your personal feedback. You can do this by writing to me via:

Email: dlybooks15@gmail.com
Website: www.dly-books.weebly.com
Twitter: @ly70473845

Thank you,
David Lawrence-Young

About the Author

David Lawrence-Young is a retired English and history teacher and lecturer who has written twenty-five historical and crime novels. He loves writing and researching about quirky aspects of English history, the British monarchy, Shakespeare and military history. This book about the *Mary Celeste* is an obvious exception to the above!

When he is not writing, he enjoys reading historical novels, thrillers and books about Shakespeare. He plays the clarinet badly and is a keen photographer. When he has the opportunity, he likes travelling abroad, especially to places that he is writing about. He is married and has two children and four grandchildren. This is the fifth book he has had published by Cranthorpe Millner.

Bibliography

In order for this landlubber author to get the key facts as accurate as possible about the *Mary Celeste*, the *Dei Gratia*, Captains Briggs and Morehouse, the names of the crews and the long, drawn-out enquiry that followed in Gibraltar, I have based many of the details regarding the *Mary Celeste*, the *Dei Gratia* and their crews on Brian Hicks's excellent book, *Ghost Ship*. In addition I have also referred to *Mary Celeste: A Centenary Record* by Macdonald Hastings, *The Mysterious Case of the Mary Celeste* by Graham Faiella, *The Mary Celeste: An Unsolved Mystery from History* by Jane Yolen and *The Mary Celeste* by Brian Freemantle (publishing details below). In addition, I used J. Dispenza's excellent article, *Ghost Ship Found What Happened on the 'Mary Celeste'* and various other relevant internet sites.

Anon, *The Mary Celeste and SS Baychimo: The Unsolved Mysteries of History's Most Famous Ghost Ships*, Ann Arbor, Michigan, Charles River Editors, post 2007 (exact publication date not stated)

Begg, Paul, *Mary Celeste: The Greatest Mystery of the Sea*, London, Longman, 2006

Bryan, George Sand, *Mystery Ship: The Mary Celeste in Fancy and in Fact*, Philadelphia, Penn, USA, J.B. Lippincott, 1942

Faiella, Graham, *The Mysterious Case of the Mary Celeste: 150 Years of Myth and Mystique*, Cheltenham, Glos., The History Press, 2022

Fay, Charles Edey, Mary Celeste: *Odyssey of an Abandoned Ship*, Salem, Mass., USA, Peabody Essex Museum, 1942

Freemantle, Brian, *The Mary Celeste*, Edinburgh, Canongate Books, 1999

Furneaux, Rupert, *What Happened on the* Mary Celeste, London, Parrish, 1964

Hastings, Macdonald, *Mary Celeste: A Centenary Record*, London, Michael Joseph, 1972

Hicks, Brian, *Ghost Ship: The Mysterious True Story of the* Mary Celeste *and her Missing Crew*, New York, Ballantine Books, 2004

Jessup, Morris Ketchum, *The Case for the UFO*, London, Arco, 1957

Keating, Laurence J., *The Great* Mary Celeste *Hoax: A Famous Sea Mystery Exposed*, London, Heath Cranton Ltd., 1929

Lockhart, John Gilbert, *A Great Sea Mystery: The True Story of the* Mary Celeste, London, P. Allan, 1927

Martin, Valerie, *The Ghost of the Mary Celeste*, London, Weidenfeld & Nicolson, 2015

Maxwell, John, *The Mary Celeste: One of the Most Intriguing Mysteries of the Sea*, London, Hamlyn, 1980.

Regan, Ellen, *The Mystery of the Ghost Ship Mary Celeste*, Cork, Ireland, Mercier Press, 2000

Scribner, Vaughn, *Merpeople: A Human History*, London, Reaktion Books, 2020

Wallace, Frederick William, *In the Wake of Wind Ships*, New York, George Sully, 1927

Yolen, Jane & H.E. Yolen Stemple, *The Mary Celeste: An Unsolved Mystery from History*, New York, Aladdin Paperbacks, 2002

If you enjoyed this book, why not try my other books published by Cranthorpe Millner?

Colonel Blood – Soldier, Robber and Trickster has it all: royalty, aristocrats, love affairs, lusty wenches in taverns, war and fighting. But most of all, an incredible robbery. This is the life of self-styled 'Colonel' Thomas Blood, the seventeenth century swashbuckling Anglo-Irish adventurer who achieved fame by (almost) succeeding in stealing the Crown Jewels from the Tower of London in 1671.

But Blood did much more. He changed sides from being a Royalist cavalier to a Roundhead during the Civil War, before becoming involved in several treasonous plots. In addition, he also dramatically saved a friend from being hanged and twice attempted to kidnap his longtime enemy, the Duke of Osborne. But despite being caught after his failed jewel robbery, he was saved by King Charles II. Why was the king so magnanimous? What hold did Blood have over the 'Merry Monarch'?

In *Villains of Yore*, take some twenty British villains. Then add their dastardly crimes and their miserable backgrounds. Mix in some nefarious conversations and combine all this to produce this exciting collection of stories.

This book describes in an entertaining way through facts and conversations how criminals, from Richard Pudlicott in 1303 up to the twentieth century Elephant Gang, operated on the wrong side of the law to make their fortunes. Reading your way through these 700 years, you will meet other well-known characters including Dick Turpin, Burke and Hare and Moll Cutpurse, as well as some lesser known but equally nasty villains such as Colonel Blood, Mary Carleton and Jonathan Wild, the 'Thief-taker General'.

Being the ruler of England has always been fraught with danger. In ***Kill the King*** you will see that many people wanted to assassinate you! At least two plots were aimed at Henry VII and George III, four against Elizabeth I, and more than three against James I. Queen Victoria survived eight plots while the Queen Elizabeth II has survived three. William II was accidentally(?) killed hunting while two Anglo-Saxon kings were also murdered – one of them while he was in the loo!

Several of these stories, such as the Gunpowder Plot, are well-known, but how many people know about the Ridolphi or Babington plots? Would history have changed if Guy Fawkes had succeeded?

Kill the King describes over thirty murderous plots in a serious but light-hearted way, and this book should shed much light on your understanding of England's murderous history.

A Hungarian countess allegedly bathes in the blood of her victims; a pair of female pirates outfight the rest of the crew; and a Roman empress has several senators and members of her family killed so that she can fulfil her sexual desires. These are just four of the thirty-six *Wicked Women of Yore* who 'star' in these pages.

This book describes in an entertaining way through flashbacks and conversations how women such as Ilsa Koch, the bestial Nazi concentration camp commander, Bonny (of Bonny and Clyde), 'Princess Caraboo' and Queen Isabella, the 'She-Wolf of France', murdered, conned and blackmailed their way into history and infamy.

D. Lawrence-Young has written over twenty historical

novels. In this companion volume to his *Villains of Yore*, this book will open your eyes to the fact that the fair sex was not always so fair. From now on you will look at women, young and old, beautiful and ugly, in a completely new and different light.

www.ingramcontent.com/pod-product-compliance
Lightning Source LLC
Chambersburg PA
CBHW030544080526
44585CB00012B/250